ATHENA

To
Nicole Heather and Michael Luke,
my beloved children and cherished friends.

Athenagoras
Philosopher and Theologian

DAVID RANKIN
Trinity Theological College, Brisbane, Australia

LONDON AND NEW YORK

First published 2009 by Ashgate Publishing

2 Park Square, Milton Park, Abingdon, Oxon OX14 4RN
711 Third Avenue, New York, NY 10017, USA

Routledge is an imprint of the Taylor & Francis Group, an informa business

First issued in paperback 2016

British Library Cataloguing in Publication Data
Rankin, David Ivan
Athenagoras : philosopher and theologian
1. Athenagoras, 2nd cent
I. Title
270.1'092

Library of Congress Cataloging-in-Publication Data
Rankin, David (David Ivan), 1952–
Athenagoras : philosopher and theologian / David Rankin.
p. cm.
Includes bibliographical references and index.
ISBN 978-0-7546-6604-2 (hardcover : alk. paper)
1. Athenagoras, 2nd cent. I. Title.

B654.Z7R36 2008
270.1092—dc22

2008023033

ISBN 978-0-7546-6604-2 (hbk)
ISBN 978-1-138-26587-5 (pbk)

Contents

Acknowledgements

It was my friend and teacher, the late Revd Professor Eric Osborn (1922–2007), who first suggested that I write on Athenagoras. He discussed the work with me at great length in its early stages – I will recall forever draft pages spread across his hospital bed – and made a number of comments reflective, as ever, of his wisdom and insight. That he died during this project is a matter of profound regret as well as of sadness to me, for I know that he would have loved to see this work through to its conclusion. To him I owe far more than I can ever speak of or repay. His wife Lorna remains for me a great encourager and friend and I acknowledge now what I should have acknowledged long ago: my profound debt to her. To my colleagues – both faculty and staff – and to my students at Trinity Theological College here in Brisbane and at the ecumenical Brisbane College of Theology I also owe a great debt. Their support of my work has been consistent and unfailing. Professor Bernard Pouderon of the University of Lyons, the outstanding Athenagoras scholar of this generation at least, has read some of my drafts and made many useful comments. As always, the faults remain all my own. My appreciation goes also to Sarah Lloyd, my publisher, and the editorial staff at Ashgate. My children Nicole and Michael, whom, since the death of our wife and mother, I have watched with great pride grow into fine young adults, have been my principal companions on the journey through this project. To them I owe more than mere words can express; and to them I dedicate this book.

List of Abbreviations

ACW	Ancient Christian Writers
A-NCL	Ante-Nicene Christian Library
CH	*Church History*
CPh	*Classical Philology*
HTR	*Harvard Theological Review*
JECS	*Journal of Early Christian Studies*
JEH	*Journal of Ecclesiastical History*
JTS	*Journal of Theological Studies*
LCL	Loeb Classical Library
MSR	*Mélanges des sciences religieuses*
RAC	*Reallexikon für Antike und Christentum*
REAug	*Revue des études Augustiniennes*
REG	*Revue des études grecques*
RHE	*Revue d'histoire ecclésiastique*
SC	*Sources Chrétiennes*
SP	*Studia Patristica*
VC	*Vigiliae Christianae*

Chapter One
Athenagoras: philosopher and theologian

By way of preface it would be appropriate to set Athenagoras both in the context of Greek apologetics of the second and early third centuries of the Common Era and in that of a more specific Christian engagement with the Greco-Roman philosophical discourse of the same period.

Christian Greek Apologetics

Robert Grant declared that '[a]pologetic literature emerges from minority groups that are trying to come to terms with the larger culture in which they live'.[1] Frances Young argues that the 'primary motive' of the Greek apologists of the second century

> was justification, justification of their unpopular – indeed, potentially dangerous – decision to turn their backs on the classical literature inherited from anitiquity and the customs of their forefathers, thus abandoning the comfortable ethos of the Graeco-Roman synthesis into which they had been born, nurtured, and educated.[2]

'What is increasingly clear', she continues, 'under the head of "apologetic" is that a group that regards itself as a people is fighting for social and political recognition' and that '[i]t is this common self-justificatory content that links the second-century Greek apologists, rather than a sharply defined literary form'.[3] Among the Greek apologists of the second century – many of whom wrote works more protreptic than apologetic in nature – a number of key themes emerge. In their various defenses of the faith (and these were the defenses of a minority religious culture in the midst of a dominant culture which was either hostile or indifferent towards it), the apologists see a need to address accusations of atheism made against Christians; to explain why they choose not to participate in the worship of the Greco-Roman gods; to refute accusations of the most heinous immorality – often of cannibalism, incest and other forms of sexual deviance; and to explain their failing to accord the emperor his religious due. Other apologetic pieces –

---

[1] R.M. Grant, *Greek Apologists of the Second Century* (Philadelphia, 1988), p. 9.

[2] F. Young, 'Greek apologists of the second century', in M. Edwards et al (eds), *Apologetics in the Roman Empire. Pagans, Jews and Christians* (Oxford, 1999), p. 81.

[3] Ibid., p. 92.

for instance Irenaeus in the *Adversus haereses* and works such as the *Epistle to Barnabas* or Justin Martyr's *Dialogue with Trypho the Jew*, both belonging to the *Adversus Judaeos* genre of Christian writing – are not of particular concern here. Athenagoras, in the *Legatio* at least, writes neither of heretics nor of Jews.

Justin Martyr, in his *Apology*,[4] appeals to the emperors against the prejudice (I.2) and rumour (I.3) which bedevil the Christian cause. He complains that Christians are unfairly targetted and condemned merely for the name they bear (I.4). He refutes the accusation of atheism levelled against them (I.5) – an accusation based on their refusal to worship the pagan deities; argues that Christians hold themselves to the highest standards of morality (I.7); and condemns the idolatry implicit in pagan worship (I.9). The *Apology* (or *Apologies*) was 'an apologetic piece, or set of pieces, intended to explicate the Christian faith and thus secure for Christians fair treatment before the law as a genuine philosophy'.[5] Justin's pupil Tatian, whose approach is offensive more than defensive, attacks from the outset the immorality of pagan philosophers in his *Oration to the Greeks* (2f.), challenges (by implication) the accusation laid against Christians of atheism, affirms the Christian God as the Creator of all (5) and repudiates pagan worship as demonic (10f.). The author of the *Epistle to Diognetus* explains at the beginning of his treatise that he will address 'the mode of worship prevalent among Christians … what God they trust in, and what form of religion they observe' (1), making clear that they neither honour the gods reckoned as such by the Greeks nor hold to the 'superstition' of the Jews. He attacks pagan idolatry (2) and implies that, in their relationship to the world, Christians are like resident aliens.[6] In his three-volume *To Autolycus*, Theophilus of Antioch rises to the challenge of his friend, who 'boasts' of his own gods of wood and stone (I.1) and demands of him, Theophilus, that he in turn may explain (or 'show') his own God (I.2). In response, Theophilus speaks at length of the nature of the Christian God (I.3–4), of that God's invisibility (I.5) and of his role as Creator (I.6f.). He speaks of the Christian belief in resurrection (I.8), and condemns pagan idolatry (I.9 and II.2) and emperor worship (I.11). He declares Greek literature to be of little or no value (III.2), speaks of the inconsistency and immorality of Greek writers (III.3) and wonders how educated persons could possibly believe the accusations of atheism, sexual impropriety and cannibalism made against Christians (III.3f.). He, in response, accuses pagan philosophers of contravening to laws on sexual behaviour (III.6) and of contradicting themselves concerning the divine being (III.7ff.). He speaks of the Christian commitment to the Ten Commandments (III.9) and of the superior moral conduct of Christians (III.15). Good argues that the apologetic intent of the work is 'to secure the

---

[4] This can be understood as two separate but related works or as one work in two parts. This is not a major issue here.

[5] See my own *From Clement to Origen* (Aldershot, 2006), pp. 95f.

[6] This reflects what Grant has to say above about Christianity as a minority culture struggling to come to terms with the dominant culture of its time and place.

credibility of the Christian religion'.[7] Clement of Alexandria, in his *Protrepticus* (which is, of course, protrepticmore than it is apologetic), urges his would-be converts to abandon idolatry, speaks of the absurdity and impiety of the pagan mysteries (2.11.1f.), condemns sacrifices (3.43.1f.) and idolatry (4.49.1f.), but recognizes, however, that sometimes pagan philosophers and poets come near to the truth about God – although not quite (5.65.1ff.). He argues that true belief is found in the Prophets (8.77.1f.), and he responds to the criticism that Christians have abandoned the customs of their forebears, in particular the latter's gods (10.89.1f.). They say (in his words) that 'it is not to the credit of Christians to subvert the customs handed down to us from our fathers' (10.89.1); but he argues that 'custom, which has made you taste bondage and unreasonable care, is fostered by vain opinion' (10.99.1).

It was, then, in this context of second century Greek apologetics – a context of defending their co-religionists against charges of atheism, of immorality of all kinds, and of disloyalty to the state – that Athenagoras mounts his own defence and explication of the faith.

Christian Engagement with Philosophical Discourse

As I pointed out in the conclusion to my book *From Clement from Origen*,[8] the pre-Nicene Fathers, particularly Athenagoras' predecessors and contemporaries, differ considerably in their attitudes towards Greco-Roman philosophy and in the uses they made of it. Both Tatian and Theophilus of Antioch display a great deal of antipathy towards pagan learning, fearing that it might compromise Christian truth, while Tertullian, Justin Martyr, Clement of Alexandria and Origen are 'clearly immersed in philosophical enquiry'.[9] Both Justin and Clement indeed begin to see philosophy even as a kind of preparation, for the Greeks, of the coming Gospel – much as the Law and the Prophets were for the Jews. Justin saw Christianity simply as a superior form of philosophy. Origen speaks of the 'auxiliary' value of the study of philosophy – auxiliary to that of the Scriptures. Irenaeus displays the marks of some philosophical enquiry but finds it difficult to see beyond the notion of philosophy as the source of heresy. Tertullian likewise seems to have regarded philosophy as the 'fount' of heresy and philosophers as the 'patriarchs of heretics', and to have repudiated speculative forms of philosophical enquiry; but his indebtedness to Stoicism and his obvious respect for Plato are too well documented to be ignored. In the West in particular – although eastern Christianity is not untouched by it – Stoicism influences the thought of Clement of Rome, Hermas, Minucius Felix and Cyprian, as well as that of Tertullian.

---

7 D. Good, 'Rhetoric and wisdom in Theophilus of Antioch', *Anglican Theological Review* 73 (1991): 323.

8 Rankin, *From Clement to Origen* (above, n5), pp. 144f.

9 Ibid., p. 144.

It is generally understood that the cosmology of *1 Clement* is influenced by Stoicism,[10] though some would suggest that a Jewish provenance is just as likely.[11] The Stoic virtues of healthy living and self-reliance are evident in the *Pastor* of Hermas of Rome;[12] and Minucius Felix, the North African advocate practising his craft in Rome, evidences both a Ciceronian Academic Scepticism and, like Clement above, a Stoic-like concern for an ordered universe and physical world.[13] Minucius Felix also makes use of Plato's famous words at *Timaeus* 28c3–4 – a passage on the difficulty of finding the creator and father of the Universe, and a favourite text among the Christian writers of the time – in order to support his own argument concerning the oneness of God.[14]

Although Justin is at times profoundly critical of Greek philosophy, its influence on his thought is undeniable. Apparently he wore the philosopher's *pallium* (*Dialogue with Trypho the Jew* 1) – even Tertullian eulogizes this garb in the *De pallio* – and he regarded Christianity as the perfect philosophy, as he himself had progressed from Stoicism to Aristotelianism, Pythagoreanism and then Platonism (*Dialogue* 2), then came finally to Christian teaching.. He had some regard for Plato, whom he believed to come near to the truth at times, though not near enough. His reflections on the Logos are clearly influenced by Stoic thought (*1 Apology* 46); his thinking on the matter of the soul shows some engagement (though ultimate disagreement) with Plato; he regards Socrates with approval (*1 Apology* 5); he alludes positively to Plato's words at *Timaeus* 28c3–4 on the Creator and Father of the Universe (*2 Apology* 10.6; see above); his understanding of free will at *1 Apology* 28.3–4 is consistent with that of Plato at *Republic* 617e; and he chooses to see a doctrine of the Trinity at *Epistle* 2.312e (*1 Apology* 60.6–7).
Tertullian, despite his infamous question at *De praescriptionibus* 7.9 – what has Athens to do with Jerusalem? – and despite his comparison at *Adversus Marcionem* 2.27.6 of the Marcionite God, 'invisible and unapproachable and inactive', with the God of the philosophers, makes extensive use of philosophy and is profoundly influenced by it. Like Justin, he can speak of Christianity as a sort of philosophy (*De pallio* 6.2). While at *De anima* 3.1 he speaks of philosophers as the 'patriarchs of heretics' and the treatise is in some ways anti-Platonist, its reflections on the soul and its corporeality, for example, are markedly Stoic in origin. His *De patientia* is Stoic in outlook, and his reflections on the relationship between nature and reason and on the ideal of living in accordance with nature at *Adversus Praxean* 5 and *De spectaculis* 2f. display the clear marks of that school. Theophilus of Antioch

---

[10] W. Ullmann, 'The cosmic theme of the *Prima Clementis* and its significance for the concept of Roman rulership', *Studia Patristica* 11 (1972): 87.

[11] W.C. van Unnik, 'Is 1 Clement 20 purely Stoic?', *Vigiliae Christianae* 4 (1950): 185.

[12] Rankin, *From Clement to Origen* (above, n5), p. 38; see also Cicero, *Tusculan Disputations* 5.40.1, 81-2 on the Stoic notion of self-sufficiency.

[13] Rankin, *From Clement to Origen* (above, n5), p.44f.

[14] *Octavius*, 19.14 and (by allusion) 26.12.

demonstrates a wide knowledge of philosophical thought and is profoundly critical of the Stoics. He believes that Plato and his followers – he alludes to *Timaeus* 28c3–4 – have got it right in claiming that God is both uncreated and the Father–Creator, but wrong in regarding matter as likewise uncreated. In this schema, he says, a God who is not, alone, the unique sovereign cannot be God.

The deep engagement of Clement of Alexandria with Greek philosophy is not to be doubted, and indeed too extensive to be dealt with adequately here. This is particularly so in his *Stromateis* (all citations hereafter will be from this work), though in the *Protrepticus*, too, he deals more than favourably with contemporary thought as containing at least a partial grasp of the truth. Philosophy provides for the Greeks a preparation for the Gospel (6.6.44.4). 'Pythagoras and Plato, listening to the inner voice and with the help of God, have reached the truth' (1.7.37.1). Clement makes positive use (at 5.12.78.1 and 5.14.92.1–4) of *Timaeus* 28c3–4 on the nature of God, and also of *Epistle* 2.312e (at 5.14.103.1); of *Laws* 4.715e–716a (at 2.22.132.2 and 7.16.106.3); and of *Epistle* 7.341c (at 5.12.78.1). His reflections on the Logos also demonstrate some measure of influence from Plato and the Platonists and from Aristotle (4.25.155; 5.11.73; 4.25.156). Stählin lists, from Clement's extant works, some 1,273 borrowings from the Apostle Paul and 618 from Plato.[15]

The engagement with Greco-Roman philosophy – particularly with Platonism and Stoicism, and not at all uncritically – on the part of Christian theologians, both predecessors and contemporaries of Athenagoras, is wide-ranging and often quite profound, and it includes matters of cosmology, theology (God as a transcendent being, the Logos and the Trinity), ethics, human psychology, and the relationship between reason and nature.

Who Was Athenagoras?

This chapter will address the questions of the who, where and what in relation to Athenagoras. Apart from the unreliable testimony of Philip of Side, a fifth-century Christian historian, little of anything certain is known about Athenagoras. A later historian declares, in *Codex Bodleianus Baroccianus* 142, fol. 216 [*Patrologia Graeca* vi. 182], that

> Philip of Side says in his twenty-fourth book [of his *Christian History*]: Athenagoras was the first director of the School at Alexandria; his *floruit* was about the time of Hadrian and Antoninus, to whom he dedicated his *Embassy* on behalf of the Christians. He was a man who professed Christianity while still wearing the philosopher's garb and was the leading man in the Academy. Before Celsus did so he had planned to write against the Christians, but, reading the Holy Scriptures to make his attack the more telling, he was so won over by

15 *Clemens Alexandrinus*, ed. O. Stählin (Leipzig, 1905–36), pp. 1–66.

> the Holy Spirit as to become, like the great Paul, a teacher and not a persecutor of the faith he was attacking. Philip says that Clement, author of the *Stromateis*, was his disciple and Pantaenus Clement's. Pantaenus too was an Athenian, being a Pythagorean in his philosophy.

Even what I have previously written on this matter[16] I would now largely discount, giving virtually no credibility at all to Philip's testimony. There is no independent support for the unlikely notion that Athenagoras was either the head of the Alexandrian school or a leading figure in the Academic school. Clement of Alexandria was certainly not his pupil, but rather that of Pantaenus (rather than the other way around). Athenagoras almost certainly comes from the latter part of the second century and not from its middle years (see below). Pantaenus was probably a Stoic.

Athenian?

Where Athenagoras comes from is a matter of some dispute. In the manuscript title of the *Legatio* he is called 'Athenagoras the Athenian'. This is done in the earliest known codex containing his work – codex Parisinus Graecus 451 (A), copied out in 914CE by Baanes – secretary to Arethas, archbishop of Caesarea in Cappadocia – with annotations by the archbishop himself; and it recurs in later manuscripts – codex Mutinensis 126 (N), codex Parisinus 174 (P), codex Parisinus 450 (C), Argentoratensis 9 (S) and a number of others[17] – all of which follow, directly or indirectly, 451. This is of key importance for understanding his writing in the context, and against the background, of contemporary philosophical conversations, particularly those to do with the matter of the divine (being). The particular philosophical–theological conversation in which he was engaged in the *Legatio* (see Chapter 3 for more detailed discussion of this matter) may also provide a pointer to where he comes from.

Athenian Middle Platonism

From the latter part of the first century CE into the second, we see that in Athens itself – though one does not need to subscribe to the notion of the existence of a formal

---

[16] See, for example, the section on Athenagoras in Rankin, *From Clement to Origen* (above, n5), p. 119.

[17] *Athenagoras: Legatio and De Resurrectione*, ed. W.R. Schoedel, with translation and notes (Oxford, 1972), p. xxxv, says that there are four 'of lesser importance' and ten 'unimportant' ones. B. Pouderon, *Athénagore: Supplique au sujet des chrétiens et sur la résurrection* (Paris, 1992), p. 35, identifies some 24 manuscript copies in addition to A, N, P, C and S, including six deriving from N, ten from P, one from C, five indirectly from A, and others whose provenance is not so clear.

Middle Platonist 'School of Athens'[18] – there are philosophers associated with the city (either native Athenians or non-Athenians who had taken up residence there): figures such as Plutarch, Nicostratus, Calvenus Taurus, Atticus, Harpocration and Severus, who reflect a particular understanding of the divine being which might help inform our understanding of the thought of Athenagoras.

'We must never', says Dillon, 'underestimate the simplicity and informality of the arrangements in any ancient philosophical school'.[19] Indeed he declares: '[a]fter 86 BC, I do not believe that there was any such thing as an official Platonic Academy, until (perhaps) Marcus Aurelius founded his Regius Professorships in 176 AD'.[20] We note, for example, that it is so-called members of the alleged 'School of Athens', like Plutarch of Chaironea writing towards the end of the first century CE and Atticus in the second, who identify the supreme divine entity with the Creator–Father entity of the *Timaeus*. And they do so, possibly in company with Apuleius of Madaura (associated with the so-called but historically improbable 'School of Gaius'[21]) and with the Neopythagorean Nicomachus of Gerasa (early second century?), against the likes of Harpocration of Argos – himself a pupil of Atticus (on which see Proclus, *In Timaeum* I.305.6), who had previously come under the influence of Numenius. Harpocration distinguishes the two entities, the 'Father' and 'Creator' of the *Timaeus*, as does the Middle Platonist Alcinous (second century CE?) and the Neopythagoreans Moderatus of Gades (first century CE) and Numenius (second century). (Roughly speaking, the Neopythagoreans are Platonists who identify Plato essentially as a disciple of Pythagoras.) These two latter figures clearly distinguish the Supreme God–Father from the Creator figure of the *Timaeus*, whom they recognize as a second god at best.

The identification (or not) of the Creator entity with the Supreme God is also important because, for those like Plutarch, Atticus and Nicomachus, identifications

---

18 See J. Dillon, *The Middle Platonists 80 BC to AD 220*, rev. edn (London, 1996), pp. 231ff. In his paper 'The Academy in the Middle Platonic period', *Dionysius* 3 (1979): 63–77, Dillon comments that Plutarch in the mid-first century CE 'records himself as studying under Ammonius [in Athens]' (p. 66), but that '[i]f he joined a material Academy ... it was no more than Ammonius' school, which seems to have been a fairly simple foundation' (ibid.). He then says that in the mid-second century CE Gellius speaks of L. Calvenus Taurus not as being the head of any formal Academy, but as '*vir memoria nostra in disciplina Platonica celebratus*' (*Noctes Atticae*, 7.10), 'implying simply that he was the leading Platonist of his time in Athens' (p. 68).

19 Dillon, 'The Academy in the Middle Platonic period' (above, n18), p. 76.

20 Ibid..Dio, in the epitome (or summary) of his *Roman History*, tells us that 'when Marcus [Aurelius] had come to Athens ... [he], for the benefit of the whole world, established teachers at Athens in every branch of knowledge, granting these teachers an annual salary' (31.3–32.1). Atticus, the leading Platonist in Athens in his time, was the [first?] 'Regius Professor' of Platonism there according to J. Dillon, '"Orthodoxy" and "eclecticism": Middle Platonists and Neo-Pythagoreans', in J. Dillon and A.A. Long (eds), *The Question of Eclecticism: Studies in Later Greek Philosophers*. (Berkeley, 1988), p. 114.

21 See Dillon, *The Middle Platonists* (above, n18), pp. 266f.

of the supreme principle with the Creator also apparently led them to distinguish the God–Father–Creator from the Logos (that is, to see the Logos not merely as an attribute of God but as a distinct entity, an assimilation perhaps of the Platonic Demiurge to the Stoic Logos), which fulfilled an intermediary role between the intelligible and the sensible world.[22] Dillon comments that 'God, thus established [by Plutarch as Supreme Being, Real Being, the Good and the One], must relate to the world through suitable intermediaries, of whom the first is, not surprisingly, the Logos'.[23] At *De Iside et Osiride* 377e–378a, Plutarch speaks of 'the one *logos* which orders (or regulates) all these things [*sc.* the sun, the moon, the heavens, the earth and the sea], the *providence* which watches over them, and the subordinate powers which are set over them'. This may not be, for Plutarch himself, the Logos of Philo and of the Christians, but it does provide a point of reference for the latter. So, rather than seeing the Logos as merely an attribute or aspect of, and thereby indistinguishable from, God, they propose the Logos as an entity distinct from, though subordinate to, him. This is crucial perhaps for Athenagoras' articulation of the relationship of the Logos to the Father (God) and to the process of creation. In addition, Plutarch, Atticus and (this time) Harpocration – even though he takes a different position on the Father–Creator identification: a hangover perhaps of the influence of Atticus – understand Platonic creation in the *Timaeus* as being temporal or taking place in time, against those like Calvenus Taurus, Alcinous, Apuleius, and others in the 'Platonist' tradition, all of whom regard creation as atemporal (that is, as not happening in time and as shaped in language simply 'for the sake of instruction', μαθήσεως χάριν).[24] Thus, if Athenagoras does come from Athens (and did much of his work there), he will more likely be writing within and against the background of this tradition, which emerges (reactively?) in the late first and in the second century in Athens and which takes a particular position on matters such as the identity of the Father–Creator, the Logos, and the temporality of creation,against others within the broader (Middle) Platonist tradition, particularly as represented by Neopythagoreans like Moderatus and Numenius. Athenagoras' placement in this context might also help, at least in part, to explain Athenagoras' reference at *Legatio* 7.2 to the 'first principles' of those poets and philosophers who have gained no more than a 'peripheral understanding' of God because they have relied upon their own resources and

---

22 The question of the influence, if any, of Philo Alexandrinus on Athenagoras, given that precisely these very issues are addressed in the writings of the former, is a crucial one. If, as I say below (see my Chapter 2), the *De resurrectione* is from the hand of Athenagoras, then our author will have spent some time in Alexandria, will almost certainly have gained some acquaintanceship with the writings of Philo and may well have been influenced by him at least in this matter. It must be said, however, that in many other ways, particularly in the choice of language, there is much that divides Athenagoras and Philo.

23 Dillon, *The Middle Platonists* (above, n18), p. 200.

24 See D.T. Runia, *Philo of Alexandria: On the Creation of the Cosmos According to Moses* (Leiden, 2001), p. 17 and Dillon, *The Middle Platonists* (above, n18), p. 242.

not upon God himself and have thereby come up with different doctrines about God, matter, the forms and the world. These four are the very issues at the heart of Middle Platonist discourse in the first and second centuries of the Common Era. And then, at *De resurrectione* 1.2, Athenagoras refers to the matters which others have misrepresented; and it is not improbable that this was designed to point back to the subject matter of the *Legatio*, which he identifies in passing as the 'nature of God, the 'knowledge [of God]', and the 'activity [of God]'. These were all topics at the centre of the Middle Platonist conversation in Athenagoras' time.

An Alexandrian Connection?

Some sources point to a possible connection between Athenagoras and Alexandria. So does for instance Philip of Side, and somewhat fancifully (and thus his testimony, wrong on many other details, should be at least discounted, if not dismissed outright – see above); but others, let it be said, do it more convincingly. There are some internal pointers (including an interest in Egyptian religious matters (see *Legatio* 1.1 and 14.2 on Egyptian zoology; 22.8 on Isis and Osiris; and most of chapter 28 on Egyptian deities) – information which could, of course, be accessed by anyone in the empire at the time (especially the quotations in chapter 28 from Book II of Herodotus) – which might suggest at least some time spent in Alexandria. (There is of course the intriguing reference to 'camels' at *De resurrectione* 12.2 which suggests that the author of that work at least had some familiarity with the region.) I believe, however, that there is in fact no substantial evidence at all – apart from the testimony of Philip – to suggest, let alone prove, any period of residence in, or even a significant sojourn to, Alexandria. How any theologian, Christian or otherwise, who had spent some time in that city could fail, as is the case with the author of the *Legatio*, to demonstrate some acquaintance with the writings of Philo is difficult to explain.[25] There is in fact no reasonable *prima facie* case for any substantial Alexandrian connection whatsoever. It is time, in my view, to take more seriously the description 'the Athenian' and the suggestion of Athenagoras' probable engagement with the Athenian Middle Platonist scholarship of his era – as well as his ownership of that engagement (see Chapter 3 below).[26] *If* Runia is right, of course – and I believe he is – that terms such as ἀγαλματοφορεῖν (at12.6) and

[25] See D. Runia, '*Verba philonica*, αγαλαματοφορεῖν, and the authenticity of the *De resurrectione* attributed to Athenagoras', *Vigiliae Christianae* 46 (1992): 313–27.

[26] L.A. Ruprecht, 'Athenagoras the Christian, Pausanias the travel guide, and a mysterious Corinthian girl', Harvard Theological Review 85 (1992): 35–49, posits the environs of Corinth as the natural habitat of Athenagoras on the basis of Athenagoras' understanding of sculpture and related art matters (commonly sourced with the travel writer of antiquity, Pausanias); but, again, even someone domiciled in Athens could surely reflect a similar knowledge and competence in such matters. There are no other pointers to this claimed geographic connection. There are, then, no sufficient grounds to advance this particular suggestion, intriguing and thought-provoking though it is.

συνδιαιωνίζειν employed by the author of the *De resurrectione* (at 12.6, 15.8, and 25.4) are *verba philonica* and can really only have come into patristic usage via Philo and Alexandria;[27] and *if* it is also true that the *De resurrectione* is from the hand of Athenagoras (a thesis which, for the record, Runia himself does not accept[28]) – then Athenagoras may have spent at least some time in Alexandria, and enough for him to imbibe some Philonic language.

The Athenagorean Corpus

One needs from the outset to deal with the matter of texts and, as I will argue more extensively in Chapter 2, I side with those who are inclined towards a 'not proven' verdict on the authenticity of the *De Resurrectione* and therefore, on the basis of the *status quo* (the attribution by Arethas in the tenth century and the majority opinion since that time), I also side with those who see the need to include this treatise in any account of Athenagoras' thought. In this work, however, I will keep consideration of the two writings, the *Legatio* and the *De Resurrectione*, somewhat separate as I explore the various themes in Athenagorean thought. This is, of course, something relatively easy to do, given the very different primary themes of the two works (see the monographs of both Barnard[29] and Pouderon[30] for evidence of this). My primary starting point in the consideration of a particular Athenagorean theme or sub-theme will almost invariably be the *Legatio*, while any material from the *De resurrectione* which deals with the same or a similar theme or sub-theme will be included in parentheses, for the sake of recognition. I will offer, where appropriate, an interpretation of the material from both writings.

Up until the middle of the twentieth century, the *De Resurrectione* was almost universally accepted as authentic on the basis of a marginal ascription in a tenth-century manuscript and of a reading of *Legatio* 37.1; and thus it was not seriously challenged. Grant changed all that in the early 1950s, though his own arguments were somewhat specious.[31] The fact is that, now when the debate has been opened, scholars need to stand back and ask whether there is any real evidence (internal

---

27 Runia, '*Verba philonica*' (above, n25), passim. Some have suggested to me that a majority of scholars believe that Numenius of Apamea drew his 'He who is' in frg. 13 from Philo – and that therefore it was possible to have drawn from his work from outside of Alexandria – but it is also possible that Numenius himself spent some time in Alexandria. Dillon, *The Middle Platonists* (above, n18), p. 368, note 1, is adamant, however, that in frg. 13 Numenius was not using the phrase 'He who is' in the Philonic sense.

28 Runia, '*Verba philonica*' (above, n25), p. 324.

29 L.W. Barnard, *Athenagoras: A Study in Second Century Christian Apologetic* (Paris, 1972).

30 B. Pouderon, *Athénagore d'Athènes: Philosophe chrétien*. (Paris, 1989).

31 R.M. Grant, 'Athenagoras or Pseudo-Athenagoras', *Harvard Theological Review* 47 (1954): 121–9.

or external) for making even a *prima facie* case for the Athenagorean authorship of the *De resurrectione*; and if there is not, do these two works, when looked at afresh, actually suggest any authorial resemblance? Both Barnard and Pouderon operate on the assumption of the authenticity of the *De resurrectione* and may then appear to establish what they already accept as given. But do they have grounds for their *prima facie* acceptance of authenticity (or at least the acceptance of a verdict of 'not proven' on the matter of authenticity and the maintenance of the *status quo*)? My initial inclination was to accept the argument that making a *prima facie* case was the responsibility of those wishing to establish authenticity rather than its lack. On this ground I took the view that the different themes of the two writings, their different styles and their consistently different use of language pointed to a lack of authenticity. I have now been persuaded – in private correspondence with Prof. Pouderon and through my own re-reading of the evidence – that the ascription of the *De resurrectione* to Athenagoras (though not that of the somewhat dubious reading of *Legatio* 37.1: a point which Pouderon himself has conceded from the outset in his magisterial deliberations on Athenagoras) provides suitable grounds for making a *prima facie* case for authenticity, even if definitive evidence from within both writings does not exist to allow us to approach any level of real certainty or proof beyond that. Nicole Zeegers-vander Vorst seeks to demolish Pouderon's argument for authencity (Barnard's arguments need no challenge in my view) but, while demonstrating that a number of Pouderon's linkages are either non-existent or – at best, in Zeegers' own words – 'banal', she does not in my view provide sufficient proof to overthrow the *prima facie* case. While the two works do address different themes and have virtually nothing in common as to substance, the existence of a *prima facie* case for authenticity and the absence of compelling and irrefutable evidence to overturn it mean that a 'not proven' verdict must be read in favour of the *status quo* authenticity, for the sake of this project at least (again, see Chapter 2 for a fuller treatment of this important question).

Influences

Important here, too, would be some initial reference to the matter of influences, both Christian and non-Christian, on Athenagoras' thought.

The Legatio

Biblical references are relatively sparse throughout the *Legatio*, but this is, after all, an apologetic work addressed nominally to an imperial audience for whom the claimed authority of the scriptures will mean nothing. Indeed, only slightly less than half of these biblical references relate to a Christian ethics.[32] Other Christian

[32] Indeed, seven out of the eleven biblical references which relate to the matter of the oneness, creatorship and providence of God are taken from the Old Testament, while all

authors – for instance Justin, with whose work Athenagoras was clearly familiar – are influences, but the former's framework is not that of Athenagoras and his claim to philosophical scholarship may indeed not be as well made as that made for for Athenagoras. The latter, in my view, is in any case both philosophically and theologically more sophisticated and nuanced (see Chapter 7 below). With respect to non-Christian sources (I have indicated that I do not believe that Philo is significant here at all, though I will reference this more in Chapter 7), the Middle Platonist tradition is generally more important for Athenagoras than any other. I believe that, notwithstanding Athenagoras' acknowledgement, in chapter 6 of the *Legatio*, of his use of doxographies, he may well have had more direct access to, and may have made greater use of, copies of some contemporary texts. He almost certainly has a clear acquaintance with Alcinous' *Didaskalikon*, or at the very least a common sourcing of ideas, and there is clear evidence of his knowledge and use of Stoic thought and language (on both these themes, see Chapter 7 below). Daniélou also suggests the possible influence of Aristotle's *Protreptikos* on the *Legatio*.[33]

The De resurrectione

As in the case of the *Legatio*, there are very few references, by quotation, citation or allusion, to the scriptures. This is somewhat unusual, given that the work is addressed to a primarily Christian audience. A number of the few texts employed relate, not unexpectedly, to resurrection and after-life (see Chapter 7 for a fuller discussion of this). Athenagoras' use of other Christian authors is, as in the *Legatio*, occasional, but more marked – which is not unusual, given that this writing is more clearly part of an intra-Christian conversation. There is evidence of at least common positions between Athenagoras and Justin, pseudo-Justin, Irenaeus, Theophilus and Tertullian, although this does not necessarily equate with influence from them; and this is particularly so with the works on resurrection by pseudo-Justin and Tertullian (again, see Chapter 7). The Athenagoras' use of non-Christian sources in the *De resurrectione* is not significant and occurs primarily in the area of language rather than of concept (with the exception of a possible use of Galen on the human body's digestive processes; again, see Chapter 7).

The Scholarship of Athenagoras[34]

Athenagoras' scholarship and his intellectual sophistication are also frequently challenged by scholars who are dismissive of his contribution to the development

except one relating to a Christian ethics (9 references) come from the New Testament.

33 J. Daniélou, *Gospel Message and Hellenistic Culture* (London, 1973), p. 11.

34 See Chapter 7 below for a fuller discussion of Athenagoras' scholarship and of his use of contemporary sources.

of Christian thought generally. Opinions vary on Athenagoras among modern scholars. Schoedel believes that he 'left no deep mark on the life and thought of the ancient Church'[35] and that his argumentation is 'sometimes superficial and arid',[36] although his 'acquaintance with literature and mythology is somewhat more profound [*sc*. than that with Greek philosophy]',[37] as he cites Homer eighteen times and Plato only seven in the *Legatio*. Homer (*Illiad* 16.672) is alluded to only once in the *De resurrectione*, namely at 16.5, a passage on sleep as the 'brother of death'; Herodotus (1.107–119) is alluded once, at 4.4, on the Median feast; and Plato, clearly a minor influence (see above), is neither quoted not cited. Athenagoras is an 'amateur philosopher'[38] whose 'carefully controlled apologetic aim' contributed little to theology.[39] These claims have some measure of truth to them, but they do not thereby necessarily devalue his scholarship. It is a truism of sorts that Athenagoras appears to have left no great mark on the early church. He is mentioned only by Methodius –chapter 24 of the *Legatio* is mentioned in the latter's *De resurrectione* – and not at all by any of the great church historians of the fourth and fifth centuries. Eusebius considers Athenagoras not worth a single footnote! But this proves neither that Athenagoras left no mark nor that his thought is, at best, second-rate. Schoedel's claim that Athenagoras' argumentation is 'sometimes superficial and arid' is probably reasonably accurate with respect to parts of the *Legatio*, but not to the whole of it, and certainly it is not true of the *De resurrectione*. The claim made with respect to Athenagoras' knowledge of poets and philosophers can be substantiated on the basis of a comparison between the respective number of citations from each group; for it is the quality of his employment of the philosophers – especially of Plato in the *Legatio* – which is the true test. Athenagoras makes little use either of poets or of philosophers in the *De resurrectione*, but his audience there was largely co-religionist and the poets and philosophers did not rate highly with that audience. He probably could be called an 'amateur philosopher' – Schoedel employs the phrase here not technically but pejoratively – but then so were many intellectuals in antiquity. The claim that he contributed little to theology through his 'carefully controlled apologetic aim' cannot be proven either way. Citation is a useful indicator, but not the sole determinant of influence. Athenagoras' Greek culture, says Schoedel, 'dazzled his vision and prevented him from grasping the realities about him'.[40] This is an overstatement and lacks credible argumentation. It merely states, but it does not prove. He 'fails to note', Schoedel continues, that Christian monotheism was still more radical and hence more unyielding than anything in Greco-Roman

[35] *Athenagoras*, ed. Schoedel (above, n17), p. v.

[36] Ibid., p. vi.

[37] Ibid., p. xix.

[38] W.R. Schoedel, 'Christian "atheism" and the peace of the Roman Empire', *Church History* 42 (1973): 309.

[39] Ibid.

[40] Ibid.

thought.[41] Who can say, with such certainty, what someone might or might not 'note'? Athenagoras' apparent identification of philosophical monotheism with the Christian version of monotheism may in fact be more apparent than real. He employs the Pythagoreans, the Stoics and Aristotle among his witnesses for the unity of God, but he clearly also knows that their deity is not necessarily his own and that of his co-religionists. He seeks simply to demonstrate that the notion of the 'one God' is not itself foreign to contemporary poetic and philosophical thought. Mansfeld says that Athenagoras' learning 'is not too impressive'.[42] Yet on what grounds is such a sweeping statement made? Athenagoras' own claim – explicit and implicit – to be both 'philosopher and Christian' needs indeed to be taken seriously. Whatever the deficiencies of the *Legatio* – and I suggest that they are overstated by its modern critics – the *De resurrectione* is itself a well-written and closely argued work, which more than holds its own with contemporary works on the same theme – Tertullian's *De resurrectione mortuorum* and pseudo-Justin's *De resurrectione* among them. Schoedel himself comments on Athenagoras' *De resurrectione* that '[o]ur author's rhetorical training has equipped him well for a polemical situation of the kind that we have imagined'.[43] That the two works survived at all – even if they lay largely undisturbed for around 700 years until they were discovered by the Cappadocian archbishop – is testimony to the fact that someone thought them to be of some value. Part of the purpose of the present work is to demonstrate that the thought of Athenagoras articulated in the two works is perhaps underrated.

The Framework of the *Legatio*

In the *Legatio* Athenagoras operates within a clearly defined and well-informed philosophical framework, and he does so (as I will demonstrate in more detail later) within a particular philosophical conversation of the second century concerning the nature of the divine – more than in the context of a specifically and exclusively intra-Christian conversation about the nature of the *kerygma*. Yet he is Christian, and demonstrably so. Athenagoras writes – and he is justified in doing so – as a philosopher to philosophers, and he is one of the first (after Justin) to name Christianity a 'philosophy'.[44] He is probably an eclectic thinker drawing

---

41 Ibid., p. 316.

42 J. Mansfeld, 'Resurrection added: The *interpretatio christiana* of a Stoic doctrine', *Vigiliae Christianae* 37 (1983): 227.

43 *Athenagoras*, ed. Schoedel (above, n17), p. xxix.

44 Bernard Pouderon has pointed out to me (in private correspondence) that many Jewish writers had already by this time spoken of Jewish thought as a 'philosophy'.

from many streams,[45] but so was every philosopher, and indeed probably every philosophy, in the second century CE.[46]

The Framework of the *De resurrectione*

It is reasonably clear that Athenagoras in his treatise on resurrection writes primarily against Christians (or heretical Christians like the Gnostics or Marcionites) whose profoundly dualist position likewise prevents any suggestion of an after-death existence of the body. The basic structure of the treatise is the traditional rhetorical one of a *refutatio* followed by a *confirmatio*. In chapter 1 he speaks of the two forms of argument, the one on behalf of the truth (which is largely apologetic and is addressed to those who are hostile to the truth) and the other concerning the truth (which is largely didactic and addressed to those who normally embrace the particular truth gladly). While, he says, it is normal for an argument 'concerning the truth' to precede that 'on behalf of the truth' – one considers the contours of the truth and then argues for it – in the present case one needs to argue first on behalf of the truth. Thus Athenagoras' audience here is largely seen as hostile and disbelieving, or at least as confused and vulnerable.

The Goals of this Monograph: What are the Questions I Wish to Explore from this Point On?

In Chapters 2 and 3 I seek to situate Athenagoras in his time and context. First I offer a detailed exploration of the matter of the *authenticity or non-authenticity* of the *De resurrectione*, so that we can be clear about the texts we are dealing with, and then I offer a consideration of the layout of the argument of both works in greater detail than has been offered here (Chapter 2). Then (in Chapter 3) I explore the question of the *theological–philosophical conversation* in which

---

45 See A.J. Malherbe, 'The structure of Athenagoras, "Supplicatio pro Christianis"', *Vigiliae Christianae* 23 (1969): 1.

46 We might also, however, note the argument of A.H. Armstrong, 'Pagan and Christian traditionalism in the first three centuries A.D.', *Studia Patristica* 15 (1984): 414–31, which claims that most thinkers, Christian and pagan, of the first centuries of the Common Era 'would hold, that is, that there was one traditional authority which was an authority in the full sense, a body of teaching in which the fullness of universal truth was contained and with which it was not permissible to disagree, though of course it had to be interpreted rightly and intelligently' (p. 414), and that '[t]he so-called "eclecticism" of the philosophers of our period [*sc.* the first three centuries of the Common Era] is in most cases, where the more serious thinkers are concerned, a matter of this sort of critical selection and adaptation of useful material from other traditions' other than the 'one traditional authority', be it the Christian Bible, Plato, or whatever (p. 416).

Athenagoras is engaged, particularly in relation to the *Legatio*. Is he, for example, participating in a very much intra-Christian conversation about the nature of the Christian *kerygma* – a conversation which is had both with the orthodox and with the heterodox and is presented most obviously in summary form in the so-called 'Rules of Faith', which begin to emerge in the second century with Justin, Irenaeus, Tertullian and Clement of Alexandria, within a discussion of what constitutes the essence of the Christian message? Or is he engaged in a particularly philosophical conversation about the nature of the divine and its relationship to matter, created or merely unformed – a conversation which, in the latter part of the second century of the Common Era, engaged both Middle Platonists and Neopythagoreans, many of them associated in some way with the city of Athens, the spiritual home of much Greek philosophy? To identify the particular 'conversation' Athenagoras was engaged in is to understand better the nuances of the articulation of his own thought against a particular background. In Chapter 4 I will explore the *epistemology* of Athenagoras and seek to understand how this may have informed the development of ideas within his thought. Next, we embark on the major part of this work by exploring Athenagoras' 'first principles', particularly his *doctrine of God* (Chapter 5), then other themes as they emerge in the treatise – the Son/Word, the Spirit, the Trinity, ethics, anthropology and so on (Chapter 6) – and then the different sources exerting influence on Athenagoras' thought: biblical, patristic and philosophical (Chapter 7).

Method

Notwithstanding my belief that the case for or against the authenticity of the *De resurrectione* must remain 'not proven' and that therefore the *status quo*, the *prima facie* case, that of its authenticity, must prevail for the moment, I have chosen to treat the reflections on a variety of themes within both the *Legatio* and the *De resurrectione*, for the most part, quite separately in the body of this work, and I will deal jointly with aspects of the two works only when there are indications either of similar treatments or of treatments which are utterly at odds. Both Barnard's and Pouderon's monographs on Athenagoras have demonstrated that, given the very different matters dealt with in the two works, the very different approaches and the very different contexts – the *Legatio* is for example very clearly set within a philosophical debate not at all intra-Christian, while the *De resurrectione* is very clearly set against the background of a conversation, and a very heated one, between Christians, and shows very little interest in non-Christian views on the matter – such a separate treatment can be applied without compromising the consideration of Athenagoras' thought.

Chapter Two
Athenagoras' corpus: one lump or two?

The question of the authorship of the *De resurrectione* is an important starting point for any study of Athenagoras – even if simply to determine the actual material to be studied – and has dominated Athenagoras scholarship since Grant contested the work's authenticity in the 1950s[1] – to the detriment, it must be said, of any serious consideration of Athenagoras' place in patristic literature and in the development of Christian thought in the pre-Nicene period. Only when a decision is made on this matter can one begin to look with confidence at a genuine Athenagorean corpus. Notwithstanding this, both Barnard and Pouderon – both of whom accept the work as authentic – take the two works (the *Legatio* and the *De resurrectione*) to be largely unrelated (for the most part dealing with very different subjects) and therefore treat them separately. With a little 'cutting and pasting', Pouderon's fine monograph, for example, could have been transformed into two equally fine monographs on different texts.

The vexed question of the authorship of the *De resurrectione* – that is, the question of whether it is from the same hand as the *Legatio* – will probably never be fully resolved. Part of the difficulty in making even a provisional assessment is that of determining which party is in greater need of making their case: those who argue for authenticity or those who argue for non-authenticity. Previously,[2] my own position was as follows. The traditional arguments in favour of authenticity seemed to me very weak, They consisted, first, in the ascription, by Archbishop Arethas or his secretary Baanes in the tenth century, of a codex – Codex Parisinus graecus 451 – containing the *De resurrectione* to Athenagoras, author of the *Legatio*, through the phrase τοῦ αὐτοῦ; and, second, in the claim that a statement of Athenagoras at 37.1 of the *Legatio* that 'we should allow our discussion (λό γος) concerning the resurrection to be set aside for the present' is a reference to the present treatise on the resurrection). Hence in my view a *prima facie* case had not been made for authenticity; the onus of proof sat upon scholars like Barnard and Pouderon in particular; and those arguing for non-authenticity had to do no more than merely to raise reasonable doubt about their opponents' case. I believed

---

1 Of the articles published on Athenagoras since the Second World War, nearly 40 per cent are concerned with the authorship of the *De resurrectione*. The first effectively to challenge the traditional position on the authenticity of the *De resurrectione* was R.M. Grant, 'Athenagoras or Pseudo-Athenagoras', *Harvard Theological Review* 47 (1954): 121–9.

2 See D.I. Rankin, *From Clement to Origen: The Social and Historical Context of the Church Fathers* (Aldershot, 2006), p. 119.

that people like Grant and (more extensively) Nicole Zeegers-Vander Vorst had done this, and therefore the case for authenticity had effectively collapsed.[3] I have now been persuaded by Professor Pouderon[4] that the witness of the tenth-century archbishop must count for something – even if the *Legatio* 37.1 argument does not by itself breed the conviction that a *prima facie* case for authenticity does exist and that the onus of proof must therefore lie upon Grant, Zeegers-Vander Vorst and others of a similar mind (as Pouderon himself acknowledges that it does not). My present view on the matter is that authenticity is 'not proven' either way and that therefore the *status quo* – the traditional view that the *De resurrectione* came from the hand of Athenagoras – must be allowed to stand. I would also want to say, however, that, if the witness of Arethas did not exist, virtually no-one would as much as consider that the *Legatio* and the *De resurrectione* had come from the same hand, and that, notwithstanding my view that the verdict must be 'not proven' and therefore the *status quo* must remain, those arguing against authenticity have probably maintained a stronger case (for what it is worth) than those who have argued in favour of it. Alongside the traditional arguments in favour of authenticity – the Arethas ascription and *Legatio* 37.1 – there is a very useful one against it, apart from the evidence of the texts of the two works themselves; and that is the failure of the late third-century Christian theologian Methodius, who does mention the *Legatio* (specifically quoting from 24.2–3 of that work at *De resurrectione* I.37.1–2), to make any reference at all to the very well written and closely argued *De resurrectione* in his own work of the same title.

The most substantive arguments mounted on either side of the debate have been offered by Bernard Pouderon in favour of authenticity[5] and by Nicole Zeegers-Vander Vorst against it.[6] Both make out impressive cases, though I think that Zeegers-Vander Vorst's is perhaps the stronger one; but neither conclusively proves his or her own case, and therefore, in my view, that of Pouderon must prevail, even if by default. My only general comment, before embarking on a more detailed (though largely summary) account of their arguments, is that Pouderon too regularly overstates his case (which favours authenticity) through an overuse of such terms as '*frappant*' to describe claimed points of similarity between the two works in question, when the similarity at best moderate; while Zeegers-Vander Vorst too often characterizes her opponents' claims as 'banal',

---

3 An example of how easily this repudiation of Athenagorean authorship has taken hold can be seen when even J. Daniélou, *Gospel Message and Hellenistic Culture* (London, 1973), p. 26, note 41, can say without further argument that '[i]t is impermissible to look for [Athenagoras'] ideas in the *De Resurrectione* which is attributed to him. R.M. Grant … has shown that the work cannot be by him.'!

4 In a private communication.

5 B. Pouderon, 'L'Authenticité du traité sue la résurrection attribué à l'apologiste Athénagore', *Vigiliae Christianae* 40 (1986): 226–44.

6 N. Zeegers-Vander Vorst, 'La Paternité Athénagorienne du *De Resurrectione*', *Revue d'Histoire Ecclésiastique* 87 (1992): 337–74.

'minor', 'not pertinent', or 'incidental', when they are clearly worthy of more serious consideration. Her persistent argument that claimed divergences cannot be dismissed on the grounds of there being different themes, contexts and audiences, while sometimes possibly correct, is not always necessarily so. My intention is, first, to summarize very briefly Pouderon's arguments apart from those referring to the Arethas ascription and then to summarize Zeegers-Vander Vorst's arguments in greater detail and, where appropriate, over against those of Pouderon.

Pouderon's first point, after he has usefully summarized the arguments from both sides of the debate to date[7], is that a lexical comparison of the two works – he considers some 30 words employed more than once in both works, out of some 397 words drawn from the Schwartz index[8] – demonstrates a high probability that the two works come from the same hand.[9] He claims the same with respect to the demonstrative methods employed in both works – '*la succession d'alternatives avec réduction de chacune d'elles par l'absurde*'; '*la réfutation d'objections successives*'; '*un anti-procédé*' whereby one rejects as '*vaine l'argumentation développée et à en venir à un argument de simple évidence, capable à lui seul d'emporter l'adhésion*'; the appeal '*successivement aux plus grands systèmes philosphiques*'; and '*le souci constant de la rigeur méthodique*'.[10] He does the same also with reference to a small but common set of references from Homer's *Illiad* (16.672 at *Legatio* 12.3 and at *De resurrectione* 16.5) and from Paul (*1 Corinthians* 15.32 at *Legatio* 12.3 and at *De resurrectione* 19.3),[11] with reference to a common set of concepts and doctrines – the philosophical idea of the 'common conception', that of creation from unformed matter (from Plato's *Timaeus* 51a), of immanence expressed as divine providence, of the notion of the divine being 'free from need', of the τέλος of human being shared and not shared with the rest of the animal world, and various matters to do with a doctrine of the resurrection.[12] These latter he describes, in my view unfortunately, as '*plus convaincantes*'.[13] Then he argues thatdifferences arise from genre, '*ton*' and '*manière*'.[14] Much of this, in my view, though it is not without value, is sometimes simply and regrettably overstated.

Zeegers-Vander Vorst's approach is one of confrontation, and at times unnecessarily dismissive. Yet she does make some very useful points, and more often than not strikes her mark. But does she make a case strong enough to overturn the *status quo* and the *prima facie* case for authenticity? She dismisses rather quickly both the Arethas ascription – primarily on the basis of the divergent states

7 Pouderon, 'L'Authenticité du traité' (above, n5), pp. 226–32.

8 See E. Schwartz, *Athenagorae libellus pro Christianis, Oratio de resurrectione cadaverum* (Leipzig, 1891).

9 Pouderon, 'L'Authenticité du traité' (above, n5), pp. 232–4.

10 Ibid., pp. 235–7.

11 Ibid., pp. 237–8.

12 Ibid., pp. 238–41.

13 Ibid., p. 241.

14 Ibid.

of the two manuscripts, which suggest very different travels and therefore an accidental appearance together in the archiepiscopal collection[15] – and *Legatio* 37.1[16] (which, again, even Pouderon dismisses); and she makes much of the silence of Methodius.[17] On the question of common lexical usage, she declares that the 30 words of Pouderon are all 'banal',[18] and she wonders why '*mots rares*' have not been considered.[19] She points to some words like δύναμις, ἐνέργεια and τὰ φαινόμενα[20] and says that, despite different contexts, these are the same words used with very different meanings in the two writings. Her comment, made more than once, that there is no evidence of Trinitarian thought in the De resurrectione[21] is inconclusive and indeed somewhat irrelevant, given that there is no natural place for this theme in the work – unlike in the Legatio, which is all about the person and the work of God. It is also my view that Zeegers-Vander Vorst gives insufficient weight to the very different contexts and themes. Her list of lexical divergences[22] – which include ζωή, σοφία, and στοιχεῖον – is of some interest, but much of it is pedantic and inconclusive. Out of Pouderon's five claimed similarities in demonstrative method (see above), Zeegers-Vander Vorst ignores the first one, that of the 'succession of alternatives'; she dismisses the second and the third – the 'refutation of successive objections', which in my view has some claim, and the 'anti-process', where she ignores the marked similarity in language between *De resurrectione* 11.2 and *Legatio* 24.1 (which Pouderon does point to[23]); and she also dismisses the argument of Pouderon that the author(s) of both works make appeal to the great philosophical systems and employ a similar rigor of method in his/their argument.[24] With respect to these latter 'similarities' – Pouderon's fourth and fifth – Zeegers-Vander Vorst makes a solid case and shows up Pouderon's arguments to be extremely thin on both counts, though this is not necessarily fatal to his thesis. The very noticeable difference between the works with respect to the clear rigour of argument in the *De resurrectione* and the relative lack of it in *Legatio* is not, for example, without significance (see below). Zeegers-Vander Vorst then introduces what is, for her, marked divergences in method.[25] These have to do with the argument by consequentiality of causes (ἀκολουθία and εἱρμός) in

15 Zeegers-Vander Vorst, 'La Paternité Athénagorienne' (above, n6), pp. 333f.

16 Ibid., p. 333.

17 Ibid., p. 334.

18 Ibid., p. 337.

19 Ibid.

20 Ibid., pp. 338–9.

21 Ibid., p. 338.

22 Ibid., pp. 340–44.

23 Ibid., p. 345.

24 Ibid., pp. 346–7.

25 Ibid., pp. 347–9.

the *De resurrectione* (14.2),[26] but not in the *Legatio*; with the use of ridicule in the *Legatio* (at 4.1 and 14.1, for example), but not in the *De resurrectione*; with a desire for exactness (ἀκρίβεια), similarly used;and with an alleged difference between seeking after 'likeness', 'probability' and 'reasonableness' (εἰκός at *Legatio* 23.1; 31.4 and 36.2) and seeking after the 'clear' and the 'manifest' in the *De resurrectione* (where εὔδηλον and words of a similar meaning are used seven times) . Oddly enough, Zeegers-Vander Vorst does not provide references for this latter claim, but they are present in the treatise.[27] At 1.2 and 2.2 our author also challenges arguments on the basis that they merely appear 'likely' to their proponents (τὸ δοκοῦν). This is not, however, in my view, necessarily a very telling argument. Other, lesser and less detailed, claims of divergence from Zeegers-Vander Vorst make no great difference. With respect to Pouderon's claim of there being a set of similar references to Homer and to the Apostle, Zeegers-Vander Vorst makes the important and telling point (though hardly fatal to Pouderon's argument) that the first refences to Homer are set in very different contexts and the references to Paul are mere commonplaces in Christian literature.[28] Indeed, Zeegers-Vander Vorst introduces some evidence that there are marked divergences in the use of classical and biblical texts[29] and that these reflect '*une mentalité différente*'[30] behind the two works; these can, in my view, be explained quite often through the fact that, while the *Legatio* was clearly addressed to educated pagans and was an attempt to participate in a particular Middle Platonist conversation of the late second century concerning the divine, the *De resurrectione*, while almost certainly including some pagans in its intended audience, was primarily directed to Christians whose faith was vulnerable to heretical suggestion and against Christian heretics, namely the Gnostics or Marcionites. Both Pouderon and Zeegers-Vander Vorst make far too much of the evidence they claim to see here. Zeegers-Vander Vorst also points to what she regards as significant divergences in '*habitudes stylistiques*',[31] but these are not major. She is deeply critical of Pouderon's claim to see a great convergence between the two works in terms of concept and theology.[32] She argues that the use of the Stoic notion of 'common conceptions' in the two works is simply contradictory[33] but fails, in my view, to give sufficient weight to the fact that in the *Legatio* Athenagoras dismisses such conceptions as evidence for the existence of God (15.1) and in the *De*

26 Athenagoras speaks at 14.2 of a 'logical sequence in argument' (τῆς φυσικῆς ἀκολουθίας) and a 'natural order of argument' (τὸν φυσικὸν εἱρμόν)'.

27 At *De resurrectione* 2.3 our author employs φανερόν and at 6.5, 9.2 and 11.1 εὔδηλον.

28 Zeegers-Vander Vorst, 'La Paternité Athénagorienne' (above, n6), pp. 350–51.

29 Ibid., pp. 352–4.

30 Ibid., p. 354.

31 Ibid., pp. 355–6.

32 Ibid., pp. 356–63.

33 Ibid., p. 342.

resurrectione he simply understands them as widely held principles of argument (14.1–2). She says nothing of the notion of a creation from unformed matter and she declares that the notion of a divinity 'free of need' is 'banal'[34] and that the relative absence of privative ἀ- adjectives for God in the *De resurrectione* betrays '*des mentalités différentes*'[35] from the author of the *Legatio* in the presentation of a doctrine of God. Context and theme, in my view, are decisive here, and Zeegers-Vander Vorst asks too much of the author of the piece on the resurrection. She says that the notion of providence linked to creation offers a possible similarity (though '*ténue*' and, again, '*banale*'), and she declares that the lack of a 'two providence' and 'providential delegation' concept in the *De resurrectione* suggests a different hand.[36] Again, context and theme indicate that this argument is inconclusive. Zeegers-Vander Vorst claims that the argument for a resurrection 'from necessity', found in both works, is a commonplace;[37] that a resurrection assuming a goal for human existence common to all beings[38] – death – and one distinct from that of other animals – resurrection – has a different sense in the *De resurrectione* and in the *Legatio* and therefore suggests two hands;[39] and that the modalities of the resurrection encompassed in both works are unoriginal – they are also present in Irenaeus, Tertullian and pseudo-Justin – and in any case 'banal'![40] She also claims that divergences in the language of resurrection and at significant points in both arguments are critical. In my view, again, both Pouderon and Zeegers-Vander Vorst read too much in brief and almost incidental references to resurrection in the *Legatio*, where the main theme is the nature of the divine, over against a whole treatise which is dedicated to a careful and well argued treatment of the doctrine of the resurrection. Zeegers-Vander Vorst also points to what she sees as other divergences.[41] The different treatments of the image of God as 'potter' and of matter as 'clay'[42] – to be found positively in the *Legatio* (15.2–3) and negatively, as blasphemy, in the *De resurrectione* (9.1)[43] – cannot be explained simply by

---

34 Ibid., p. 357.

35 Ibid.

36 Ibid., p. 358.

37 Ibid., pp. 359–60.

38 Pouderon, 'L'Authenticité du traité' (above, n5), p. 239, suggests that this found at *Legatio* 25.4 and 31.4 and in the *De resurrectione*, passim.

39 Zeegers-Vander Vorst , 'La Paternité Athénagorienne' (above,n6), pp. 358–9.

40 Ibid., pp. 360–61.

41 Ibid., pp. 363f.

42 Ibid.

43 At *Legatio* 15.2–3 Athenagoras uses the analogy of the subservience of the clay – matter – to the potter – God – to argue that matter is not worthy of more honour than (or even of the same honour as) its maker. At *De resurrectione* 9.1 our author challenges the parallelism between the pairs God–potter/matter–clay when it is employed to demonstrate that God would be unlikely to wish to resurrect a dead and decomposed body. See a more detailed discussion of this analogy in Chapter 5 below.

context.[44] In my view, however, it is not this image (or parallel) that the author challenges in the latter text, but its alleged particular use to demean God. Different understandings of the particular responsibilities of the soul and of the body for good and evil acts are present in the two works,[45] but again, different contexts, different themes, and the different needs of the argument can easily explain these. Nevertheless, Zeegers-Vander Vorst is attractive here, although she could have been more accepting of the fact that at *De resurrectione* 12.8 the soul is said to 'govern' the impulses of the body. Her claim that the two works testify for different valuations of our life on earth[46] in relation to our life to come, one showing contempt (*Legatio* 12.3 and 33.1) and the other appreciation (*De resurrectione* 13.1), do not give appropriate weight to the claim, made in the latter, that any characterisation of earthly life as needy and corruptible (hardly ringing endorsements!) is set within the framework of accepting that such a life is suited for our present existence. Zeegers-Vander Vorst's final claim that the primary arguments for authenticity are 'banal', minor, not pertinent, or incidental[47] does not give many of them sufficient weight – but Pouderon's frequent claim that the evidence for similarity is 'frappant' perhaps invites such a response to a certain extent.

I start therefore with an acceptance of the *status quo* of authenticity. Yet has Zeegers-Vander Vorst done enough to shift the balance? Much of her argument certainly points very strongly towards this, but in the final analysis it is not beyond the realms of reason that these two very different works, differently themed, differently argued, differently toned, written in completely and utterly different styles, are yet from the same hand. Yet my study of the thought of Athenagoras will be shaped, in part, by the niggling thought that they might not be! We need, then, to examine the nature of each work and a number of related matters: dating, audience, genre, rhetorical structure, purpose, major lines of argument and basic structure.

The *Legatio*

Date of the Legatio

There is a very broad consensus which places this work towards the end of the reign of Emperor Marcus Aurelius (somewhere between 177 and 180 CE). Grant places it before the summer of 177.[48] He accepts the emendation of Mommsen

---

44 As Zeegers-Vander Vorst claims: 'La Paternité Athénagorienne' (above, n6), pp. 363–5.

45 See ibid., pp. 365–71.

46 Ibid., pp. 367–8.

47 Ibid., p. 370.

48 R.M. Grant, 'The chronology of the Greek apologists', *Vigiliae Christianae* 9 (1955): 28–9.

(followed by Schwartz), who reads Γερμανικοῖς instead of Ἀρμενιακοῖς in the titles of the emperors in the preface of the work; he notes that the joint rule of the two emperors, father and son, commenced on 27 November 176 CE; he claims to see, in the 'profound peace' mentioned at 1.2 (βαθείας εἰρήνης), that period marked by the *pax eeterna* which was inscribed on some coins issued between 10 December 176 and 9 December 177; and he argues that Athenagoras' claim, at 35.3, that no slave owned by Christians had ever testified about the cannibalism practiced by Christians must pre-date the record of slaves doing just this during the persecution of Christians in Lyons (Eusebius, *Historia Ecclesiastica* 5.1.14).[49] He therefore presupposes a date of composition after November 176, but before the summer of 177. Barnard suggests a date between November 176 – the beginning of the emperors' joint rule – and March 180 – the death of Marcus Aurelius.[50] He accepts the use of the title Ἀρμενιακός by both emperors; he says that the phrase 'profound peace' was a rhetorical commonplace and therefore does not necessarily provide any sort of date; but he maintains that there can be no greater precision than to say that the treatise was written sometime between 176 and 180. Schoedel suggests a date between 176 and 178.[51] He also accepts a date beyond November 176 (beginning of joint rule) and speaks of the relative calm in the empire between 175 and 178, but he also acknowledge that Commodus did not become 'Augustus' until 177. Pouderon suggests a composition date in 177,[52] on the basis of a *terminus post quem* in November 176 (beginning of joint rule) – a period of relative calm between the autumn of 175 (the end of the revolt of Avidius Cassius) and the beginning of 178 (the commencement of the Second Germanic War) – and the granting of the title 'Augustus' to Commodus in 177. Barnes also, like most others, suggests a date between late 175 and May 177, but offers September 176 as the more likely period.[53] He does so on the basis that the composition must be placed after the end of the revolt of Avidius Cassius and before the beginning of the Second Germanic War, but also before Commodus became 'Augustus' in August 177. Marcus Aurelius and his son Commodus came to Athens in the late summer of 176, and this would have provided the appropriate setting in which Athenagoras might have composed this writing, whether he actually intended it for the emperors or not. This date, of course, might seem to be precluded by the fact that the joint rule did not begin officially until November of that year, but its

[49] In my view this last argument is somewhat weak, but this does not affect the argument particularly.

[50] L.W. Barnard, 'The Embassy of Athenagoras', *Vigiliae Christianae* 21 (1967): 88–92.

[51] *Athenagoras: Legatio and De Resurrectione*, ed. W.R. Schoedel, with translation and notes (Oxford, 1972), pp. xi–xii.

[52] B. Pouderon, *Athénagore d'Athènes: Philosophe chrétien* (Théologie Histoire 82), (Paris, 1989), pp. 38–40.

[53] T.D. Barnes, 'The Embassy of Athenagoras', *Journal of Theological Studies* 26 (1975): 111–14.

anticipation would have been quite acceptable in the political climate of the day, given that Marcus Aurelius had made it clear for some time that he intended to share his rule with his son.

Intended Use of the Legatio

Was the *Legatio* intended for delivery before the emperors, was it actually delivered, or was it simply a literary piece shaped by the demands of an actual plea (which may or may not have been designed at least to be read by the emperors or their officials)? The general consensus among scholars – although there are some dissenting voices on the matter – is that the piece was probably neither delivered nor intended to be delivered in person: it would have been too long such a purpose, and the various attempts to find evidence of 'real-time' delivery in the text itself, by way of style and language, would fail to identify commonplace rhetorical devices. My own view is that the work cannot have been actually delivered to the emperors in 'real time', but a copy may have reached them – particularly if Athenagoras was, as we have suggested, an Athenian domiciled in his home town. Hence I do not believe that the work was either actually delivered before the emperors or intended to be; I think it was, in all likelihood, a 'lettre ouverte' (in Pouderon's felicitous phrase)[54] or a 'purely literary event' (to use Schoedel's description).[55] Barnard,[56] Barnes[57] and Grant[58] are on the side of the argument which favours the view that the work was either delivered in person before the emperors or intended to be so, and Schoedel,[59] Pouderon[60] and Buck[61] are against it. The work is, of course, shaped by the demands of rhetorical form.[62]

Genre of the Legatio

The work itself is clearly apologetic, being shaped in part by the demands of rhetorical form, which includes many rhetorical features. It seeks to provide an

---

54 Pouderon, *Athénagore d'Athènes* (above, n52), p. 62.

55 W.R. Schoedel, 'Apologetic literature and ambassadorial activities', *Harvard Theological Review* 82 (1989): 59.

56 Barnard, 'Embassy' (above, n50), p. 92.

57 Barnes, 'Embassy' (above, n53), p. 114.

58 R.M. Grant, 'Five apologists and Marcus Aurelius', *Vigiliae Christianae* 42 (1988): 8f.

59 Schoedel, 'Apologetic literature' (above, n55), p. 59.

60 Pouderon, *Athénagore d'Athènes* (above, n52), p. 62.

61 P.L. Buck, 'Athenagoras' *Embassy*: A literary fiction', *Harvard Theological Review* 89 (1996): 209ff.

62 See P. Keseling, 'Athenagoras', in T. Klauser, *Reallexikon für Antike und Christentum*, Vol. 1 (Stuttgart, 1950), p. 881; *Athenagoras*, ed. Schoedel (above, n51), p. xvi; and Buck, 'Athenagoras' *Embassy*' (above, n61), *passim*.

articulation of Christian teaching, primarily on the nature of God, to a largely non-Christian audience represented (in fact or form) by the philosophical princes, the imperial father and son; and it would have been incomprehensible to the many poorly educated or non-educated Christians of whom Athenagoras speaks with some warmth and appreciation in the treatise. Malherbe sees it as an attempt to speak to the Christian doctrine from a Middle Platonist framework.[63] I believe, however, that this does not do proper justice to Athenagoras' overall purpose. Athenagoras is, clearly, philosophically trained; he is aware of the issues in which contemporary philosophical discourse and conversation were engaged, in Athens and elsewhere in the second century of the Common Era – the nature of the divine being, the relationship between that being and creation, and so on – and he sees this conversation as one in which the Christians needed to be involved. His is not, then, simply the case of a Christian apologist employing the language of the marketplace and target audience to provide access to a Christian world-view; rather, he sees himself as being engaged in a broader conversation (broader than a simply intra-Christian one), but doing so very much as a Christian. He owns the language of contemporary thought; he does not merely use it but it is his own, and he uses it naturally and without pretence. He therefore seeks to contribute to that conversation on its own terms and on those of the faith which he is proud to uphold and defend. Thus this work is more than simple apologetics.[64] Pouderon's suggestion that the *Legatio* would be primarily protreptic in nature – '*l'ensemble de l'ouvrage s'apparente plutôt au genre protreptique, destiné à gagner sinon l'adhésion, du moins la sympathie de l'empereur et du public païen*'[65] – is rather implausible, because the *Legatio* does not seek the conversion of the emperors but simply a better treatment for the faith of the community to which Athenagoras belongs. In fairness to Pouderon, however, this is probably not what he is suggesting, as he employs '*protreptique*' in a general rather than a technically correct sense.[66]

Rhetorical Structure of the Legatio

Whatever its actual intended use, it is, however, in the form of a rhetorical piece composed in the ambassadorial style. It evidences the contemporary conventions of Hellenistic rhetorical style and structure. The preface and the first chapter combine to create an *exordium* in which Athenagoras seeks the goodwill of the emperors

[63] A.J. Malherbe, 'The structure of Athenagoras, "Supplicatio pro christianis"', *Vigiliae Christianae* 23 (1969): 1–20.

[64] This matter will be given even more detailed attention in Chapters 3 and 4 to follow.

[65] Pouderon, *Athénagore d'Athènes* (above, n52), p. 303.

[66] Justin Martyr's *Apologies* are sometimes also described as protreptic in nature but can only be seen as such in a broad sense, as seeking to elicit the sympathy of the jury rather than to convert.

by referring to them as the 'greatest of kings', as 'philosophers', and as peaceable and humane. This opening also contains the beginnings of a *narratio* in which the author points to the manifest injustice of the treatment of the Christians by the state. In chapter 2 he continues this *narratio*. Then he offers a *partitio* in which he outlines the three main allegations or charges laid against Christians – those of atheism, of cannibalism, and of promiscuity and incest. In chapter 4 he begins his *probatio* with a lengthy defence against the charge of atheism, which occupies the bulk of the treatise (chapters 4–30). He employs scripture as witness for his case and points to the evident good character of the Christians as proof of their piety. From chapter 14 on he embarks on an attack on pagan religion (a *refutatio*), which continues until chapter 30. At chapter 31 he begins a brief dismissal of the charges of cannibalism, incest and promiscuity, and he offers a more detailed defence against them from chapter 32 to chapter 36. In the final chapter, 37, he concludes with a *peroratio* which summarizes his central thesis that the Christians, far from being atheistic and promiscuous, are indeed 'godly, mild and chastened in soul', and he exhorts the emperors to treat them more appropriately.

Purpose of the Legatio

Essentially, what Athenagoras is seeking to do (and he does this from the outset, in good rhetorical style) is to identify himself as a fellow philosopher with his addressees. Malherbe also suggests that Athenagoras, when describing as 'philosophers' the emperors to whom he is formally writing, does so in contexts where he 'implicitly describes Christian doctrine as being philosophical'.[67] Malherbe is probably correct in this evaluation (the emperors' learning and wisdom are enlisted for a formal *apologia* of Christianism); but I would suggest that chapter 18 does not truly fit the argument, whereas 24.1, 31.3 and 37.1 could be taken to support Malherbe's claim, given that there Athenagoras juxtaposes claims of the emperors being learned with references to Christian doctrine. Athenagoras wants to create a sense of empathy and identity between himself and his principal readership. This is, of course, a common rhetorical device, but it is, in my view, even more substantial for Athenagoras here. Athenagoras writes as a philosopher – and he is justified in doing so – to other philosophers, and he is one of the first (after Justin) to name Christianity a 'philosophy'. He is probably an eclectic thinker,[68] but so was every philosopher, and indeed probably every philosophy, in the second century CE.[69]

---

[67] 2 passim; 9.1; 11.3; 17 passim; 18 passim: Malherbe, 'Structure of "Supplicatio"', p. 6, note 37.

[68] Ibid., p. 1.

[69] I have neither the time nor the space to deal with the vexed question of eclecticism in the second century CE, but a useful discussion may be found in the collection of essays edited by J.M. Dillon and A.A. Long, *The Question of 'Eclecticism': Studies in Later Greek Philosophy* (Berkeley, 1988). In their introduction, the editors suggest that, while

The Argument of the Legatio

In the opening two chapters of the *Legatio* Athenagoras makes a plea to the emperors for a more just treatment of Christians. At 2.6 he urges the emperors not to 'be carried away and prejudiced by low and irrational rumour', so that they 'will not go wrong through ignorance' about Christian belief and practice; and he speaks of beginning his 'defence of our teaching'. At 3.1 Athenagoras lists the three accusations commonly made against Christians: atheism, cannibalism and incest. If these are true, he says, then deal vigorously with the guilty, who would therefore be living like wild animals. But if the accusations be false, he continues, then, as evidence of that natural principle or divine law by which evil opposes virtue and opposites war against each another, at the very least treat the Christians as you would treat any of their persecutors.

At 4.1 Athenagoras begins his lengthy refutation of the charge of atheism (which takes up the bulk of the treatise: chapters 4 to 30). In these chapters, the *probatio* of his work, he argues for the distinction between God and matter (chapter 4), for the oneness of God (chapters 5–9), for the Christian doctrine of the Trinity (chapter 10), for an ethics founded on the Christian belief in their God (chapters 11–12). He acknowledges the appropriateness of the historical judgement on Diagoras of Melos, of having been an atheist, but he challenges its application to the Christians at 4.1. For 'we', he argues, distinguish God from matter, demonstrate that matter is one thing and God another and that the difference between them is immense. At 4.2 Athenagoras speaks of the 'signs conducive to piety' available to Christians in the order, harmony, magnitude, colours, shapes and arrangement of the world. If we, Christians, agreed with Diagoras, notwithstanding all the pointers to the contrary, then we would properly be condemned, says Athenagoras. He then speaks of the Christian teaching that there is one God maker of the universe as mirroring the famous statement of Plato at *Timaeus* 28c3–4.

In chapters 5 and 6 he speaks of poets and philosophers who were not regarded as atheists, on account of giving attention to matters concerning God (see Chapter 5 below). He speaks of Euripides' perplexity over those whom 'common preconception' ignorantly names as gods, and then of his setting out his own teaching on the existence of God through 'rational insight' (see Chapter 4 below). In chapter 6, Athenagoras begins to marshall the support of the philosophical schools for his argument that the true God is one. In 6.1 he deals with the Pythagoreans and their teaching on the Monad; at 6.2, with the teachings of Plato (quoting both *Timaeus* 28c and 41a); at 6.3, with those of Aristotle, and at 6.4 with the doctrine of the Stoics on the nature of God as One.

'neither the word nor the concept it expresses is attested before the Roman period' (p. 4), in the Platonic–Sceptical Academy of the first century BCE and later, '[e]clecticism, as in Antiochus, suggests that disagreements between philosophers are merely verbal and that at bottom the doctrines of superficially discrepant systems are compatible' (p. 6).

At 7.1 Athenagoras begins to speak explicitly of the first principles of the universe (see Chapter 5 below). In the preceding chapters he had spoken of God and matter (4), of God and unqualified matter as ὑποκειμένον (5), and of God and world (6). Now he summarizes chapters 5 and 6 in particular, by concluding that all (that is, the poets and philosophers surveyed) recognize, even if reluctantly, that the divine being is one. He then inquires why, when the Christians insist that the one who ordered the universe is God and they establish with compelling proofs and arguments the correctness of what they believe, that God is one, they should have a law applied against them, while others should enjoy the freedom to speak and write about God without restraint. At 7.2 Athenagoras declares that, although the poets and philosophers have concluded rightly that God is one, they have done so 'by guesswork'. They have derived this idea solely through some 'affinity' with the 'breath' (or Spirit?) of God. They have relied upon their own resources, and not upon God, to learn about God. For this reason they came up with a wide variety of first principles. The Christians, however, have the advantage, argues Athenagoras – in that they have the prophets as witnesses to their thoughts and beliefs about God. The prophets spoke out about God and the things of God through a divinely inspired Spirit (7.3).

In chapter 8, Athenagoras deals in a purely logical way with the matter of God and the world and argues logically for the oneness of God. In chapter 9 he confirms his conclusions from chapter 8 with reference to the unimpeachable witness of the prophets, but he acknowledges that, if all he had were the logical arguments of chapter 8, then Christian teaching would be merely a human construct and his arguments mere 'concepts' ('thoughts', as he puts it). But he has the scriptures and the prophets moved by the Spirit to provide not only confirmation of his argument but in fact its very basis.

In chapter 10 Athenagoras offers his first formal presentation of the doctrine of the Trinity (see Chapter 6 below). He concludes his arguments from chapters 4–9 on the oneness of God and thereby the proof that Christians are not atheists, then he begins a particular, Christian treatment of the theme of the divine being as Three. He speaks of the Son of God, a notion which, he says, is not ridiculous; he speaks of this Son as the Word of the Father in *idea* and in *energeia*. He speaks of the Spirit as active in those who speak prophetically and as an effluence of God, flowing out and returning like a ray of the sun (10.4). He speaks of the unity of Father, Son and Holy Spirit and of the host of angels brought into being through the Word to administer the elements, the heavens and the world and to provide for their good order (10.5).

In chapter 11 Athenagoras argues that a Christian ethics based on love is grounded in scripture (see Chapter 6 below). He further contends, over against any claims which pagan religion might make, that teachings based on syllogisms, on the elimination of ambiguities and on the tracing of etymologies cannot provide for the happiness and contentment of their followers, while a life lived in accord with the Christian virtues of love, blessing and prayer for the other, a life based on deeds and not on words, will do so (11.3). Indeed, he says, there are Christians who cannot eloquently articulate their beliefs but whose lives exemplify them (12.4). In chapter 12 he shows how the omnipresent attention of the Christian God encourages a virtuous life. He claims, as Plato did, that evil will be punished by God (12.2). Christians, he continues, are those who consider this life as of little account and who are accompanied on their journey solely by the knowledge of the one true God – a knowledge grounded in the communion of the three divine persons (12.3).

In chapter 13 Athenagoras begins his *refutatio*, his attack on the beliefs of his immediate opponents. He attacks them for their ignorance of any true understanding of theology and condemns their reliance on sacrifice as something pleasing to God (13.1). The Creator and Father of the universe, he counters, requires no sacrifice, but only the knowledge of who he is and what he has done (13.2). It is from observation of the wonders of God's creation that one can gauge something of his greatness. In chapter 14 Athenagoras mocks the varieties of worship among the pagans and asks why it is that Christians should be condemned for not conforming to this non-conformity (14.3). In chapter 15 he returns to his primary theme of distinguishing between God and matter – equating the former with being, the uncreated and the intelligible, and the latter with non-being, the created and the perceptible – and employs the images of the potter and the clay to make his point. In chapter 16 he continues his argument, but this time he draws a comparison between God and the world as ordered matter. At 17.1 Athenagoras begins an examination of the naming of the pagan gods – gods made by human beings – as part of what he calls 'defending my cause'. Here he seeks to demonstrate how images of the gods can be no older than the artisans who made them. At 18.1 he notes the claims of some – presumably those who make no suggestion that the statues themselves are divine – that the statues only represent these gods and that it is less dangerous to worship the images than to approach directly the gods whom they represent. At 19.1 Athenagoras challenges this 'version' of the creation of the gods and the universe. He suggests that, since each of the pagans' 'gods' has a beginning, each must also be perishable; then, in support of his position, he refers to Plato's dichotomy between the uncreated/intelligible and the created/perceptible (*Timaeus* 27d) and he presents the Stoic ontology of the two causes – the active and the passive, God and matter. At 20.1 he speaks of 'the non-persuasivness of their theology', 'they' presumably being those against whom he has been contending from chapter 13 onwards. He repeats his assertion that that which is created must be subject to dissolution – again, he seeks to contrast God and matter – and would have been content to leave things there. In chapter 21 he ponders upon the attribution of emotions to the pagan deities – particularly of lust, grief and anger – and suggests that these are inappropriate for the divine being. He continues this theme in chapter 22. Perhaps, he begins, this is all just a poetic deceit and there is a scientific or natural explanation for such descriptions. Again, he seeks to contrast God as something uncreated and eternal with matter as something created, perishable and unstable. In chapter 23 Athenagoras, once again acknowledging the wisdom of the emperors, attempts an explanation of why the statues associated with some pagan deities seem to 'do things', if this is not the activity of gods (which he denies). He then draws on the support of Thales and Plato for a preliminary exploration of the division between the uncreated God and the created divinities on the one hand, the demons on the other. At 24.1 Athenagoras makes reference yet again to the erudition of the emperors and observes how unnecessary it is for them either to bring to mind the views of the poets or to examine other opinions. It would be sufficient for him to say that, even if the poets and philosophers had not recognized God as one and had not had crucial understandings about the other 'gods' – for some understood them as demons, others as matter, others as human beings who had lived before – it would still make no sense to condemn the Christians, who distinguish between God and matter and between their respective 'beings'. In the course of this chapter Athenagoras also revisits the doctrine of the Trinity, which he has introduced in chapter 10. He also introduces here the notion of a particular providential oversight, given to the angels by God, and the notion of a universal and general providence, reserved for God himself.

From chapter 25 to chapter 27, Athenagoras argues that 'fallen' angels busy themselves with air and earth and are no longer able to rise to the super-celestial realms. The souls of the giants – the giants who were the result of the union of the fallen angels and maidens referred to at 24.6 – are now the demons who wander about the earth. Athenagoras repeats his earlier assertion that the prince of matter acts in a manner opposed to God's goodness; then he quotes Euripides in support of this idea. These angels-as-evil-demons influence the souls and the behaviour of the human beings who fall into their clutches (25.3). In chapter 27 Athenagoras draws on the language of Stoic psychology to demonstrate precisely how human beings are drawn away from their perfected natures into sin, through the delusion and fantasy resulting from their inattention to the things of God and from their orientation towards things associated with matter.

From chapter 28 to chapter 30, Athenagoras rounds off the argument he began at chapter 13. He begins with a few comments on the names of the gods. He draws from the testimony of Herodotus, whom he quotes extensively in this chapter, on the making of men into gods. In chapter 29 he continues this theme, adding the support of the 'wise' among the poets and historians of Greece; these include Homer, Hesiod, Euripides and Pindar. The divine, he says, needs nothing and is above all desire. Therefore, if these 'gods' of the pagans are ignorant and greedy, then they must be human (that is, non-godly). At 30.1 he speaks of the detestable and hateful character of those named 'gods' and provides yet more examples. He compares them yet again with God, who alone is eternal. At 30.6 he concludes this lengthy section of his polemical apology with the claim that he has offered proof that the Christians are not atheists: they recognize the maker of the universe and the Word which proceeds from him. (Schoedel's translation of the final words of this last section, 'and the Word proceeding from him as God', has no basis in the transmitted text.)

Having dealt to his own satisfaction with what he clearly sees as the primary allegation against Christians – that of atheism – from chapter 31 on Athenagoras moves to deal with the other two accusations made against them: the Thystean banquets (3.1: called there 'godless meals') and the Oedipean unions (3.1: called there 'unions among ourselves'). In chapter 32 Athenagoras points out the immorality of the pagan gods. In chapter 33 he repeats that the Christians hope for eternal life. On this ground, they will despise other pleasures of the soul. Given that Christian life is so chaste and pure, it seems strange, he says – and employs an otherwise unknown proverb – that the harlot (that is, the pagan) should presume to teach the chaste (34.1). From chapter 35 onwards he addresses that particular allegation – though briefly; for, no matter whether Athenagoras intended to write a further work on the topic and whether the *De resurrectione* is actually his, it is not his intention here so much to write on the Christian doctrine of resurrection as to use it as a background for his refutation of the charge of cannibalism. At 36.1 he questions whether a person who believes in resurrection would allow his body to become the tomb for (other) bodies, also destined to rise from the dead. He even offers a post-resurrection scenario where the 'eaten' seek their bodies from within those of the 'eater'. At 37.1 he determines to put aside the Christian teaching on the resurrection for the time being. He reminds the emperors that they are good, moderate, humane and worthy of their office, and he urges them to acknowledge that he has proven his case before them. He seeks from the emperors a just outcome for the Christians on the basis of his representations and of the fact that Christians pray for their reign, for a proper succession, and for their growth in power as increasing numbers become their subjects (37.2). This would be to the advantage of the Christians, whom peace and stability can only benefit and whose ongoing loyalty and obedience is affirmed.

The basic structure then of the *Legatio* is as follows:

Chapters 1 and 2	Opening plea to the emperors for a fairer treatment of the Christians.
Chapter 3	Outline of the primary charges made against the Christians.
Chapters 4–12	Argument in support of the claim that the Christians are not atheists but indeed believe in the one true and eternal god (*probatio*).
Chapters 13–22	Demolition of pagan claims about the divine (*refutatio*).
Chapters 23–30.5	Exploration of demons and of their impact on human psychology.
Chapter 30.6	Summary of argument from chapters 4–30.
Chapter 31	Introduction to the defence against the other charges.
Chapters 32–4	Defence against the charge of immorality.
Chapters 35–6	Defence against the charge of cannibalism.
Chapter 37	Conclusion and final appeal (*peroratio*).

The *De resurrectione*

Date of the De resurrectione

Part of the problem concerning both the authorship and the date of the *De resurrectione* is that, as Barnard himself says, this work is 'totally unknown in Christian antiquity'.[70] It is, for example, not mentioned by Methodius in his treatise on resurrection written in the latter part of the third century (which is, of course, one of the reasons advanced for not accepting it as a second-century work). Judgements on the date of this treatise are largely influenced, as is natural, by whether one believes it to be by the hand of Athenagoras or not, although the matter of its possible dating does contribute to that particular controversy itself. Grant, who does not believe that the *De resurrectione* is Athenagorean and who sees it as part of the opposition to Origenist views on the resurrection,[71] places it in a period from the mid-third to the early fourth centuries.[72] Schoedel, who also doubts the authorship of Athenagoras and places the work in the anti-Origenist camp, places it similarly in a later period.[73] Barnard, who argues for authenticity, dates it between 176 and 180;[74] and Pouderon, again arguing for authenticity, says that it must come *c.* 180, but after the *Legatio*.[75] Runia, who challenges authenticity on the grounds that the use of Philonic language in the *De resurrectione* would suggest a different author from that of the *Legatio* (a work with no obvious connection with Alexandria), suggests a dating beyond the second century.[76] But even if Athenagoras wrote it, it must of course come after the *Legatio*; otherwise he would have made clearer reference to it in the latter work.

Intended Use of the De resurrectione

There is no doubt that the *De resurrectione* is in part addressed to the Christians, given that Athenagoras says at 1.5 that the ones he speaks for in the treatise include those who 'accept our basic assumptions' but 'are doubtful' on the matter of resurrection. This also implies, of course, that the addressees may include non-believers: both the actively hostile and the indifferent. The treatise is shaped by a division – as Athenagoras himself says – into arguments *on behalf of the* truth and arguments *concerning the truth*; this division represents what Alcinous calls (at 6.3.158.19f.) the process of refutation and of demonstration: the refuting of false

---

70 L.Barnard, 'Notes on Athenagoras', *Latomus* 31 (1972): 432.

71 Grant, 'Athenagoras or Pseudo-Athenagoras?' (above, n1), pp. 123f.

72 Ibid., pp. 128f.

73 *Athenagoras*, ed. Schoedel (above, 51), p. xxviii.

74 Barnard, 'Notes' (above, n70), p. 420.

75 Pouderon, *Athénagore d'Athènes* (above, n52), p. 81.

76 D.T. Runia, 'Verba philonica, ἀγαλματοφορεῖν, and the authenticity of the *De resurrectione* attributed to Athenagoras', *Vigiliae Christianae* 46 (1992): 324.

statements through investigation and the demonstrating of true ones through a type of exposition. Grant maintains that the treatise is 'only partly' directed against pagans,[77] which implies that it is in part addressed to other Christians. Schoedel claims that the main audience is made of Christians who are in doubt, and offers as evidence our author's use of the scriptures, of 'the Apostle' (18.5) and of the Law (23.2).[78] It is, he says, an 'intramural debate'. Barnard calls the work a 'public lecture' directed to pagans, anti-resurrection Christians and doubters from the same camp.[79] Pouderon offers (in my view) the most comprehensive and well argued overview of this matter and I am happy largely to summarize his arguments here. Part of the context of the *De resurrectione*, Pouderon says, is the challenge to the Christian doctrine of resurrection which was coming from pagan critics.[80] We see this in Origen's challenge to the second-century critic Celsus, who in his own treatise *De vera religione* argued thoughtfully against this particular belief (*Contra Celsum* 5.14). Indeed Athenagoras' argument in favour of God having the capacity to effect a resurrection of the dead may well be intended as a direct challenge to Celsus' claim that such an action is not only contrary to nature but impossible. Pouderon points to the reports of the massacre of Christians in Lyons in the time of Athenagoras as it was recorded in Eusebius (*Historia Ecclesiastica* 5.62–3), and to the apparent claims of the pagans on that occasion that their destruction of the bodies of the martyrs, which they threw into the Rhone, was in part intended to deny the Christians the possibility of their God ever being able to restore them.[81] Pouderon also points to the testimony of Lucian of Samosata, in his *Peregrinus*, that the doctrine of resurrection was understood by the pagans as sitting at the centre of Christian belief and was thus a fit subject for attack;[82] and he calls our attention to the obvious attempts of Latin church fathers like Tertullian and Minucius Felix, near-contemporaries of Athenagoras, to combat pagan challenges to this particular Christian doctrine,[83] – the former in his own *De resurrectione*, in the *Aopologeticum* and in the *Adversus Marcionem*; the latter in the *Octavius*.

A second audience is then explored by Pouderon, and he identifies it as consisting of other Christians (non-Gnostic).[84] Celsus by all accounts recognized this division within (orthodox) Christianity (Origen, *Contra Celsum* 5.14), while Tertullian, at *De resurrectione* 2.11, spoke of the need to convince one's orthodox fellows ('those in the camp of the Creator'), the uneducated, the faltering and the

---

77 Grant, 'Athenagoras or Pseudo-Athenagoras?' (above, n1), p. 123.

78 *Athenagoras*, ed. Schoedel, p. xxix.

79 L. Barnard, 'The authenticity of Athenagoras' *De resurrectione*', *Studia Patristica* 15 (1984): 43f.

80 Pouderon, *Athénagore d'Athènes* (above, n52) pp. 89f.

81 Ibid.

82 Ibid., p. 91.

83 Ibid., pp. 91f.

84 Ibid., pp. 92f.

weak-minded. This, of course, matches the concern of Athenagoras at 1.5, at least in the first part.

According to Pouderon, the third component in Athenagoras' audience was represented by the Gnostics.[85] Tertullian identifies this group in his own work on resurrection (2.2), as did Polycarp (7.1), Irenaeus (*Adversus haereses* 5.13.2-3), and pseudo-Justin (*De resurrectione* 2.588).[86] Here, says Pouderon, Christians polemicists addressed not only the Gnostic challenges to a physical resurrection, but also the general Gnostic condemnation of the flesh and of the physical world – a stance clearly influenced by Platonist dualism.

Here, then, are the three audiences for Athenagoras: pagans, doubting and wavering Christians, and Gnostics. But who is the primary audience of the *De resurrectione*? Pouderon dismisses rather quickly any suggestion that the pagans may fit the bill.[87] He argues that the primary audience of the treatise consists in educated persons who may be contemplating conversion to Christianity or may even have signed up for it, but for whom the doctrine of resurrection presents at least one near-insurmountable barrier.[88] However, his primary target, as opponents, are the Gnostics. The treatise, Pouderon says, does not set out to persuade anyone of the fact of survival after death in some form, nor of the '*qualité*' of the risen flesh, but rather of the fact of a resurrection of the body in all its members and parts.[89] Its purpose is to establish the resurrection of precisely that flesh which has been the flesh of specific human beings during their earthly existence. The treatise is addressed, Pouderon says, to those neophytes influenced and challenged by 'those who honour the sowing of spurious seed to the destruction of the truth' (1.1). These, he declares correctly, are the heretics, not the pagans.[90] Thus Athenagoras argues in the *De resurrectione* that the whole human being is a composite of immortal soul and body: the human being is not solely soul (15.6; 20.3; 23.2). As a way of supporting this hypothesis, Pouderon then proceeds to compare the different arguments of Athenagoras on this matter with those of other Christian authors of the period whose works were more explicitly directed against the Gnostics.[91] He compares, for example, Athenagoras' comment at 10.5 on the claim that no person of sense would suggest that the soul is in any way wronged in resurrection with similar points in pseudo-Justin (12.592) and Tertullian (*De resurrectione* 4.2). He then compares Athenagoras' view (although it is expressed in the *Legatio* (34.2)) that the present world, as the creation of the good creator, is thereby good with the Gnostic need to establish a second god as a creator, in order

---

[85] One might wish to say, of course, that this could also include 'hidden' Gnostics, whom one does not properly include among the Gnostics.

[86] Ibid., pp. 95f.

[87] Ibid., pp. 98f.

[88] Ibid., pp. 101f.

[89] Ibid., p. 104.

[90] Ibid., p. 105.

[91] Ibid., pp. 106ff.

to explain a less than perfect world.[92] Next, Pouderon addresses the admitted fact that the dualism of the Gnostics (against the relativistic anthropological monism of the orthodox) is shared with Platonists. Is the latter also the target of the treatise? The dependence of the Gnostics on Platonist dualism was well accepted in contemporary orthodoxy. The employment by Athenagoras of the biblical analogy of the wheat and the tares (though only implicitly) to represent the adulteration of the truth by the heretic (at 1.1 and 11.5) is evidence, says Pouderon, that his primary (if not sole) target is the Gnostic.[93] Pouderon also argues that the use of the term παραφύεσθαι ('to grow beside') to characterize the error which he identifies at 1.1 'indique bien que l'erreur, le "mensonge" (ψεῦδος), pour être plus exact, s'est développé *en marge* du christianisme, et non extérieurement à lui'. This, he rightly says, can only accommodate the Gnostics, not the pagans.[94] He suggests that other terms, perjoratively employed in the treatise, can only be directed at heterodox Christians and not, in this context, at pagans: ἀκόλαστοι ('intemperate') at 2.2; βλασφημεῖν ('to speak ill of, to blaspheme') at 2.3; μιξό θηροι ('half-beasts') at 8.5; and οἱ χείριστοι ('the worst, the last of the last, the scum of earth') at 9.1. Pouderon argues that his conviction in this matter is based on his own reading of the writings of pseudo-Justin, Tertullian and Gregory of Nyssa on the subject. Their preoccupations are the same and the arguments they employ are different from those employed to respond to Celsus.[95]

Genre of the De resurrectione

The work itself is both polemically apologetic and didactic, being shaped in part by the demands of rhetorical form, as it includes many rhetorical features. It is not classically protreptic in that it is not intended or directed towards the conversion of anyone, particularly not of unbelievers, or towards a particular point of view – save perhaps to convince wavering Christians to hold more clearly to orthodoxy and to place more trust in traditional doctrine.

Rhetorical Structure of the De resurrectione

The influence of rhetorical forms on this treatise is unmistakeable. Its opening chapter is an obvious *exordium*, intended to place the author alongside his primary audience, the wavering and hesitant and vulnerable believers, to encourage them and to put to them as forcefully as possible that those who might seek to convince them of the unacceptability of certain aspects of Christian teaching are not only wrong but dangerously so. In chapters 2 to 4 Athenagoras offers a *narratio* of sorts, which outlines his theme – namely God's power and will to effect the resurrection

92 Ibid., p. 106.

93 Ibid., p. 107.

94 Ibid., p. 108.

95 Ibid., p. 109.

of human beings – and foreshadows his own positive arguments (3.1–3) and at the same time gives a *précis* of the sort of arguments his opponents will most probably raise (4.1–4). In chapter 5 he begins his *probatio*, which consists both of a *refutatio* of his opponent's position (5.1–9.2) and of a *confirmatio* supporting his own (10.1–11.2). He then offers his primary didactic piece, in which he first divides up the topics for discussion (11.7) and then provides a two-fold argument: one main argument from first principles (12.1–17.4), which deals with the creation of the human being just for its own sake (12.1–13.2) and then with the nature of that being (13.3–17.4); and then a set of two secondary arguments (18.1–25.5), namely from the providence of God and the judging of the human being (18.1–23.6) and from the end of the human being (24.1–25.5). Somewhat oddly, there is no clear *peroratio*, first to offer a summary of the arguments and then to provide a final appeal to the audience, and this may add some weight to Pouderon's speculation that what we have is not the whole treatise. Yet, notwithstanding this omission, the treatise is clearly shaped, at least in part, by the demands of rhetorical form, as was the *Legatio*.

Purpose of the De resurrectione

Pouderon's claim is undoubtedly correct: the *De resurrectione* does not lay out a doctrine of the resurrection of the body but seeks rather on the one hand to refute the objections of those who would say that resurrection is impossible and unworthy of God, and on the other hand to provide grounds for a positive argument for both for the possibility and for the worthiness of resurrection by God through an account of the creation, the nature, the judgement and the end of the human being.[96] Likewise is Pouderon's assertion that Athenagoras defends the doctrine of the resurrection '*mais il ne la développe pas*'.[97] Whether, however, the treatise is, in its present form, incomplete – particularly with respect to the absence of a fuller doctrine of the resurrection – is less certain (as Pouderon himself acknowledges).[98] The purpose of the treatise, then, is clear. It seeks to argue that God is both able and willing to raise the dead – that such action is not unworthy of him – and thereby to strengthen the faith of the faltering believer.

The Argument of the De resurrectione

The theme of resurrection is at the heart of the whole treatise. At 2.3 Athenagoras acknowledges that there are those who doubt – these can be both Christians and non-Christians –that God is either able or willing to reconstitute dead bodies (including those utterly decomposed) and to restore them to being the very same persons they had previously been. Yet 'it is impossible for God, however, to be

[96] Ibid., p. 110.

[97] Ibid.

[98] Ibid., p. 111.

ignorant of the nature of our bodies, which are destined to arise' (2.5). He knows 'every part and member in their entirety'. He knows where everything goes and 'what part of the appropriate element receives what is decomposed and dissolved into its own kind' (ibid.). He knew beforehand the nature of the elements yet to be created from which human bodies arise, and he knew the parts of the elements from which he planned to select in order to form the human body (ibid.). 'The creation of our bodies [in the first place] shows that God's power', he says, 'suffices for their resurrection' (3.1). God both wills and is able to raise the dead. God can also restore to risen bodies parts and elements which have been lost at sea and devoured by fish, devoured by animals, oe even eaten by members of their own species (3.3f.). Bodies which arise are reconstituted from their own parts (7.1) and can never be fused with others of the same kind (7.4 and 8.2). The parts of the body 'are united again to one another and occupy the same place as before so as to restore the harmonious composition of the body and effect the resurrection and the life of the body that has died and has totally decomposed' (8.4).

Athenagoras deals, too, with the claim that raising humans from the dead is unjust and unworthy of God – unjust towards those whom God does not resurrect: angels and animals (10.1f.). Yet the resurrection of human beings does no harm to the purely rational natures (presumably angels and demons), for it brings no impediment to their existence; nor to those creatures with neither reason nor soul (animals), for they, being soul-less, will not exist after resurrection (10.2). In addition, given that animals cannot discern justice, there are no creatures on whose behalf a charge of injustice might be brought (10.4). And the work of resurrection – to reconstruct decomposed bodies – cannot be a work unworthy of God, given that the prior and lesser work – the creation of corruptible and passible bodies – was not (10.6).

The human person, says Athenagoras, came into existence neither by chance nor without purpose (12.1). He did not come into being for the sake of the Creator nor for the sake of any other creature. He came into being so that 'after his creation he should live and endure in accordance with the nature with which he was created' (ibid.). God did not make the human being for his own use; for God does not need anything. Neither did God make the human being for the sake of any other of his created works (12.3). God made the human being for her own sake, and out of the goodness and wisdom which is reflected throughout creation. God made the human being simply for the survival of such creatures themselves: that they should not be kindled for a short time, then entirely extinguished (12.5). The Creator has decreed an unending existence to those who bear his image in themselves, are gifted with intelligence and share the faculty of rational discernment (λογικῆς κρί σεως), so that, knowing their Creator and his power and wisdom and complying with the demands of law and justice, they might live without distress, eternally, with the powers by which they governed their former life, even though they were in corruptible and earthly bodies (12.6).

And what is without purpose can have no place among the things created by God. As for that which was created simply for the sake of existing and living in accordance with its own nature, there can be no reason for it ever to perish entirely, since the very reason for its existence is comprehended by its nature and is seen to be simply and solely this – to exist (εἶναι) (12.7). 'Since, then, the reason is seen to be seen to be this, to exist for ever, the living being with its natural active and passive functions must by all means be preserved; each of the two parts of which it consists makes its contribution' (12.8). God made the human person of an immortal soul and a body and endowed her with intelligence and an innate law to safeguard and protect the things he gave her which are suitable for intelligent beings with a rational life (βίῳ καὶ ζωῇλογικῇ)' (13.1).

Some of the arguments for the resurrection of the human person, reconstructed both in body and in soul, are primary – those which are grounded in the work of creation – and some are secondary – those which are grounded in divine providence and the judgement of God (15.1). Human nature, universally considered, is constituted by an immortal soul and a body which has been united with it at creation (15.2). Human beings are thereby composed of both soul and body.

> There is one living being composed of two parts, undergoing all the experiences of soul and body, and actively carrying out whatever requires the judgement of the senses and reason. (15.2)

Yet – asks Athenagoras – do death and corruption put an end to 'permanence' for the human person, composed as it is of an immortal soul, but also of a corruptible and thereby mortal body? It is not 'worthwhile in the case of men', he answers, 'to look for the undisturbed and changeless permanence that characterizes superior beings [= angels]; for the latter were created immortal from the beginning and were made to survive for ever simply by the will of God, whereas men were created to survive unchanged only in respect to the soul, but in respect to the body to gain incorruptibility through a transformation' (16.2). A 'certain of lack of continuity characterizes the 'permanence' of humans (16.4). This 'human nature has been allotted discontinuity from the outset by the will of the Creator … it has a kind of life and permanence characterized by discontinuity and interrupted sometimes by sleep, sometimes by death' (17.1).

Athenagoras concludes this work on resurrection by observing that 'the end of humans must certainly be seen in some other state of the same composite creature' (ἀνάγκη πᾶσα κατ' ἄλλην τοῦ συναμφοτέρου καὶ τοῦ αὐτοῦ ζῴου σύστασιν τὸ τῶν ἀνθρώπων φανῆναι τέλος) (25.2) and that 'it is impossible for the same men to be reconstituted unless the same bodies are united with the same souls' (25.3). 'The *telos* of a life capable of prudence and rational discernment' (ἔμφρονος καὶ λογικῆς κρίσεως), he says, 'is to live eternally without being torn away from those things which natural reason has found first and foremost in harmony with itself, and to rejoice unceasingly in the contemplation of their Giver and decrees' (25.4).

The basic structure of the *De resurrectione* is as follows:

Chapter 1	Introduction to the two modes of argumentation.
Chapters 2–3	Arguments on behalf of the resurrection.
Chapter 4	Summary of objections to the resurrection.
Chapters 5–9	Refutation of arguments against the doctrine.
Chapters 10–11	Arguments for God being both able and willing to effect a resurrection of human beings.
Chapters 12–17	Primary arguments for resurrection drawn from the purpose and nature of the human being.
Chapters 18–25	Secondary arguments for resurrection drawn from the requirements of divine providence and judgement and from the end of human being.

Chapter Three
Athenagoras and contemporary theological and philosophical conversations

Introduction

In this chapter we will situate Athenagoras, specifically in relation to the *Legatio*,[1] in the context of one or more of the contemporary theological–philosophical conversations,[2] be those intra-Christian or broader. The primary issue is, in my view, whether Athenagoras consciously participates in a primarily intra-Christian conversation about the content and direction of a specifically Christian *kerygma*, particularly as it developed during the second century of the Common Era; or whether he–intentionally – participates in a broader conversation which involves a philosophical framework addressing specific problems. Foremost among these would be the Middle Platonism of the second century – and this would also encompass so-called Neopythagoreanism[3] – which dealt with the nature of the divine; with a a supreme divine entity and the relationship (if any) between it and a creator entity;or with creation itself; with the extent of divine providence; and with the existence and form of entities acting as mediators between the intelligible and sensible realms, between the worlds of being and becoming, and so on.

[1] It is reasonably clear (see Chs 1–2 and below) that the *De resurrectione* is situated within an intra-Christian conversation and on one of the key themes of second-century Christian apologetics. That in this treatise he demonstrates only passing and largely indirect interest in pagan thought on the subject is clear even from a superficial reading of the text.

[2] I employ the word 'conversation' quite deliberately, because what we are considering here is not formal debates or controversies but a series of exchanges between thinkers and writers on matters of shared interest having to do with the principal 'problems' of second-century theological–philosophical thought. Some of these exchanges would be consciously engaged in; others simply occurred, and posterity offers perhaps the only perspective from which one can delineate or even identify the particular conversation.

[3] Like all such formulae, 'Middle Platonism' and 'Neopythagoreanism' should be employed with due care and discretion. It is perhaps helpful to regard Neopythagoreans like Moderatus and Numenius, who are often associated by scholars with the Middle Platonists, as virtual Platonists who regard Plato himself as having been the pupil of Pythagoras; this was the fashion of the day. Theologically there is much in common between Middle Platonists and Neopythagoreans, although on the matter of the divine being the latter are normally seen as anticipating the Neoplatonists in their view of the supreme god as utterly transcendent.

Athenagoras may, in fact, be engaged in both these conversations. But which one is primary for him, consciously or otherwise? Now it is clear that the position which Athenagoras takes with respect to the proclamation of the Christian God has its own integrity and does not need to be seen as part of a broader conversation in order to achieve any sort of legitimacy. It is, however, useful to situate him in the context of one or the other of these conversations (if not both, or even more), at least in order to understand some of the nuances of his language and thought.

The Christian Conversation: The Rules of Faith

What we see in the Christian tradition, particularly in the second century (with theologians such as Clement of Rome, Hermas, Justin, Tertullian, Irenaeus, Tatian or Theophilus) and leading into the third (with figures such as Clement of Alexandria and Origen), is a particular conversation, which is primarily concerned with the content of the *kerygma*: that is, it deals with issues such as the unity, the essential goodness, the creativity and the providence of God, but it also puts forward a coherent account (or summary) of God's saving plan – which is summed up, fulfilled and effected in Christ and declared in the Holy Scriptures – and of the offer of and participation in that salvation for all.

While there is not, in any of Justin Martyr's extant works, anything which approximates to a formal credal statement – a deliberately articulated 'rule of faith' such as one finds in Irenaeus, Tertullian[4] and Origen – it is important to consider Justin Martyr, both because his works are full of minor credal statements (at least on various aspects of the *kerygma*) and because it is clear that Athenagoras was familiar with his work and probably borrowed from it. Justin speaks of the most true father of righteousness (*1 Apology* 6), the unchangeable and eternal (*1A* 13), the good and the unbegotten (*1A* 14; *2 Apology* 6), the Father and Creator of all (*1A* 12), the maker of all things in heaven and earth (*1A* 58), who created and arranged all things out of unformed matter (*1A* 10; 20 and elsewhere), who arranged the heavenly elements and appointed the divine law (*2A* 5), who created us when we were not (*1A* 10); of the Word (as first begotten Son (*1A* 23)) who took shape and became human for the sake of the human race (*1A* 63) and was called Jesus Christ (*1A* 5), our Saviour, made flesh by the word of God for our salvation (*1A* 66; *2A* 13), bringing us healing (*2A* 13), predicted by the prophets (*1A* 58), born of a virgin, crucified, dying and rising again and ascending into heaven (*1A* 31), through whom things were created, arranged and ordered (*2A* 6) – this very Son of God who is the first-born of every creature, who became human through the Virgin, who suffered and was crucified under Pontius Pilate, who died, who rose from the dead and ascended into heaven (*Dialogue with Trypho the Jew* 85

4 See L.W. Countryman, 'Tertullian and the regula fidei', *Second Century* 2 (1982): 208–27. Countryman says that these 'rules' are intended as a 'specific summary of the faith' rather than as a 'criterion of the truth' (p. 208).

– the closest to a formal creedal statement in Justin; *1A* 6 and at least thirty other times).

Irenaeus of Lyons, in the *Adversus haereses*, speaks of the church receiving from the apostles and their disciples this (rule of) faith: (faith) in one God, the Father Almighty, who made the heaven and the earth; in one Christ Jesus, the Son of God, who became incarnate for our salvation; and in one Holy Spirit, who proclaimed through the Prophets the dispensations and the advents. This Christ Jesus would raise up anew the flesh of the whole human race. Irenaeus also speaks of a just judgement for all, and of conferring immortality, as an act of grace, on the righteous and holy, who would be surrounded with everlasting glory (1.2–3).

Like Justin, Theophilus of Antioch does not have an explicit, formal rule in his *Ad Autolycum*, but he does address the matter of the *kerygma* throughout that work. Christians 'acknowledge a god, but only one, the Founder and Maker and Demiurge of this whole universe' (3.9). At 1.2 Theophilus speaks of God as 'he who can be seen by those capable of seeing him'; as nevertheless ineffable and expressible; as Light, Logos, Mind, Spirit and Wisdom (1.3). He is 'father of the righteous', uncreated, immutable (1.4). He is 'creator and maker of the universe' and makes everything out of what did not exist (1.4 and 2.4), God is seen 'through his providence and his works' (1.5). He 'sets the universe in order' (2.6). God remains perfect, is full of power, intelligence, wisdom and immortality (2.15). God heals and gives life through Logos and wisdom, and he made everything through Logos and wisdom (1.7).[5] God has the Word innate 'in his own bowels, has generated him together with his own wisdom before all else' (2.10). Both wisdom and the Word are always present with God (2.10). God's triad is made of God himself, his Word and his wisdom [= the Spirit here?]. God's command, 'Let us make!', refers to Godself, his Word and his wisdom (2.18). Yet it is through the Word that God made all things. He assumed the role of the Father in Paradise and spoke with Adam. The 'voice' of God was the Word. The Word is always innate in the heart of God. Originally, God was alone and the Word was in him (2.22). All things are taught us by the Holy Spirit, who spoke through Moses and the other Prophets (2.30). God brings about a general resurrection of all humankind (1.13). God is not contained but is himself the *locus* of the universe (2.3).

Tertullian of Carthage, in the *De praescriptionibus*, speaks of a 'rule of faith' taught by Christ and of the content of 'that which we defend', prescribing what the Christians should believe: that there is only one God, none other than the Creator of the world, who produced all things out of nothing through his own Word; his Son, brought down by the Spirit and Power of God into the Virgin Mary, was made flesh and preached a new law and a new promise of the kingdom of heaven; instead of himself, God sent the power of the Holy Spirit with glory, to take the

5 Theophilus is unusual in this coupling of Word and wisdom for the purposes of creation, though the identification of Word with wisdom was itself not unusual among the early Fathers.

saints to the enjoyment of everlasting life and of the heavenly promises, after resurrection and the restoration of the flesh (13).

For Clement of Alexandria, God is the Creator of the world, God and Father (*Stromateis* 4.13). He is the only true God who exists in the invariableness of righteous goodness (7.3.15.4). He is without beginning, the perfect beginning of the universe, the producer of the beginning. He is being; the first principle in the department of action; good; mind; the first principle of reasoning and judgement (4.25). He is the absolute first and oldest principle, the cause of all things, father of the universe, the One, indivisible, infinite, being without dimension, not having a limit; the good; mind; absolute being; father, creator and lord (5.12.81.6–82.2). The Son of the most high Father, the instructor of men, is alone teacher (4.25). He is Saviour and Lord (7.2.7.6), and also leader (7.7.35.1) – an activity of the Father (πατρική τις ἐνέργεια) (7.2.7.7); he is the true only-begotten, the express image of the glory of the King and Father (7.3.16.5).

Although Origen of Alexandria falls outside our immediate period, it is also instructive to listen to his version of a 'definite line and unmistakeable rule' and *kerygma* of the church – which, he claims, is preserved unaltered from the time of the apostles: God is one; he created and set in order all things; he caused the universe to be from nothing; he sent Lord Jesus Christ, first for the purpose of calling Israel, and secondly, after the unbelief of the people of Israel, for the purpose of calling the Gentiles too; this just and good God and Father of our Lord Jesus Christ gave the law, the Prophets and the gospels; the pre-existent Christ, begotten of the Father, was made man, was made flesh, born of a virgin and of the Holy Spirit; the Holy Spirit is united in honour and dignity with the Father and the Son; and so on.

There is here, then, a generally common approach on the part of these Fathers to what constitutes the authoritative Christian *kerygma* and this approach significantly constitutes, shapes and informs what they write. The approach is to state that there is a God who is one and creator and (re)former of all things. There is his son, Christ Jesus; the Word, incarnate for our sakes and for our salvation; and a Holy Spirit, not infrequently speaking through the Prophets. And there is the promise to all who believe of a glory to be had after a resurrection of the dead. It might also be said that all of them – particularly Justin, Irenaeus, Tertullian and Origen – are informed in what they say, at least in part, by their clear desire to differentiate what they regard as authoritative, orthodox Christian teaching from what they regard as heterodox. Thus their understandings of God, of Christ the Son, of the Spirit, of the Holy Trinity, of the meaning of resurrection, of redemption, are at least in part moved by the express need to refute the heretical teachings of the Docetists, Marcionites and Gnostics – to name a few. There is also, however, a desire to articulate the beliefs of the Christians in comprehensible terms, for the benefit of the educated pagan – who is indifferent, curious or hostile to the faith; and this desire is reflected at its best in apologetic and protreptic writings of the early Fathers (see particularly Justin, Theophilus, Tertullian, Clement of Alexandria and Origen). This, again, is *the primary conversation* in which the

Fathers find themselves: the articulation of orthodoxy both in the face of pagan incomprehension and hostility and in the face of heterodox error.

Athenagoras does not put forth an explicit or formal kerygmatic statement in the *Legatio* (nor for that matter in the *De resurrectione*) – a *rule of belief*, as it were, or a philosophical canon or criterion by which claims to orthodoxy and truth might be evaluated – as do many of his contemporaries in the faith; but, if he had, what might it have looked like? Among his co-religionists, Athenagoras would certainly assert the following beliefs:

We are not atheists, for we distinguish God from matter (4.1), the uncreated from the created (14.1), the intelligible from the perceptible (15.1); this God is uncreated, eternal (indeed alone eternal (30.3)), ever self-same (22.3), impassible (10.1), indivisible (8.3), invisible (10.1), incomprehensible (10.1), infinite (10.1), and does not consist of parts (8.3); a perfect fragrance, he has no need of anything from within or without (29.3), is inaccessible light, is totally light, a complete system (κόσμος), spirit, power (16.3) and reason, immortal, immovable, and unchangeable (22.6), one of a single nature and good, and can be contemplated by thought and reason alone (23.7); He is eternal mind; He is one and Maker and Father of this universe (and He has ordered this universe and now governs it); He is uncreated Being (τὸ ὄν) (rather than created non-being) (4.2), and without His Providence the elements are without use, no matter how beautifully they may be ordered; He has a universal and general providence over all things (24.3); He has a Son/Word (the ἰδέα and ἐνέργεια of the Father) (10.2; 10.3), by whom all things were created or came into existence, by whom the universe is ruled, who issues/proceeds from God and who is the Mind and Reason of the Father (10.2)) and inseparable from the Him; and a Spirit, the effluence (ἀπόρροια) of God (10.4), who upholds all things and gives them coherence and who provides the power and the unity for the Father and the Son; and we await a life far better than words can tell if we are brought there pure from all blame; we hope for eternal life and we believe in a resurrection; we believe that we will render (to God) an account of our present life.

In the *De Resurrectione* Athenagoras deals, of course, almost exclusively with the doctrine of the resurrection of the dead, but at 1.2 he makes a reference to some issues which some persons have 'not left free from misrepresentation'. These include the 'nature of God', '[God's] knowledge', and '[God's] activity (τὴν ἐνέ ργειαν)'. It is possible that these are references back to the primary themes of the *Legatio*. At 19.1, after Athenagoras has introduced the 'secondary' argument for the resurrection of the dead in body and soul (namely that from divine providence and the requirement of divine judgement), he speaks of 'those who recognize providence and accept the same first principles as we do, and then for some strange reason repudiate their own presuppositions' (τῶν οἰκείων ὑποθέσεων). He then refers to the 'fundamentals' (τῶν πρώτων) at 19.2 and speaks of 'laying down another principle anterior to [such fundamentals]'. And from Athenagoras' next words this prior principle would appear to be that of the purpose of the creation and the role of the Creator as 'overseer of his creatures who stands over all that is, or will be, and as a judge of both our deeds and our schemes'. Thus for the author of the *De resurrectione* it is important that God should be acknowledged as the providential overseer and judge of his creation.

Then Athenagoras does not deal with all the aspects of the primitive apostolic *kerygma* as they were addressed by other Christian writers of the second and third centuries. We need to be careful here, of course: given the – perhaps narrow – range (or focus) of apologetic aims in the *Legatio* and the doctrinal bent of the *De resurrectione*, Athenagoras was not here defending the Christian *kerygma* in its entirety. Yet when we look at the *Legatio* it is obvious that some aspects of this debate – this conversation, if you like – are present; and my observation would be that these are aspects which the Christian *kerygma* has in common with the philosophical discourse of the time (see especially Chapter 5 to follow). Athenagoras certainly deals with the unity of God (particular attention is given to this theme in chapters 5, 6, 7, 8, 9, 10, 12, 23 and 24, and primarily in a trinitarian context in chapters 6, 10, 12 and 24); with the essential goodness of God (chapters 23, 24, 25 and 26); with God as Creator and Father (principally chapters 6, 13 and 27); and with the Providence of God (principally chapters 8, 22, 24 and 25). Yet there is, by way of example, no obvious mentioning in the *Legatio* of any coherent saving *oikonomia* or plan of God fulfilled in Christ – in fact, apart from the one brief allusion to the Incarnation at 21.4 (which is employed as a subordinate prop to another unrelated argument), the earthly Christ as Jesus of Nazareth plays virtually no part at all in Athenagoras' discourse[6] nor is there is in Athenagoras any particular reference to salvation. There is nothing in Athenagoras to be compared with Justin's declaration that 'Word became human for our sake'; that he is called 'our Saviour'; 'that he was made flesh by the word of God for our salvation'; or with Irenaeus' declaration that Christ 'became incarnate for our salvation'. One might hardly know, from reading the *Legatio*, that the Christian gospel is at least primarily concerned with God as Saviour. Indeed, Athenagoras may well have borrowed from Justin, but his principal concerns are often very different from those of his co-religionist. There is, it must be said, no apparent concern in Athenagoras with the Christian experience of God's intimate engagement with people which informs much of the biblical account and presentation of a doctrine of God.

Some might protest that I am being unduly harsh here. For example at 11.3, when speaking of the love principle – indeed of the Christian virtues of love for the enemy, blessing for the reproachful and prayer for those who threaten death and violence – Athenagoras talks about the εὐδαιμονία promised to the Christians. This may perhaps have some connection with the notion of human salvation, but the connection is, in my view, not explicit. In chapter 12 he clearly talks about the ethical life of the Christian being shaped and informed (motivated even) by

[6] We note, however, Michel Spanneut's comment that, apart from Aristides, Justin and Tertullian, no other contemporary Father *'nomme Jésus'*, but all of them rather focus on and speak of the Logos–Word (*Le Stoïcisme des pères de l'église de Clément de Rome à Clément d'Alexandrie* (Paris, 1957), p. 296).

a recognition of the coming judgement: Christians, he maintains, choose a life of moderation which shows care for the other, given that they will be required to render an account of all their life to the God who made both them and the world; and great gains are to be had in the next life for a life which is gentle and kind now. At 12.3 Athenagoras speaks of the Christian neighbourly love being rooted in the expectation and recognition of potential rewards in the afterlife; for the Christians, he says, behave and live now so as to escape condemnation in the next life and believe that the life awaiting them is beyond words if they 'come there pure from all blame in this one'. Yet, while Athenagoras says at 12.3 that, in his living of a pure life, the Christian is attended only by the knowledge of him who is truly God and of the Word who issues from him – hence by a knowledge of God, Father, Son and Holy Spirit – there is nothing in this passage to suggest that the rewards in the next life are in any sense founded in Christ; rather, they are simply a *quid pro quo*: life lived well now – rewards later.

This much one can find in the philosophers. Indeed, much of what Athenagoras says concerning Christian ethics could be seen as a counter-argument to the Stoic insistence on fate and on the potential lack of personal moral responsibility. At 31.2 Athenagoras speaks of the 'good reputation' which Christians have with God, and at 31.3 he says that they live their lives taking God as their measure, 'so that each of us may be blameless and faultless before [Him]'. At 31.4 he declares that if Christians live virtuously in this life they will 'live another life better than that here', a heavenly life of abiding with God and being aided by him to remain 'changeless and impassible in soul as though we were not body'. And, conversely, if Christians 'fall with the rest of humankind, we shall live another life, worse than that here, in the realms of fire'. 'Since we hope for eternal life, we despise the things of this life, including the pleasures of the soul' (33.1). This is not salvation in Christ, or through Christ, or by Christ. It is salvation earned by the virtuousness of our present existence. The pagan would have found nothing unusual here. This is the standard *quid pro quo* by which the natural human being lives.

At *De resurrectione* 14.5, Athenagoras speaks of divine providence as 'the reward or punishment owing each person in accordance with just judgement and the end that befits human life'. At 18.2 providence as reward or punishment forms part of his secondary argument for the resurrection of the dead. At 25.5 he concludes the treatise with the comment that '[e]ach person will be examined in these matters individually, and reward or punishment will be distributed in proportion to each for lives lived well or badly.

Yet it must be said, regardless of whether Athenagoras is speaking of human salvation or not, that in any case he is not primarily concerned with a contemporary Christian ethics; for, in the *Legatio*, his dealing with a Christian ethics is intended to demonstrate how only the belief in a Christian God and the fear of judgement and condemnation in the next life impose an ethical conduct on believers; and, in the *De resurrectione*, it aims to show how the providential and just judgement of a human being requires such an entity to be, both in this life and in a renewed or resurrected one, a composite of body and soul. The consideration of ethics is therefore subordinated in the *Legatio* to the proper study of theology and of the proofs for the oneness and existence of God, and in the *de Resurrectione* to a proof for the resurrection of human beings from death.

The thought of second-century theologians such as Justin, Irenaeus and Tertullian is primarily set against the background of the Christian *kerygma*, which is expressed most neatly in the various rules of faith, part didactic, part apologetic and part polemical. The polemical part is designed both against pagans and against heretics – the latter (and particularly the Gnostics) being associated with what was seen as perversions, or adulterations, of the Christian teaching. Of this polemic against fellow 'Christians' we see no evidence in the *Legatio*. There is no talk there of particular perversions of Christian teaching; there is only a unified front for the faith. A fight against heresy is not what Athenagoras is on about here, this is not what the conversation he is engaged in is about. That conversation is not primarily (if at all) conducted with other Christian thinkers; it is predominantly a conversation with non-Christian thinkers, represented (in fact or at least in principle) by the philosopher–emperors. The *De resurrectione* is, of course, a whole other matter. It is clear from the text of this treatise that, while pagans are not entirely ignored, it is primarily the Gnostics (and the Marcionites?), with their challenge to the notion of a physical resurrection from the dead,[7] that are targeted in this work – whereas other, otherwise orthodox or 'right-believing' Christians vulnerable to Gnostic argument constitute the intended audience. Athenagoras shares this feature with those Christian writers of his own era who wrote predominantly for the sake of the community of faith and against those who would make it vulnerable by challenging its sure grasp of the hope and promise of the *kerygma*.

The Philosophers' Conversation

Dillon says that Plato did not bequeath his successors a system as much as a set of problems.[8] Yet, according to the same scholar elsewhere, Plato did leave behind him a group of clear and 'positive' principles which shaped his thought, as would be obvious from the dialogues and from the 'unwritten doctrine'.[9] These included the doctrines of the two levels of reality, Being and Becoming;[10] of the benevolence

[7] Note, however, in a Gnostic work like the *Epistle to Rheginos*, that Gnostic writers can attest to a belief in a resurrection, even if not of the physical body.

[8] J. Dillon, 'Logos and Trinity: Patterns of Platonist influence on early Christianity', in G. Vesey (ed.), *The Philosophy in Christianity* (Cambridge, 1989), p. 2.

[9] J. Dillon, *The Middle Platonists: 80 BC to AD 220*, rev. edn (London, 1996), pp. 1–11.

[10] One is also mindful of the three γένη of *Timaeus* 50c ff., where matter is implicitly included as the unformed 'receptacle' given form.

of the Deity; of the purposiveness of the universe; of the theory of Forms; and of the immortality of the soul.

We know that the second-century Middle Platonist and Athenian L. Calvenus Taurus[11] wrote commentaries on some of Plato's dialogues and in the one on the *Timaeus* he 'wrestled with the problem of Plato's meaning at *Tim.* 28b when he states that the world is created'.[12] Spanneut declares that the three themes '*qui constituent le centre de la pensée religieuse au IIe siècle*' were '*Dieu, l'homme, et le monde*'.[13] Dillon comments that '*the conflict between the doctrines of God's providence and human free will* [my italics] is perhaps the most burning philosophical and spiritual issue in second century Platonism'.[14] This gives a good picture of the Middle Platonist universe. *Daemons* and other mediating entities, too, are a major issue in Middle Platonist thought, particularly in the period under consideration (see, for example, Plutarch, *De defectu oraculorum* 416c ff. and *De genio Socratis* 593d ff.). Russell, with particular reference to Plutarch, speaks of 'a religious sentiment characteristic of the age: [namely] *the demand for mediators between god and man* [which] we may plausibly see … as a natural consequence in an anxious age, in an anxious population, of the distancing of the divine from ordinary experience that followed from the Hellenistic diffusion of philosophical ideas'.[15] Dillon concurs, remarking that '[t]he more transcendent the Supreme God becomes, the more he stands in need of other beings to mediate between him and the material world, over which, in Platonism, he always exercises a general supervision (*pronoia*)'.[16] Plutarch himself says that

> [o]n the boundary, as it were, between gods and men there exist certain natures susceptible to human emotions and involuntary changes, whom it is right that we, like our fathers before us, should regard as daemons, and, calling them by that name, should reverence them … [and[those who refuse to leave us the race of daemons make the relations of gods and men remote and alien by doing away with the 'interpretative and ministering nature' as Plato [*Politicus* 260d, *Symposium* 202e] has called it'. (*De defectu oraculorum* 416c ff.)

And the trend towards an increasing focus or emphasis on the absolute transcendence of the supreme divine entity, and thereby on the need for a mediator

---

11 Gellius calls him 'vir memoria nostra in disciplina Platonica celebratus' (Noctes Atticae 7.10).

12 J. Dillon, 'The Academy in the Middle Platonic period', *Dionysius* III (Halifax, 1979), p. 69.

13 Spanneut, *Le Stoïcisme des pères de l'église* (above, n6), p. 73.

14 J. Dillon, 'Plutarch and Second Century Platonism', in A.H. Armstrong (ed.), *Classical Mediterranean Spirituality: Egyptian, Greek, Roman.* (New York, 1986), p. 225.

15 D.A. Russell, *Plutarch*, 2nd edn, with foreword and bibliography by Judith Mossman (Bristol, 2001), p. 77.

16 Dillon, *The Middle Platonists* (above, n9). p. 216.

of sorts between the intelligible and the sensible, is particularly marked with the Neopythagoreans.

Athenagoras and the Philosophers' Conversation

What needs here to be investigated is the extent to which the thought of Athenagoras is influenced or shaped by particular philosophical conversations of the second century of the Common Era over against the possible influence or shaping by a more specifically and narrowly Christian one, one concerned primarily with the core content of the *kerygma*. Athenagoras' language and, what is more, his thought are very obviously influenced by the former conversation – particularly that of the late first and of the second century and more specifically Middle Platonism, or even Athenian Middle Platonism – and not only (if at all) for protreptic purposes, that is, for employing the language of the audience merely in order to make himself heard and understood but without also adopting it for himself. It might also be noted that, when Athenagoras at *Legatio* 7.2 speaks of poets and philosophers coming up with different doctrines on God, the Ideas, matter and the world, he is very probably not only referring to the three (plus one) ἀρχαί of the Middle Platonists, but also has in mind those particular themes which mark his own engagement with a conversation among Middle Platonists. This conversation includes the question of God (is God both transcendent and a creator?); that of the Ideas (what are Ideas – are they merely the thoughts of God?); that of Matter (is Matter properly to be regarded, like God, as a first principle?); and that of the world (has it been created in time or not? What is its relation to God, and does God care for it, does he make provision for it, when Aristotle and Epicurus seem to suggest that He does not?). And for this reason an Athenian connection for Athenagoras would be most appropriate. An Athenian he most certainly was and one who probably spent much of his time at home, where there is clear evidence of a lively and ongoing engagement in his time with philosophical problems concerning the divine, the creation, and the connection between the two.

Athenagoras is concerned, particularly in the *Legatio*, with what largely shapes his presentation of the nature of God – remembering that his primary purpose in the work is to refute allegations that the Christians are atheists:

> with the contrast between God as uncreated, eternal and intelligible Being and with Matter as created, perishable and perceptible non-being (or becoming) (see *Legatio* 4.1; 10.3; 15 and 16 *passim*; 19.2 and 19.4);
> with the nature of the world and the relationship of this world to the Creator entity (as God or not);
> with the concept of Platonic Ideas (the Son at *Legatio* 10.2 and 10.3 is described as the Idea and Energeia of the Father) and Forms (that is, forms in matter – a notion found explicitly in Alcinous and implicitly in the *Timaeus* (50e–1a), where the unqualified 'receptacle' (= matter) is said to

receive the forms), and the relationship of the Forms to matter (see *Legatio* 15.4; 22.5; 22.9; 24.2; 24.5);
with daemons (see *Legatio* 18ff.);
with the notion of the existence of intermediate and mediating entities between God and creation (such as the Logos and the Spirit – although his dealing with the latter is probably more influenced by Stoicism than by Middle Platonism; on the other hand, it is also clear that many Middle Platonists of this period drew their Logos doctrine from the Stoics, as a way of providing for a mediating entity between the intelligible and sensible worlds) (see *Legatio* 10, *passim*; 24.2);
with the argument over the temporal or non-temporal nature of creation (see on this particularly Plutarch, that 'bit of a maverick',[17] and with him Atticus (*fl.* 175), the 'Regius Professor' of Platonism at Athens and a rabid anti-Aristotelian – see his *Against those who Claim to Interpret the Doctrine of Plato through that of Aristotle*, whose reasons for postulating the creation of the world in time are tied more to the preservation of divine providence[18];
and with the the relationship between the supreme God and the Creator of the universe (with particular attention given to the Father–Creator entity of *Timaeus* 28c3–4).

All these were themes under investigation both in second-century Middle Platonism (as is clear in particular from Plutarch and Alcinous) or, to a lesser extent, in second-century Stoicism (which at this date was probably more concerned with ethics; although, as we saw above, Spanneut speaks of the three themes which constitute the centre of second-century thought – God, man and the world – particularly in relation to the Stoics[19]). We will now look at some of these key Middle Platonist themes broadly in the order outlined by Dillon above and we will examine the apparent engagement of Athenagoras with them, particularly in the *Legatio*.

Being and Becoming

From the outset of his campaign to refute the primary charge of atheism leveled against the Christians by their detractors, Athenagoras situates his apologetic endeavours squarely within the framework of the notion of God as uncreated, eternal, immutable and incorruptible over against that of matter as created, perishable and mutable. As we shall note in an later chapter, of course Plato himself – and those who for the most part claim later to follow him – seems to

---

[17] J. Dillon, '"Orthodoxy" and "eclecticism": Middle Platonists and Neopythagoreans', in J. Dillon and A.A. Long (eds), *The Question of Eclecticism: Studies in Later Greek Philosophy*. (Berkeley, 1988), p. 113.

[18] Ibid., p. 117.

[19] Spanneut, *Le Stoïcisme des pères de l'église* (above, n6), p. 73.

have regarded matter (though he does not employ the term himself) as at least on a par with God with respect to its uncreatedness. It is almost certain that he does not include matter among the perceptibles at *Timaeus* 28a which come into being and do not exist always – matter indeed probably does not figure at all in that portion of the dialogue – but rather regards Matter as the third γένος, the formless 'receptacle' of *Timaeus* 48e, alongside the Paradigm (as the intelligible and ever uniformly existent) and the Copy of the Paradigm (as subject to becoming and visible). Thus Athenagoras' implicit claim that matter is to be regarded as included in the Platonic notion of the 'becoming' is not entirely faithful to Plato himself. At 4.1 he declares, from the outset of his defence of Christian theism, that it is not rational to call atheists those who, like the Christians, distinguish between a God, uncreated and eternal (and able to be contemplated by thought and reason alone) and matter, created and perishable. The allusion to *Timaeus* 28a (and to *Timaeus* 48e and 52a and *Phaedrus* 247c) is unmistakeable and quite deliberate, even if, as we have seen just above, not entirely accurate. He follows this up at 4.2 with a contrast between the one Creator of this universe (*Timaeus* 28c), who is uncreated and Being, and the 'other' – Matter, which is created and a non-being. At 6.2, Plato is said to understand the uncreated and eternal God as one. At 7.2 Athenagoras describes the poets' and philosophers' inability to gain more than a marginal or peripheral understanding of God as an inability to find Being – a common Platonist term for the divine. At 10.1 God is again presented as uncreated, eternal and impassible (among other attributes). In chapter 15 we return once more to an explicit comparison between God as something uncreated, intelligible and a form of being and matter as something created, sensible and a form of non-being (15.1). This ability to distinguish between the two is what separates the Christians from the mob, says Athenagoras (15.2). At 15.3 we are given a number of illustrations, principally that of the potter and his clay, which expand on this essential distinction between God and matter (see Chapter 2 above). At 15.4 Athenagoras makes the points that enmattered forms (τὰ εἶδη τῆς ὕλης: litterally 'forms-in-matter'), being perishable and corruptible, must not be equated with he who is truly God and eternal. Chapter 16 continues this theme, but now the contrast is between God as Creator, described as 'perfect', and the world and its elements (matter in an ordered form). These elements, no matter how beautifully arranged and ordered, are yet changeable and perishable insofar as they are matter (16.4). At 19.1 Athenagoras characterizes the gods as being perishable, as having a beginning (and thereby as being improperly regarded as divine); then at 19.2 he declares that there is no disagreement between himself and the philosophers on this issue and quotes *Timaeus* 27d, a passage on the distinction between that which always is and does not come into being and that which comes into being but never is, or between the eternal/uncreated/intelligible and the not-always/created/perceptible. Again, we are reminded that this is not an entirely accurate reading of Plato with respect to the nature of unformed matter. At 19.3 Athenagoras brings the Stoics into play with their distinction between God conceived of as the active cause and matter represented as the passive cause; and at 19.4 he describes the latter as that which comes into being. At 22.3 he describes matter as the ruled, the perishable, unstable and changeable, and God as the ruling principle, uncreated, eternal and ever self-same. At 22.9 he contrasts the forms-in-matter with the God contemplated by reason. At 24.1 he declares that what characterizes the Christians is their teaching, which distinguishes between God and matter. At 30.3 the uncreated God is portrayed as 'alone eternal'. The Platonic distinction between being and becoming is very much at the fore of Athenagoras' theological framework and shapes much of what he has to say in the *Legatio* about God, notwithstanding the very real fact that there is a measure of misrepresentation of Plato here. The concepts of being and becoming, construed as a context, or framework, in or against which to articulate an understanding of the nature of God, is not one found in the biblical (or generally patristic) tradition.

The Goodness of God and the Purposiveness of the Universe

The purposiveness of creation and the essential goodness of the Creator are attested in Stoic and Platonic writings and are, of course, consistent with a Judaeo-Christian understanding of ontology. In no Stoic text of which I am aware is God ever described as 'good'. This is so even in the most eloquent of the Stoic reflections upon the divine being: Cleanthes' *Hymn to Zeus*. Sandbach comments that '"good" (*agathon*) was [for the Stoics] an absolute term applicable only to moral perfection'[20] and that for the Stoics there are no degrees of good or evil. Goodness only ever seems to be spoken of in terms of human morality. Plutarch does say, however, that for the Stoics 'god is preconceived and thought of not only as immortal and blessed but also as benevolent, caring and beneficent' (*On common conceptions*, 1075e). With respect to the divine purpose in creation, Long and Sedley comment that 'physics is that part of Stoic philosophy which provides the terms and theories for understanding that the world functions according to laws of an omnipresent divine nature', which designs all its products 'according to a rational plan'.[21] For the Stoics, creation proceeds according to 'a rational of constructive growth'.[22] The Stoics ascribe to God a 'providential intelligence and creativity'.[23] In Cicero's *On the nature of the gods*, the Stoic spokesman Balbus declares that it was by the providence of the gods that the world and all its constituent parts were first compounded and then governed (2.75–6). He then adds that the world was created for the sake of the gods and humans – those living beings who use reason (2.133). Thus for the Stoics the world is no random product of irrational and chance forces but the product of a rational and providential god, who indulges in creative work for the sake of the gods and other rational creatures.

20 F.H. Sandbach, *The Stoics*, 2nd edn (London, 1989), p. 28.

21 A.A. Long and D.N. Sedley, *The Hellenistic Philosophers*, 2 vols, I: *Translations of the Principal Sources with Philosophical Commentary* (Cambridge, 1987), p. 267.

22 Ibid., p. 277.

23 Ibid., p. 278.

Plato says in the *Timaeus* that God, being good, 'desired that, so far as possible, all things should be good and nothing evil' (29e–30a). A reading of the *Timaeus* might suggest that Plato's creator created simply out of a desire to create something which, like himself, was good. But, for Plato as for the Stoics, the creation is not random but purposeful. Alcinous, quoting in part from *Timaeus* 29e, says that, God looked to the form of the world as he was creating this most beautiful of all constructions, and then proceeded "through a most admirable providence and administrative care to create the world, because 'he was good'" (12.1.167.9–15). The biblical sense of the purposiveness of creation and of the goodness reflected in that creation comes out clearly from a reading of the early chapters of *Genesis*.

At 4.2 Athenagoras declares that we can see in the order, perfect harmony and arrangement of the world 'impressive signs conducive to piety'. At 5.3 he speaks of the nature of God, which fills heaven and earth with God's beauty. At 11.3 he speaks of the blessedness, the happiness (εὐδαιμονίας) provided for those who follow the teachings of God on a life characterized by love, blessing for the other, and prayer for the persecutor. At 13.2 he speaks of the God who needs nothing – save perhaps our knowledge of his creative endeavours; the perfection of the universe; and his creation of animals and of ourselves. He is the Creator who preserves and governs over all things with knowledge and great skill. Again, at 16.1 the world is spoken of as beautiful, perfect in shape and requiring worship for its maker. The world, being God's piece of craftsmanship, is beautiful but not deserving, as God is, of our worship. The elements, he says at 22.12, are beautifully ordered, but not without the providence of God. Goodness, to which the prince of matter is opposed – he continues at 24.2 – belongs to God. It is not, however, a part of God – for God has no parts (see also 8.3) – but a quality associated with God. The good is in God's province, and with it goes virtue; vice is what men and angels sometimes choose freely. God, then, is good and what he has made is, as he has made it, good, beautiful and perfect and what he has made reflects his purpose for it and no other.

At *De resurrectione* 12.5, while our author says that God 'made human being for his own sake and out of the goodness and wisdom which is reflected throughout creation', he does not necessarily suggest that this goodness and wisdom reflect qualities of the Creator, although this would not be an unreasonable reading of the text. At 12.7 he says that 'what is without purpose can have no place among the things created by God'. At 18.2 he declares that 'those who accept God as Creator of our universe must ascribe to his wisdom and justice a concern to guard and provide for all created things'.

The Ideas and the Forms

The separate concepts of ἰδέα (translated here as 'Idea') and εἶδος (translated here as 'Form') – although these terms are sometimes interchangeable in Plato's writings – are integral parts of the Platonic framework. Yet there was a lack of clarity in Plato's presentation of this basic set of concepts, which left the way open, particularly among his followers and successors (and this was certainly true of the Middle Platonists), to make of them what they would. Dillon, to whom I am greatly indebted for much of what follows in this section, declares that we do not really know 'what stage the theory of Ideas had reached in Plato's maturest thought',[24] and much of what we think we know comes to us through the somewhat unreliable prism of Aristotle's account of his master's thought. While the term ἰδέ α is employed with the usual meaning of 'form', 'idea', 'type',[25] 'aspect', 'image', 'shape' and 'framework' all throughout the dialogues – and in this respect it is used almost interchangeably at times with εἶδος (see in particular *Parmenides* 132a3 and e4; 133c8 and d4; and 135a2 and c1, where the two terms are employed together effectively to designate the same reality) – in the *Cratylus*, *Republic* and, occasionally, *Timaeus* it is employed to designate the Forms which provide the ideal paradigm for everything created. At *Cratylus* 418e7 there is a reference to the 'Form of the Good'. But the *Republic* is the dialogue where one can find Plato's theory of Forms in its most developed formulation (such as it is). There Plato speaks at 5.479a1 of the 'Form of beauty itself always remaining the same and unchanged'. At 6.486d10 there is reference to 'the ideal reality in all things'. At 6.505a2 Plato says that 'the Form of the Good is the greatest thing to learn'. At 6.507b10 it is reported that 'the Forms can be thought of but not be seen'. And then at 6.508e3 there comes the following passage:

> This reality, then, that gives their truth to the objects of knowledge and the power of knowing to the knower, you must say is the idea of good, and you must conceive of it as being the cause of knowledge and of truth in so far as known.

At 7.517c1 it is said that

> the idea of good is the cause of all that is right and beautiful in all things, giving birth in the visible world to light, and the author of light and itself in the intelligible world being the authentic source of truth and reason.

At 10.596b7 we come across the famous reference to the Form of the couch; but there is every indication in Plato that he did not subscribe to the notion that every created item has its very own Form. The evidence of the *Timaeus*, too, is patchy but of some interest. At 39e8 Plato speaks of νοῦς perceiving Forms which exist in the living creature and says that there are four such Forms. The third of these Forms, he says at 40a1, is the εἶδος which inhabits the water. This might at least suggest a notion such as that of the Forms-in-matter (or enmattered Forms), found both in Alcinous and in Athenagoras (see below; and, for the possibility of 'enmattered' Platonic forms, see above, p. 52). At 46c8 Plato speaks of the Form of the highest

---

24 Dillon, *The Middle Platonists* (above, n9), p. 47.

25 At *Republic* viii 544c8 Plato speaks of a 'type of government' using this terminology: ἰδέαν πολιτείας.

good. There is, of course, his somewhat enigmatic treatment of the 'paradigm' or model after which the Demiurge constructed the universe (28a ff.). Nowhere in that passage does Plato employ the term ἰδέα (or for that matter εἶδος), but this is clearly what he has in mind. This paradigm is also the cause; it is uniform and self-identical; it is eternal, the best of all causes, apprehensible by thought and reason, and good; it is that living creature of which all intelligible living creatures are a portion; it is the fairest of all and the most perfect. Yet our concern here is not particularly with Plato's own understanding of the Forms, nor with that of his successors down to just before the Christian era, but rather with those Platonists with whom Athenagoras would have dealt as his contemporaries.

'With the assimilation of the Platonic Demiurge to the Stoic Logos', Dillon says, 'the situating of the Ideas in the mind of God becomes more or less inevitable'[26] and, given the increasing distinction between the first and the second Gods in the ontologies of the Middle Platonist period, 'the Ideas gravitate towards the mind of the second, demiurgic God'.[27] Antiochus of Ascalon (born *c.*130 BCE), who drew the Middle Academy away from its flirtation with Scepticism, identified the Platonic Forms with the Stoic 'cognitive perceptions'. An Antiochian in Cicero's *De oratore* speaks of an 'intellectual ideal' graspable by the mind and imagination and Cicero identifies them with Plato's '*ideai*', which themselves exist forever and are contained (*contineri*) by intellect and reason (8ff.). Loenen holds to the view that 'the conception of the ideas as thoughts of God, in a pantheistic sense ... has been introduced into Platonism by Antiochus'.[28] While it is almost certain that this notion of the Platonic Forms as the thoughts of God goes back to a stage before Antiochus, it is absolutely certain that it does not go back to Plato himself – or to any ancient philosopher for that matter.[29] The Roman philosopher Seneca (2 BCE–65 CE) speaks in his *Epistles* of what he describes as Plato's six 'existents'. These are:

> 'what is', which cannot be grasped by sight or touch or by any of the senses but by thought alone;
> 'pre-eminent being';
> those things which exist 'in the proper sense of that term', namely the *ideai* ('ideas');
> 'form';
> existence 'in the usual sense of the term' like that of cattle, human beings, and things; and

26 Dillon, *The Middle Platonists* (above, n9), p. 48.

27 Ibid.

28 J.H. Loenen, 'Albinus' metaphysics. An attempt at rehabilitation. II: The sources of Albinus' metaphysics', *Mnemosyne* IV.10 (1957): 45.

29 See R. Miller Jones, 'The Ideas as the thoughts of God', *Classical Philology* 21 (1926): 317–26 and A.N.M. Rich, 'The Platonic Ideas as the thoughts of God', *Mnemosyne* IV.7 (1954): 123–33.

what exists 'fictitiously', like void or time (58.16–22).

The items of the third class – the *ideai*, which exist 'properly' – are countless and situated beyond our sight. They are that from which and that according to their pattern of which all visible things are created. They are immortal, unchangeable and inviolable. And Plato's conception of a Form, according to Seneca, is that 'it is the everlasting pattern of those things which are created by nature' (58.19). This last statement lines up with Alcinous (9.2.163.23f.) and with Diogenes Laertius, who says that Plato 'assumes the Forms to be causes and principles by virtue of which the world of natural objects is what it is' (3.77).

Of Plato's fourth class of existents Seneca says that, while the '*idea* is the pattern from which things are fashioned, the 'form' (the *idos*) is the shape taken from the pattern and embodied in the work (58.20). This would be both Alcinous' and Athenagoras' distinction between the transcendent form – the Form – and the immanent form – the form: they may have thought they found the latter at *Timaeus* 50e and 51a (and also, but less likely, at the end of the *Phaedo*).

Dillon sees this division to be a part of a regular Middle Platonist metaphysical scheme.[30] In *Epistle* 65 Seneca says that Plato added a fifth cause to Aristotle's four, namely the '*idea*' (65.7). 'God has within himself these patterns of all things, and his mind comprehends the harmonies and the measures of the whole totality of things which are to be carried out'. In the *Parmenides* Plato indeed spoke of such forms – there he employed the term εἴδη – which exist in nature as patterns (paradigms). Philo understands the Ideas to be the intelligible cosmos taken as a whole.[31] Plutarch (*c.*45–*c.*125 CE) says that the Ideas, as transcendent and 'in themselves', are the thoughts of God (*de Iside et Ossiride* 373a–b) and, as immanent, are the content of the immanent Logos. Atticus (*fl.* 176 CE), a contemporary of Athenagoras, appears in Fragment 9 (815a ff.) to suggest that the Ideas are the thoughts (νοήματα) of God – although later on Porphyry will claim that for Atticus the Ideas are outside the divine intellect. Dillon proposes, as a solution to this dilemma, that Atticus may have regarded the Ideas (the paradigms) as external, though necessarily subject to God – who for Atticus possesses a transcendent simplicity – and may have wished to distinguish them from the very essence of God.[32] Alcinous (Albinus), according to Mansfeld, 'distinguishes between ἰδέαι, transcendental ideas separate from matter which are identified with the thoughts of the transcelestial and first intellect, and immanent εἴδη, forms which are inseparable from matter (though conceivable by our mind)'.[33] At 4.7.155.40 of the *Didaskalikos* Alcinous speaks of the primary, transcendent Ideas (αἱ ἰδέαι) and of the secondary forms in matter (τὰ εἴδη τὰ ἐπὶ τῇ ὕλῃ) which are inseparable from matter. At 9.1.163.14 he says that the ἰδέα is considered in relation to God's thought, and at 9.2.163.24

30 Dillon, *The Middle Platonists* (above, n9), p. 137.

31 Ibid., p. 158.

32 Ibid., pp. 255f.

33 J. Mansfeld, 'Three notes on Albinus', in *Théta-Pi* I (Leiden, 1971), p. 67.

that ἰδέα 'is defined as an eternal model of things that are in accordance with nature'. God, he says, is mind and 'has thoughts' (9.3.163.33). Apuleius in the *De Platone* speaks of Ideas as being simple, eternal and incorporeal, and the models of all things; but he makes no mention of them as the thoughts of God (6). He says nothing, however, which would contradict that concept. Nicomachus of Gerasa, a Neopythagorean, says that the Ideas are 'set in the mind of God'.[34] He also says that God is both a Mind and a Demiurge and, unlike the other Neopythagoreans, he does not distinguish between God and the Demiurge. In his review of Platonist thought, the Christian Hippolytus of Rome says that the Platonic Ideas are the thoughts of God (*Refutation of All Heresies*, 1.19). In the time of Athenagoras, then, it was commonplace to regard the 'Ideas' as thoughts of God and to treat the Forms as 'Ideas' immanent in matter.

At 7.2 Athenagoras acknowledges the philosophers' wrangling over first principles: he lists the traditional Platonist three *archai* – God, matter and the Forms (περὶ εἰδῶν)[35] – and then he adds a fourth one which, as we have seen with Spanneut above, was of increasing concern in the second century: the world. It is also worthy of note, as indicated earlier, that Athenagoras' listing of these four *archai*[36] may have been motivated by his desire to provide a clear statement of the topics within the Middle Platonist 'conversation' he wished to engage with, at least insofar as to provide an acknowledgement of the *archai* themselves. It is clear that Athenagoras, like Alcinous (at 4.7.155.40), distinguished the 'Ideas' (αἱ ἰδέαι) from the Forms, considered 'Forms-in-matter' (τὰ εἴδη τὰ ἐν τῇ ὕλῃ): the former would be transcendent and the latter immanent. It may in fact be that Athenagoras' employment of εἶδος rather than ἰδέα here may be a way of underlining that, for him, the philosophers did not actually know the true 'Idea' but merely those objects which are modeled in some way or other on that primary and sole 'Idea'. For Athenagoras, the Son–Word is alone the 'Idea', serving as image–model–paradigm for the creation. He alone is the perfect exemplar (10.2 and 10.3). At 10.2 Athenagoras says that the Son of God – unlike in the mythmaking of the poets, where the gods (and by implication their offspring) are no better than human beings – is the Logos of the Father ἐν ἰδέᾳ and 'in activity' (ἐνεργείᾳ), for all things come into being in his likeness (πρὸς αὐτοῦ) and through him (δι' αὐτοῦ). Thus the Son as *idea* and *energeia* is both the model or paradigm of the created order and the means by which it comes to be. And this Son is also the *nous* and *logos* of the Father, the God who can be apprehended by *nous* and *logos* alone. At 10.3 it is said that the Son is the first-begotten of the Father – the God, or eternal mind – and came forth to serve as *idea* and as *energeia* for everything material which was without qualities. This Son, then, as *idea* and as *energeia*, gives form to unformed matter, matter without quality. Matter so formed is the 'forms-in-

34 Dillon, *The Middle Platonists* (above, n9), p. 355.

35 It is not without interest here that he employs the term εἴδη rather than ἰδέαι.

36 Athenagoras actually refers to these at 7.2 as dogmas (ἐδογμάτισεν), but at 7.1 he makes clear reference to the *archai*.

matter' (τὰ εἴδη τῆς ὕλης). These immanent Forms – what Schoedel translates as 'material forms' and what we find (though not with the terminology of 'matter') in the *Timaeus* (at 50e–1a, where the unqualified 'receptacle' (matter) receives the forms) – we find at *Legatio* 15.4; 22.5; 22.9; 24.2; 24.5. At 15.4 the forms-in-matter are the product of unformed matter given articulation, form (σχῆμα), and order by God as Creator (15.2). At 22.5, in a discussion of the Stoic notion of the pervading of matter by the spirit of God, the 'composite entities' thus formed from unformed matter, the 'forms-in-matter (τὰς παραλλάξεις)', will be the body of God. At 22.9 Athenagoras condemns those who are preoccupied with 'forms-in-matter' (τὰ εἴδη τῆς ὕλης) while giving no attention to the God contemplated by reason. At 24.2 the spirit opposed to God (τὴν ἀντίθεον) was created by God and entrusted with the oversight of matter and of the forms-in-matter. At 24.5 this spirit is called the 'prince over matter and forms-in-matter'. Such forms-in-matter are perishable and corruptible (15.4 and 22.5), and their administration is entrusted to the spirit opposed to God (24.2 and 24.5); they are contrasted with God, who is contemplated by reason (22.9). Athenagoras then operates within a Middle Platonist framework, but gives it a very Christian edge. There is an *idea*, but that entity is the Son of God alone, the image and the mediator of the creative purpose and activity of God. And the Forms, as in Alcinous, are the immanent copies of the paradigmatic *idea*.

Fate, Providence and Free Will

Dillon maintains that fate and freewill were among the basic questions addressed in Middle Platonism.[37] He says that any Platonist (although he is speaking particularly of Philo) 'must resist Stoic determinism, and yet reconcile the doctrine of the freedom of the will with that of the Providence of God'.[38] He also acknowledges that few of them did it particularly well and comments that 'Philo gives us the first defence of the Platonist position, which asserts both freedom of the will and the existence of Providence against Stoic *heimarmenē* with more vigour than logical force'.[39] '[Y]et every Platonist wished to maintain the doctrine of God's Providence'.[40] While the Middle Platonists, he consistently argues, did not address the dilemma particularly well, '[o]nly Plotinus, in *Enneads* III 2–3, comes seriously to grips with the problem, and he only succeeds ultimately in demonstrating its insolubility'.[41]

Cicero declares in *On Fate* (39–43) that ancient philosophers adopted different views on fate. Some believed that 'all things came about by fate, in such a way that that fate applied the force of necessity'. This view was that of Democritus,

37 Dillon, *The Middle Platonists* (above, n9), p. 320.

38 Ibid., p. 166.

39 Ibid., p. 45.

40 Ibid.

41 Ibid., p. 211.

Heraclitus, Empedocles and Aristotle. Others, he says (though he does not name them), 'believed that there are voluntary motions of our minds, free from all fate'. Chrysippus the Stoic, he maintains, wished to drive a middle path through these two views but, although he personally inclined towards the former, he ended up 'unintentionally asserting the necessity of fate'. Alexander, in his own *On Fate* (181,13–182,20), says that the Stoics 'deny that man has the freedom to choose between opposite actions and say that it is what comes about *through* us that is in our power'. Everything one does 'is done of necessity'. Dillon comments that for Chrysippus chance and free will are illusory. Free will is 'subjective'; 'we only appear to ourselves to make decisions', there is no underlying reality.[42] The Epicurean, say Long and Sedley, would maintain 'that moral responsibility is flatly incompatible with determinism'.[43] Diogenes of Oenoanda, a second century CE Epicurean philosopher, declared that the major issue was that 'if fate is believed in, that is the end of all censure and admonition, and even the wicked will not be open to blame' (32.1.14–3.14). For the Stoics, on the other hand, determinism and moral responsibility not only are compatible but presuppose one another. For them 'moral goodness largely consists in living willingly and to the best of your ability the life assigned to you'. For Chrysippus, 'fate … is the set of external causes which, by acting upon him, work to bring about their destined effects. But since these external causes are no more than triggering causes, he cannot hold them in any strong sense *responsible* for his actions, let alone sufficient to necessitate them. The primary cause is himself'.[44] Gellius (7.2.3) reports that in book 4 of his *On Providence* Chrysippus said that 'fate is a certain natural everlasting ordering of the universe'. Quintus Cicero, defending the Stoic theory of divination, claims that 'nothing has happened which was not going to be' and that 'nothing is going to be of which nature does not contain causes working to that very thing about' (Cicero, *On Divination* 1.125–6). Fate, then, for the Stoic, is not the 'fate' of superstition but of physics. Stobaeus reports that for Chrysippus fate is 'a power of breath, carrying out the orderly government of all' and, among other things, 'the rationale of providence's acts of government in the world' (I79,1–12). 'Nothing', according to Alexander (*On Fate* 191.30–192.28), 'in the world exists or happens causelessly' for the Stoics. Long and Sedley suggest that, for Chrysippus, however, 'fate should not be seen as the entire causal nexus but merely as the set of triggering or "preliminary" causes'.[45] The Stoics, they say, faced problems similar to those confronted by Christian theologians: 'how to reconcile the existence of vice with a world providentially organized to be the best possible'.[46] They rejected the notion of original sin, but among their various defences was the notion that 'vice

42 Ibid., pp. 84f.

43 A.A. Long and D.N. Sedley, *The Hellenistic Philosophers* (above, n21), Vol 1, p. 392.

44 Ibid., p. 393.

45 Ibid., p. 343.

46 Ibid., p. 386.

is compatible with cosmic order, since without it its opposite could not exist'.[47] Pseudo-Plutarch (*De fato*) speaks of three providences: the primary, that of the thought or mind of the primordial god; the secondary, that of the inferior gods (see *Timaeus* 42d–e); and the tertiary, that of the daemons as watchers and overseers. Apuleius in his *De Platone*, says Dillon, has a primary providence, that of the supreme god, a secondary, that of the lesser gods appointed by God, and implies a third, that of the daemons (1.12).

Athenagoras has much to say, in both treatises, on the matter of providence and free will and intends thereby to construct a doctrine of accountability and, in the *De resurrectione*, of divine justice. At *Legatio* 5.3 he speaks of the God recognized by Euripides, whose spirit guides his works. At 6.2 he says that Plato recognizes the God whose Word creates all things and whose Spirit upholds them. At 8.4 he speaks of the maker of the world as being above all created things and as governing that world through the exercise of his providence over the things he has created. At 8.8 he makes the assertion that only the creator of something can exercise providence over it. At 10.1 he speaks of the God who created, adorned, and now rules the universe through his Word, and at 10.5, of the angels and ministers set by God to be concerned with the elements, the heavens and the world, along with all that is in it and its good order. At 12.1 he speaks of God presiding over the human race and declares that this provides the basis for human ethics. At 13.3 he declares that God as Creator both preserves and governs all things with knowledge and skill. At 19.3 he identifies the Stoics' active cause with God as Providence. At 22.12 he affirms that the elements, no matter how beautifully ordered, are of no value or use without the Providence of God.

From chapter 24 on of the *Legatio*, after he has indicated that the spirit opposed to God was given the administration of matter and material things, he speaks of the general and universal Providence over all things exercised by God alone and of the particular Providence which is given to angels called into existence for this purpose (24.3)[48], Athenagoras says that these angels, like human beings, have the choice of opting for vice or for virtue (thus he takes seriously the notion of *free will* both in relation to humans and in relation to angels–daemons): some take their appointed office seriously and choose virtue, while others – like the prince of matter, the ἀντίθεος – are untrustworthy and choose vice. Athenagoras would almost certainly have embraced the saying from *Republic* 10.617e, much loved by Platonists: 'The blame is with the chooser; God is blameless.'[49] Some angels, says Athenagoras, all of whom were created free by God – that is, as αὐθαίρετοι, or 'self-chosen' and autonomous – remained true to the tasks given them by God, while others violated both their own nature and their divinely appointed office (24.5). This latter category included the spirit opposed to God – the prince of matter and

[47] Ibid.

[48] Is there in Athenagoras an implied tertiary providence; the first being that of God, the second that of the lesser gods, and the third that of the daemons?

[49] This is also quoted by Justin Martyr at *1A* 44.8.

of material things (24.2), who operated wickedly – and others, stationed at the first firmament: for instance those who lusted after maidens and allowed themselves to be conquered by the flesh, and from whose union with maidens came the so-called 'giants'. Both the angels and the daemons who have fallen from heaven and can no longer rise above it – and these comprised the daemons as souls of the giants, offspring of angels and maidens, who wandered the earth – produce movements: the daemons, movements akin to their natures; and angels, movements akin to their lusts (25.1).[50] As a result, daemonic movements and activities bring in their train wild attacks; men are moved from within and from without, some one way and some another, some as individuals and some as nations, one at a time or all together. This happens because of our kinship with matter and of our affinity with the divine (*simul*, 25.3); and this is part of Athenagoras' explanation of the fact that humankind's choices are both fated (providenced) and free. Yet each element in the world is the product of reason and goes not beyond its appointed order. As a result of reason, man is a well-ordered creature *to the extent that he depends on his creator* (25.4). His nature in origin has one common reason, and his bodily form does not go beyond the law established for it. The end of life remains the same for all those who are alike. Yet, *to the extent that it depends on the reason peculiar to each individual person* and to the activity of the ruling prince – the spirit opposed to God's goodness (24.2) – and of his attendant daemons, one person is swept this way, another that, even though each has the same reasoning (λογισμός) within.

Thus does Athenagoras reconcile the impact of fate (or providence) and free will. You choose, but your choice has predetermined outcomes (see Alcinous 26.1.179.1ff.). As Dillon says of the treatment of this matter by Apuleius of Madaura, '[f]ate becomes simply a general tendency for certain consequences to follow certain actions'.[51] For Justin Martyr, 'each person goes to everlasting punishment or salvation according to the value of their actions' (*1A* 12). Justin addresses the question of whether anything that happens happens by a fatal necessity (*1A* 43). '[P]unishments, and chastisements, and good rewards', he says, 'are rendered according to the merit of each person's actions'. For if all happens by fate, nothing is in our own power. 'For if it be fated that this person, for example, be good, and this other evil, neither is the former meritorious nor the latter to be blamed' (ibid.). The human race, he says, must have the power to avoid evil and choose good by free choice. 'But this we assert is inevitable fate, that they who choose the good have worthy rewards, and they who choose the opposite have their merited awards' (ibid.). For God gave choice over good and evil (*1A* 44). Each person acts rightly, or sins, by free choice (*2A* 7.3). The Stoics, Justin says, maintained that all things take place according to the necessity of fate. But this cannot be, he protests; for God in the beginning made the race of angels and of

---

[50] At 25.2 Athenagoras maintains with Aristotle that a sub-lunar divine providence does not operate.

[51] Dillon, *The Middle Platonists* (above, n9), p. 323.

men endowed with free will (*2A* 7.4). 'And this', he says, 'is the nature of all that is made, to be capable of vice and virtue' (ibid.).

In chapters 11 and 12 of the *Legatio*, Athenagoras, speaking of the proper ethical life of the Christian, underpins the living of such a life with a reference to the fact that Christians are 'attended only by the knowledge (εἰδέναι) of him who is truly God and of the Word that issues from him' (12.3). They are, then, given the means by which they might lead the life required of them by God. God equips for what God demands. This knowledge of God, of who God is and of what God requires, is sufficient. But that humankind can go astray is equally clear, and no fault of God. For Alcinous, fate does not mean that something will happen automatically, of necessity, but rather that, if a person should choose a particular life and act in a particular way, certain consequences will automatically follow (26.1.179.1ff.). As Justin puts it, 'if the word of God foretells that some angels and men shall be certainly punished, it did so not because it foreknew that they would be unchangeably [wicked], but because God had created them so' (*Dialogue* 141). This is very much how Athenagoras resolves the issue of fate, free will and providence. It would seem that here Athenagoras takes a similar line to that of Justin, but whether he does so consciously or because both are taking part in the conversation beyond the Christian one cannot be said.

At *De resurrectione* 14.5, Athenagoras speaks of divine providence as 'reward or punishment owing each person in accordance with just judgement and the end that befits human life'. At 18.1 he develops an argument from justice to support the thesis of resurrection: it is an argument from that notion of providence according to which God judges human beings who have lived well or ill. At 18.2 Athenagoras says that those who accept God as Creator of the universe must ascribe to his wisdom and justice a concern to guard and provide for all created things; the Creator's care extends to everything, the invisible and the visible, the small and the great.

Daemons

For the first- century CE Stoic philosopher Posidonius, a daemon was to be likened to the divine ruler of the world and therefore could be called a 'god'.[52] In later Middle Platonism, the 'young gods' were regarded either as a sub-rational 'world soul' or as a class of daemons subservient to the 'world soul'.[53] Plutarch tells us in the treatise *On the Obsolescence of Oracles* (416c–d) that Xenocrates maintained that between the gods and the humans there were 'certain natures susceptible to human emotions and involuntary changes' and that these were called daemons (frg. 23). These daemons possessed therefore both human emotion and divine power. They were the mean between gods and humans, sharing in immortality with the former and in passions with the latter. But they could, according to Xenocrates as

52 F.H. Sandbach, *The Stoics* (above, n20), p. 136.

53 Dillon, *The Middle Platonists* (above, n9), p. 7.

depicted in Plutarch's treatise *On Isis and Osiris* (360e), be either good or evil, virtuous or vicious. For him, 'such phenomena as days of ill omen, and festivals which involve self-laceration, lamentation, obscenity, or such atrocities as human sacrifice can only be explained by postulating the existence of evil spirits that take delight in such things and who must be placated' (316e).[54] The Middle Platonic 'cosmos', says Dillon, 'was filled with subordinate, intermediate beings, the race of daemons'.[55] Plato himself speaks of the daemons as intermediaries between the gods and humankind and acting as interpreters from one to the other (*Symposium* 202e); their origins are, he says, too great to discover or declare, but according to the ancients they are the descendants of the gods (*Timaeus* 40d–e). They are the 'created gods'. Dillon maintains that there were two prevailing theories on daemons in the Middle Platonist period. One, represented by Xenocrates, saw them as 'permanent fixtures' in the universe, intermediate beings between gods and humans; the other, represented by Plutarch (*De Iside et Ossiride* 361c) and Apuleius, saw them as souls, either heading upwards on the way to purification (and thus divinization) or heading downwards for embodiment on the earth.[56] On both theories, daemons can be evil as well as good. Yet evil daemons, as opposed to those acting as avenging agents of God, are not really Platonic conceptions, 'but rather a concession to popular belief' or the result of Persian dualist influence.[57] The 'avenging' daemons are the more usual Platonic construct. Yet, whatever daemons may be in the Platonist universe, there is a need for intermediary entities between God and humankind, so that God may not be contaminated by contact with matter. Apuleius offers his most considered thought on the subject of daemons in his *De deo Socratis*. He regards them as composed of air (chs 9–12), but air of the purest quality. In chapter 13 he describes them as subject to passions: able to be roused to anger and pity, placated by gifts and enraged by abuse. They are 'animate, of rational mind, of spirit passionate, of body aery, of duration eternal'. They share the first three qualities with the humans, the first two and the last with the gods, so that the fourth is what is peculiar to them. Apuleius does not explicitly say that they can be evil. In chapters 15 and 16 he distinguishes three types of daemon: the human soul; souls which have departed their bodies and are good or bad (though not inherently so); and daemons which never enter bodies at all. This last type, the guardian daemon, is the most exalted of all. Its distinction from the *nous* daemon immanent in the individual is not too clearly drawn in Apuleius. For Alcinous, the *nous* daemons are the 'created gods' of *Timaeus* 41a, present in each element, some visible, some not (15.1.171.15ff.). It is to them that the administration of the entire sublunar and terrestrial spheres is assigned. They are created by God, they are his children, and all omens and presages, all dreams and oracles, all artificial divination performed by mortals derive from them (15.2.171.22f.).

---

54 Ibid., p. 32.

55 Ibid., p. 46.

56 Ibid., pp. 46 f.

57 Ibid., p. 47.

At 18.1 Athenagoras begins an exploration of the verifiable reports to the effect that there are 'activities' associated with the statues of certain gods. He then looks, from 18.2 to 22.12, at the question of the relationship between these 'gods' and their hardcopy images, while he is on his way towards concluding that it is not the 'gods' – which for him do not exist – who 'activate' the images (mainly statues), but the daemons. His particular discussion of the daemons themselves, with reference in part to the 'activities' or 'movements' associated with the statues in question, continues at 23.1, after he hasaccepted as fact that there are discernible/visible 'effects' related to the statues but that these cannot come from non-existent gods. First he explores the distinction between God and the created 'gods' and demons (23.4f.). For this purpose he brings as witnesses Thales – who distinguished God as Mind of the World, daemons as 'psychic substances' and heroes as 'souls separated from humans' – and Plato (*Timaeus* 40ab and 40de) – who distinguishes the uncreated God (and the planets and stars as created gods) from the daemons, offspring of the gods who have come into existence from the perceptible realms of earth and heaven (23.7). At 24.2, where he talks of the Trinity for the first time, Athenagoras mentions 'other powers' concerned with matter and who operate through it, together with the chief spirit opposed to the goodness of God, the ἀντίθεον); but this spirit is not to God what Strife is to Love in Empedocles, or what night is to day in nature; he was created by God, as were the rest of the angels, and he was entrusted with the administration of matter and of material things. Athenagoras describes how, in the context of this entrusting of the things of the world to angels and other ministers created for the purpose, the chief opposing angel – later called the prince of matter (24.5) – was given the administration of matter and of forms-in-matter. But this 'prince', like other angels who proved unworthy of God's trust and chose vice over virtue, violated his own nature and his divinely granted office and 'fell' from heaven (25.1). He and these other 'fallen' angels can no longer rise back to heaven, and the souls of the giants – born of the union of fallen angels and maidens – are demons who wander the earth (though I do not believe that these are, for Athenagoras, the only daemons there are, nor that all daemons are thereby necessarily evil). These demons have become the attendants of the prince of matter (25.4).

It is these evil daemons, says Athenagoras, who drag men to images (26.1) and make them usurp the names of the gods they represent (26.2). Athenagoras quotes a proverbial expression: 'When the daemon prepares evil for a man, he first perverts his mind.' Thus the 'activities' associated with the statues of the gods are caused not by the gods themselves (who in any case do not exist) but by daemons. Finally, when the souls of men attach themselves to the spirit of matter and blend with it and do not look to the things of heaven and to their maker but down to earthly things, they are ripe for exploitation by the demons and their master (27.1). When these souls are directed not by reason but by fantasy, delusion and illusory images and, as weak and docile, are ignorant, unlearned in sound teaching and unable to contemplate the truth and to understand who the Father and Creator of all things is, then the demons associated with matter exploit this situation, delude such men, and take credit for the activities associated with the statues – even the beneficial ones such as healing (27.2f.). There is, then, in Athenagoras' dealing with the matter of daemons, much that he holds in common with Middle Platonism, although his primary concern here is with those who are evil in purpose and activity.

Among the Christian theologians of the second century, Justin Martyr appears to regard all daemons as evil. He speaks of the evil daemons as having instigated the allegations made against Christians (*1A* 5), having defiled women and having corrupted boys. He says in that context that those persons who do not use reason but are struck with fear by the daemons call the daemons gods and call them by the divine names which the daemons themselves have chosen. Socrates, he says, tried to deliver men from the daemons, but the latter conspired to bring about his death. The wicked daemons, he declares, are allied to the lust of wickedness, which is in every person and leads them to vice and to the accusations against Christians (*1A* 10). Daemons imitate Christian baptism in the temples (*1A* 62). Angels, having been appointed to the care of men and of all things under heaven by God (*2A*5.2), transgressed this appointment and were captivated by the love of women (see above). They begat children by these women, children called daemons. The latter subdued the human race to themselves by various means (which he lists); and poets and mythologists, ignorant of this, ascribe their activities to God himself (*2A* 5.3). The wicked angels appoint laws conformable to their own wickedness, and the 'right reason' (= the Word = Christ) combats them (*2A* 9.4). These angels rebel against God and the 'gods of the nations are daemons', says the Psalmist (96.5) – 'the gods of the people are idols', echoes Justin (*Dialogue* 79). Athenagoras, then, whatever his affinity with the philosophers on these topics, could easily have been influenced by his co-religionists.

The *de Resurrectione* makes no mentioning of *daemons*.

There is also, among the things Athenagoras also expressed his mind about, a number of issues which were part both of a Middle Platonist conversation of the first and second centuries of the Common Era and – just as much – of the Christian conversation of the time. These issues included the relationship between the Supreme God entity and the Creator/Demiurge; and question whether these two should be identified; the problem of whether the 'creation' of the world was to be understood 'in time' or as continuously in process; and that of whether creation was to be understood as 'from nothing'.

The Supreme God and the Creator

A major aspect of the conversation within first and second century Middle Platonism is the dispute between those like Plutarch, Atticus and Nicomachus, who identify the supreme God and the Creator, and those like Harpocration, Alcinous and the Neopythagoreans Moderatus and Numenius, who distinguish, even to the extent of separating as distinct entities, the 'Creator and Father' of *Timaeus* 28c3-4. It is also broadly agreed that Plato himself, though the matter is far from clear, would have sided with those who would not regard the Demiurge as the Supreme God. For

Athenagoras, however, there could of course be no question but that the Supreme God and the Demiurge were one. He would be required to do this identification between Supreme God and Demiurge at the very least over against Gnostics and Marcionites. The fact that he does not identify the two explicitly in the *Legatio* is further testimony to the fact that, unlike many of his contemporary Christian theologians whose primary concern appears to have been to establish the Christian *kerygma* in the face of heretical claims about the divine being (in particular the separation between God and Demiurge), his primary engagement (even as a Christian) was in a Middle Platonist, not in an intra-Christian conversation. Justin Martyr, for example, in his *First Apology*, while dealing with the arguments of the philosophers in his own presentation of a doctrine of God as both supreme being and Creator, nevertheless engages also with Christian heresy, condemning Marcion of Pontus first at 26.5, for teaching that there is a God greater than the Creator and for denying (aided by demons) that God is the Creator of this universe; and then at 58.1, where he repeats that only a demonic influence could have caused his opponent to deny that God is the Creator of all things and the Christ predicted by the prophets is the Creator's Son, and to teach instead that there is another God beside the Creator and another Son beside Jesus. When one reads the *Legatio* – though this is not true also of the *De resurrectione* – one might never know that there was such a thing as Christian heresy.

Creation of the Universe 'in Time'?

Among the Middle Platonists of the first and second centuries, there was also a debate between those like Plutarch, Atticus (for whom this position is demanded by the reality of divine providence) and Harpocration – the minority temporalists – who argued that the words of Plato in the *Timaeus* were meant to suggest that the creation of the universe was an event 'in time', and those like Calvenus Taurus, Alcinous, Apuleius and others – the majority atemporalists – who believed that the language of Plato was intended 'for the sake of instruction' and not as the descriptor of an event 'in time', but rather of an event which was always in a state of coming to be. For Athenagoras, the creation of the world, as witnessed in the Christian scriptures, is an event 'in time'.

Creation out of Nothing (creatio ex nihilo)

From the time of Parmenides at least, it was clear to Greek philosophers that *ex nihilo nihil fit*.[58] And even for Jewish and Christians theologians until the latter part of the second century, talk of a 'creation out of nothing' did not necessarily imply anything different. Bray declares that '[i]t is true that Hellenistic Jews could talk of a creation by God "out of nothing", but the formula was demonstrably

---

58 G. Bray, *Creatio ex nihilo: The Doctrine of 'Creation out of Nothing' in Early Christian Thought* (Edinburgh, 1994), p. 8.

not meant in an ontological sense and in no way excluded the acceptance of an eternal material for the world'.[59] That Philo of Alexandria for example 'postulates a pre-existent matter alongside God'[60] is clear from the following passage from *De opificio mundi*:

> the passive part [as against the active cause, the perfectly pure and unsullied Mind of the universe] is in itself incapable of life and motion [but] when [it is] set in motion and shaped[61] and quickened by Mind, changes into the most perfect masterpiece, namely this world. (9)

Indeed, continues Bray, it was '[o]nly with Christians theologians of the [latter part] of the second century [that] the traditional saying, that God created the world out of nothing, takes on a principled ontological sense: the expression "out of nothing" now meant that absolutely, and excluded the idea that the creator had merely imposed form on a pre-existent material'.[62] The first Christian theologian known to have challenged the suggestion that God in his capacity of Creator must be thought of as other than a human artist (like a potter working with clay) was Theophilus of Antioch.[63] Bray declares that a number of Christian theologians – Justin, Athenagoras, Hermogenes and Clement of Alexandria – who had been trained in Platonism 'could hold that acceptance of an unformed matter was entirely reconcilable with biblical monotheism and the omnipotence of God'.[64] In the *First Apology* at 10.2 Justin declares that Christians have been taught 'that [God] in the beginning did of his own goodness, for humankind's sake, create all things out of unformed matter'. At 20.4 he says that 'all things have been produced and arranged into a world by God'; nevertheless, he may be suggesting by this that unformed matter is itself created out of nothing. At 59.1 he notes that Plato himself borrowed from the prophets 'his statement that God, having altered matter which was shapeless, made the world'. And in the *Second Apology* at 6.3 he speaks of God having through the Word 'created and arranged all things', again implying that God may have first created from nothing unformed matter which was then given form. Theophilus, Irenaeus and Tertullian (against Hermogenes and in support of the resurrection of the dead) all defended the doctrine of *creatio ex nihilo* literally understood, and with them 'the defence of the omnipotence and unity of God inevitably demands the proposition that matter is also created by God'.[65] And thus 'from the end of the second century [*creatio ex nihilo*] becomes with astonishing

---

59 Ibid., p. xi.

60 Ibid., p. 10.

61 At *Legatio* 15.2 Athenagoras speaks of God 'the potter' giving articulation, shape and order to matter.

62 Bray, *Creatio ex nihilo* (above, n58), p. 22.

63 Ibid., p. 74. See also p. 147.

64 Ibid.

65 Ibid., p. 148.

speed the self-evident premise of Christian talk of the creation'.[66] Bray's claim that 'Athenagoras understands the creation of the world unambiguously as the mere shaping of the unoriginated matter',[67] while hardly argued for beyond simple assertion, is broadly accurate.

At various points, particularly in the *Legatio*, Athenagoras argues for the createdness of matter over the uncreatedness of God (4.1; 15.1; 19.2). While this might imply that matter is created out of nothing, such implication is nowhere made explicit; the intention of the author is merely to distinguish between God and matter and to deny the latter the status of a first principle (see my chapter 5). At 6.2 Athenagoras speaks of God 'ordering' the universe through His Word; at 7.1, of 'ordering' the all; and at 10.1, of both creating and arranging it, again, through His Word. What he presents has all the marks of a creation in which form and order is given to what was previously formless and without order. At 10.3 of the *Legatio*, where Athenagoras describes the Son as the *idea* and *energeia* of the Father, he speaks of him coming forth as such for everything material, which at that point is without qualities. Again, creation is the giving of form and quality to the formless and that without qualities. At 15.2f. Athenagoras' comparison of God and matter with the potter and the clay carries with it the implication that God's dealing with Matter has less to do with creating it than with simply giving form and order to that without form or order.[68] Here God is spoken of not as creator (ποιητής) or builder (δημιουργός) – the normal words for 'creator' – but rather as craftsman (τεχνίτης) (15.2; 19.4). At 15.3 God is spoken of as providing the 'arrangement and good order of things'. At 16.4 Athenagoras speaks of God's 'craftsmanship'.

At *De resurrectione* 3.2, our author speaks of God 'giving shape to substance regarded as shapeless, [of arranging] in many different patterns that which is unstructured and disordered'.

In any case, Athenagoras nowhere speaks of a creation by God 'out of nothing'. His thought on the matter of that out of which creation takes place is undeniably influenced – as it was for most, if not all, Judaeo-Christian thinkers before Theophilus, Irenaeus and Tertullian – by the philosophical presuppositions of the day: that the world was made out of unformed matter, whose own origin is itself not speculated upon.

Summary Thus Athenagoras clearly participates either for the most part directly or at least indirectly in a conversation within the Middle Platonism of the first and second centuries. The topics of this conversation included:

the division of reality into being and becoming (as we find it in the *Timaeus*);

the goodness and purposiveness of God in creating the universe;

[66] Ibid., p. 177.

[67] Ibid., pp. 138f.

[68] At *de Resurrectione* 9.1 the author challenges the employment of the analogy of the potter and clay, but only in a context where it is being used to refute suggestions that God might wish to resurrect dead and decomposed bodies.

the Platonic Ideas and Forms;
fate, providence and free will;
daemons;
the identities of the supreme God and of the Creator;
the problem of creation in time; and
the problem of creation out of nothing.

Thus, as a Christian with concern for the *kerygma*, Athenagoras participates in a philosophical conversation of the first and second centuries, principally as it focused in Athens, notwithstanding the absence there of a formal school or Academy in his time (although it is of interest that one or three years before the writing of the *Legatio* Atticus possibly became the first person to be appointed as the first imperially funded Professor of Platonic Studies in Athens (175 CE))[69]. Athenagoras never employs the term 'philosophy' in a pejorative sense – though he may condemn some of its practitioners – because this is the game in which he is engaged. Philosophy is theology is philosophy; it is all to do with the love of truth and of certain, attainable knowledge. True philosophy is the self-revelation of God through the prophetic witness supported by reason; the imperfect seeing and knowing and grasping of others does not diminish this, nor does it deny that the imperfect is yet a grasp of some of the truth. Thus in all areas listed above it is primarily (though not exclusively) the philosophical conversation that seems to provide the framework in which Athenagoras operates – far more than the specifically and exclusively Christian one about the nature of the *kerygma*. But what is the historical *locus* in which this church Father operates?

Among the Middle Platonists of Athens in the late first and second centuries[70] we find a sharp contrast between being and becoming; the notion of God as 'real being'; and the identification by some of the supreme God-principle with the creator entity of Plato's *Timaeus* against those who wished to distinguish the supreme being from the Creator. Thus we see among them, and particularly among those in Athens, who identified the supreme God with the demiurgic entity, both this conversation and the one over the temporal or atemporal nature of the creation – which is particularly related to the question of what Plato actually intended in his account of the 'creation' of the universe in the *Timaeus* – among Middle Platonists. The language employed by Athenagoras for the most part clearly situates him

[69] J. Dillon, *The Middle Platonists* (above, n9), p. 248. The evidence for the establishment of chairs in Athens for all the major schools of philosophy under Marcus Aurelius is Dio, *Roman History* 72.31.3.

[70] With respect to the so-called (but probably non-existent) 'School of Athens', Dillon comments that 'there was [not] any such thing as an official Platonic Academy, until (perhaps) Marcus Aurelius founded his Regius Professorships in 176 AD' ('The Academy in the Middle Platonic period' (above, n12), pp. 76f.). Later Dillon speaks of 'the disappearance from the philosophic scene, after 88 BC, of the Platonic Academy as an institution' as being 'now ... an accepted fact' ('"Orthodoxy" and "Eclecticism"' (above, n17), p. 103).

primarily in this conversation rather than in the Christian one about the content and direction of the *kerygma*.

While the *De resurrectione* draws some of its language from Platonist, Stoic and Aristotelian sources and is written, at least in part, against the background of a Christian challenge to the physiological and psychological dualism of the Platonists (particularly through the Gnostics), the tract reflects mainly an intra-Christian struggle between an orthodoxy represented by our present author and a heterodoxy represented by the Gnostics (and Marcionites?); a struggle for the hearts and minds of those Christians, the 'waverers' who accepted most of the orthodox Christian teachings but baulked at a belief in the resurrection of the human being, a belief which perhaps they felt to be irrational, since resurrection would be impossible and unworthy of the Creator God.

Chapter Four
How do we know about God? Epistemology

Introduction

I have placed the 'how' before the 'what' of knowing about God – that is, I have put the matter of Athenagoras' epistemology ahead of that of his treatment of first principles and of a doctrine of God (see Chapter 5) – but I could just as easily mount an equally strong case for reversing that order. The primary issue must, however, be the 'what' – what Athenagoras understands as first principles, and particularly of God – given that the 'how' – how one knows the 'what' about God – simply indicates the entry points for the former. The 'how' may itself, of course, provide some very significant indicators to the question of the content of Athenagoras' beliefs, particularly the 'what' of God.

Knowledge of the Divine in Antiquity

Asmis declares that there are two main issues in Epicurean epistemology: 1) what is the foundation of knowledge? and 2) how is knowledge built on this foundation?[1] In Cicero's treatise *On the Nature of the Gods*, the Academic philosopher Cotta declares that Epicurus 'saw that there are gods because nature herself had impressed a notion (*notionem*) of them in the minds of all. For what nation or race of men [he said] is there that does not have a certain preconception (*anticipationem* = πρόληψις) of the gods without any teaching?' (1.43). Stoic epistemology, says Frede, 'amounts to a complex hypothesis as to how nature has endowed us with means to attain knowledge and wisdom', given that nature is provident and that therefore the knowledge which is wisdom must be humanly attainable.[2] Diogenes Laertius reported that the Stoics argued that 'while it is by sense-perception that we apprehend white and black, rough and smooth, it is by reason that we apprehend conclusions reached through demonstration, such as the gods' existence and their providence' (7.52). Schofield declares that '[t]he main thesis to which Arcesilaus [head of the Sceptical Academy] is said to have subscribed is the claim that nothing is known for certain, or more precisely that there is no such thing as what

---

1 E. Asmis, 'Epicurean epistemology', in K. Algra et al. (eds), *The Cambridge History of Hellenistic Philosophy* (Cambridge, 2005), p. 260.

2 M. Frede, 'Stoic epistemology', in Algra et al. (eds), *Hellenistic Philosophy* (above, n1), p. 296.

the Stoics called cognition'.[3] Cicero, however, himself an adherent of the Sceptical –Academy and advocate of its main positions, says that

> [o]ur position is not that we hold that nothing is true, but that we assert that all true sensations are associated with false ones so closely resembling them that they contain no infallible mark to guide our judgement and assent. From this followed the corollary that many sensations are plausible (*probalilia*),[4] that is, though not amounting to a full perception that they are yet possessed of a certain distinctness and clearness, and so can serve to direct the conduct of the wise man. (*On the Nature of the Gods* I.12)

In Cicero's *Academica*, Lucullus, the Antiochean supporter, says that, while Epicurus 'places the standard of judgement (*iudicium*)[5] entirely in the senses and in notions (*notitiis*) of objects and in pleasure', Plato 'held that the entire criterion of truth (*omnem iudicium veritatis*) and truth itself is detached from opinions and from the senses and belongs to the mere activity of thought itself and to the mind' (II.142). 'Albinus [*sc.* Alcinous]', according to Dillon, 'recognises another source of knowledge superior to sense-perception, the direct apprehension of intelligible reality, which in its pure form is the mode of perception proper to God, but which is also possible for us'.[6] This is best seen in chapter 4 of his *Didaskalikos*, from 4.6.155.21 onwards. There Alcinous says that

> intellection is the activity of the intellect as it contemplates the primary objects of intellection … intellection in the strict sense is that which takes place prior to the soul's coming to be in the body [and is] the first principle of scientific reasoning. 4.6.155.20-21

The Difference between Knowing and Opining about God

Rist, in his monograph on Augustine,[7] makes at least two very useful comments which might assist us in our consideration of the epistemology of Athenagoras against the background of ancient epistemology generally. The first is that 'indeed few in antiquity harboured doubts of a God or gods'.[8] Diagoras of Melos (a fifth-century figure), one might observe, would hardly merit the title 'the Atheist' if

---

3 M. Schofield, 'Academic epistemology', in Algra et al. (eds), *Hellenistic Philosophy* (above, n1), p. 327.

4 The Latin word probabilis in this context does not bear the sense of the English 'probable' but rather that of the Greek word πιθανός, which means 'plausible'.

5 The Latin term iudicium – here and immediately below – is the equivalent of the Greek κριτήριον.

6 J. Dillon, *The Middle Platonists*, 80 BC to AD 220, rev. edn (London, 1996), p. 274.

7 J.M. Rist, *Augustine: Ancient Thought Baptized* (Cambridge, 1996).

8 Ibid., p. 62.

such a stance were commonplace (see 4.2).[9] Yet even those who did harbour some nagging doubts concerning the divine were often persuaded to keep those doubts to themselves, because of the political and social realities of the world in which they lived. One need only consider Athenagoras' own vigorous defence of Christian theism – mounted both because the Christians were not atheists, as their opponents claimed (which was a matter of apologetics), and because it was not politically or socially acceptable or safe for them to be thought so – to see the pressure on those who were accused of atheism. The second of Rist's comments is that 'the most basic principle of Platonic epistemology is not the distinction between "intelligibles" and "sensibles" (important though that is), but the distinction between first-hand experience which gives "knowledge" (*epistēmē*) and second-hand (or other) experience which gives various sorts of more or less justified "belief" (*doxa*)'.[10]

Both the Epicureans and the Stoics, as we have seen above, suggest that there are 'criteria of truth' which allow their sages access to the reality of things. In both schools and systems of thought, an epistemology based on the concept of an infallible sense-perception enjoys a certain primacy as they both seek to combat the Pyrrhonian Sceptic view that 'neither our sensations nor our opinions tell us truths or falsehoods' (Aristocles in Eusebius, *Praeparatio evangelica* 14.18.1–5). In Epicurean epistemology opinions, as 'judgements which we make on the basis of our [sense-]impressions' (Sextus Empiricus, *Against the Professors* 7.206–10, summarizing Epicurus), can be either true or false. We judge some things correctly, Epicurus says, but others not so. Opinions therefore are fallible for the Epicurean, unlike the sense-impressions themselves. Diogenes Laertius claims that, for the Epicurean, opinion, which he says they call supposition (ὑπόληψις), is true and false; the former if attested and uncontested, the latter if unattested or contested (10.34). Opinion, then, cannot be for the Epicurean a criterion of truth. For, he says, it is sensations, preconceptions (προλήψεις) and our feelings that provide such criteria according to Epicurus; other Epicureans include perceptions of mental presentations. For the Stoic, on the other hand, no opinion can ever be true. For this reason, as Zeno is alleged to have said, '[t]he wise man would not opine' (Cicero, *Academica* 2.77). The Antiochean Varro of the *Academica* says that Zeno contrasted *scientia* (knowledge) and *inscientia* (ignorance) and claimed that opinion, as something weak and related to what was false and incognitive or unknowable, was sourced from the latter (1.41–2). Sextus Empiricus says that the Stoics differentiated knowledge, opinion and cognition (κατάληψις). The first of these, knowledge, would be cognition which is secure, firm and unchangeable

9 Philodemus, in his On Piety, says that Epicurus, in the twelfth book of his On Nature, criticized the atheism of the fifth-century sophists Prodicus of Cos, Diagoras, Critias and others and called them 'mad', like those in a Bacchic frenzy (112.5–12). This, according to A.A. Long and D.N. Sedley, *The Hellenistic Philosophers* (Cambridge, 1987), 2 vols, II, p. 151, was the 'standard list of atheists'.

10 Rist, *Augustine* (above, n7), p. 45.

by reason; the second, opinion, would be weak and false assent; and the third, cognition, comes in between and would be assent to a cognitive impression which is true and could not turn out to be false (*Against the Professors* 7.151–7). Stobaeus on the other hand reports that for the Stoics there are two types of opinion: assent to the incognitive supposition and assent to the weak supposition; both are alien to the sage (2.111, 18–112, 8).

Concerning the New (that is, Sceptical) Academy, Cicero reports that truth is effectively submerged in an abyss (according to Democritus),[11] everything being in the grip of opinions and conventions (*Academica* 1.44). While Carneades, one of the 'scholarchs' (heads) of this phase, apparently could accept the possibility of an opinion being true, Plutarch spoke of 'that only in which falsehood and deception are engendered – opinion' (*Against Colotes* 1122a–f). Cicero himself said that the wise man will never opine (2.66–7), that the highest of activities 'wars against sense-presentations and withstands opinions' (2.108), and that the wise man might opine, but will do so in such a way as to realize that he is merely opining and that there is nothing which can be grasped and cognized (2.148).

Dillon identifies four modes of cognition in Plato's thought (according to Aristotle, *De anima* 404b16ff., and also alluded to by Plato himself at *Laws* 10.894a and in the famous line simile of *Republic* 6): intuitive knowledge (*nous*), discursive knowledge (*epistēmē*), opinion (*doxa*), and sense-perception (*aisthēsis*).[12] These four are alluded to, he says, at *Laws* 10.894a and are probably referred to at *Republic* 6.511e, where Plato speaks of νόησις (reason), διάνοια (understanding), πίστις (belief) and εἰκασία (conjecture). In the *Republic* δόξα is related to the world of appearances at 6.509c ff., as it is both in the *Theaetetus* (187a–210b) and in the *Timaeus* (51d ff.); at 5.476d Plato contrasts knowledge (γνώμη) and opinion; and at 477a he places opinion between knowledge (γνῶσις) and ignorance, in a class of its own. At *Timaeus* 27d, where Plato distinguishes between 'being' – that which always is and has no becoming – and 'becoming' – that which always becomes and never is – he describes the former as apprehensible through thought aided by reason and the other as the object of opinion aided by unreasoning sensation, since it becomes and perishes and never really exists. At 51d of the same work he differentiates reason from true opinion, the one coming by teaching and the other by persuasion, one always in company with true reasoning and the other irrational, one immovable by persuasion, the other alterable by it. For Plato, according to Dillon, *doxa* in fact concerns the realm of popular opinion and customary belief[13] and the senses are the 'realm of opinion (*doxa*), where nothing is certain or clearly perceived because of its constant flux'.[14] Antiochus of Ascalon, the last member of the Athenian New Academy as we know it,distinguished between δόξα and

---

[11] Diogenes Laertius reports that Democritus declared that 'of truth we know nothing, for truth is in a well' (ἐν βυθῷ γὰρ ἡ ἀλήθεια, 9.72).

[12] Dillon, *The Middle Platonists* (above, n6), p. 6.

[13] Ibid., p. 36.

[14] Ibid., p. 92.

ἐπιστήμη, the one having to do with the senses and matters about which there is nothing certain or clearly perceived and the latter with the intellect and thereby with the Forms. Alcinous, too, says that knowledge differs from opinion (reflecting *Timaeus* 51d–2a); that their objects will be different; and that there will be primary objects of both knowledge and opinion – which, he argues, demonstrates that Forms exist (9.4.164.2f.). He also contrasts 'true' and 'false' opinion in chapter 4, but also contrasts both of them with knowledge (νόησις –4.5.154.41ff.).

Athenagoras contrasts knowledge and opinion frequently. At 7.2, for example, when he criticizes the poets and the philosophers for their marked inability to gain any more than a marginal understanding of the truth, of being, of God, he suggests that this is because they go at it through guesswork, surmisingor conjecture (στοχαστικῶς).[15] Thus Athenagoras seems to suggest that they are satisfied with a form of non-certain, unstable opinion. At 7.3, where he speaks of the superior source represented by the Spirit-inspired prophets – he actually says that 'we have prophets as witnesses to that which we think and believe' – he claims that it would be irrational (ἄλογον) to abandon belief in the Spirit which comes from God and has moved the mouths of the prophets like musical instruments and to pay attention to human opinions instead (δόξαις ἀνθρωπίναις). Thus here Athenagoras does not so much contrast knowledge (ἐπιστήμη) with opinion (δόξα) as he contrasts the latter with belief (πίστις) – although the Christian understanding of πίστις encompasses more than Platonic 'belief' and makes it indeed more akin to a form of divine 'knowledge' (knowledge of the highest kind). At 9.1 Athenagoras speaks of the testimony of the prophets confirming his arguments (λογισμούς) on the oneness of God – his logical proof of this claim in chapter 8 – and says that his principal readers – the emperors – being themselves so learned as well as eager for knowledge, will not be without understanding (οὐκ ἀνοήτους) of the teachings of the prophets on this matter. It is likely that here Athenagoras is (at least implicitly) drawing a distinction between concepts qua human constructions (ἐννοίαις ἀνθρωπικὸν ... λόγον) and hence akin to 'opinions' and arguments (τοὺς λογισμούς) of the kind that the prophets confirm (πιστεῖν bears the sense of something more than an affirmation or confirmation – rather like a guarantee or a binding), which are implicitly akin to knowledge of the highest order. His employment of the language of 'knowledge' and 'learning' confirms this hypothesis. At 11.1 he tells the emperors that he is outlining Christian teaching for them, in detail and carefully, so that they might not be carried along by common and irrational opinion (τῇ κοινῇ καὶ ἀλόγῳ γνώμῃ – on which see again the Platonic passage discussed above *Republic* 5.476d) but might instead be enabled to know the truth. Here there is a reasonably explicit distinction drawn between opinion and what, under the language of 'truth', is, clearly, knowledge

[15] One might compare Athenagoras' thought here with Plato's reference at *Republic* 6.511e (see above) to the fourth of the affections (παθήματα) occurring in the soul, that of conjecture or likeness (εἰκασίαν), which is placed lower, according to the degree to which it participates in clearness and precision.

of the highest order. As at 9.2 he again distinguishes doctrines, which he takes to be human constructions (τῶν δογμάτων ... ἀνθρωπικοῖς), from those things ordained and taught by God (θεοφάτοις καὶ θεοδιδάκτοις), the purest and highest forms of knowledge. At 12.3 he actually identifies this 'knowledge' when he says that the Christians, in their consideration of this life and of the life to come, are attended only by the knowledge (εἰδέναι) of him who is truly God and of the Word that issues from him – a knowledge of what constitutes the unity of the Son with the Father, the communion of the Father with the Son, the Spirit, the unity of the Spirit, the Son, and the Father, and their diversity when thus united. At 13.3, after he has accused his opponents of being ignorant and unacquainted with physical and theological doctrine, he speaks of God preserving and governing all things with knowledge and skill. Thus a form of 'knowledge' higher than the one available to human beings – in fact the latter's source – is that which God employs in his providing for, and ruling over, what he has created. At 24.1 Athenagoras suggests that it is now unnecessary for the emperors, as learned individuals, to call to mind the views of the poets or to examine other opinions (ἑτέρας δόξας). It is clear that here and in the next sentence, where he acknowledges indirectly that it is the teachings of the poets and philosophers that he has in mind, he regards these 'opinions' as being of much less value than the doctrine of the Christians – here, specifically, the doctine of the distinction between God and matter. At 24.6 Athenagoras contrasts the worldly wisdom of the poets and their 'partial' account (ἐκ μέρους) of the generation of the giants with prophetic wisdom. (At this point the transmitted text is lacunose and Schwartz adds καὶ τῆς προφητικῆς. Both Schoedel and Pouderon accept this emendation, while Marcovich prefers τῆς θεί ας. But nothing much hangs on it: the point is the same.) The two differ from one another, the worldly from the prophetic/divine wisdom, as truth differs from plausibility (τοῦ πιθανοῦ). Thus here Athenagoras draws a clear line between a worldly wisdom akin to 'opinion' and the divine–prophetic one, akin to the highest form of knowledge available to human being. At 25.2, in speaking of the particular providence of God, Athenagoras says that he is concerned with truth and not opinion. Truth and knowledge, for Athenagoras, are clearly identical, as one can also see at 11.1. At 27.1, a passage on the exploitation of weak and ignorant human souls by demons, Athenagoras talks of the movements of such souls being directed, not by reason, but by fantasy, which dwells 'in the realm of opinions' (περὶ τὰς δόξας). The images that such a soul gains come from matter, for this soul attaches itself to the spirit of matter and does not look up to heavenly things and their maker; it does not seek to know – whereas 12.3 suggests that knowledge underpins all Christian endeavours. Souls such as these, weak and docile, souls not directed by reason, souls ignorant and unacquainted with sound teaching, are unable to contemplate the truth (cf. 11.1) and unable to know (ἀπερινόητοι) who is the Father and Creator of all things (cf. 12.3). Such a soul has impressed upon itself false opinions (ψευδεῖς δόξας) concerning itself and is thus exploited and misled by the demons associated with matter. Thus here, near the end of his defence of Christianity against the charge of atheism, Athenagoras provides a robust articulation of the epistemological basis of Christian teaching in knowledge-as-truth, knowledge given by God and to be identified with God – over against the human constructions produced by opinion and conjecture.

Thus Athenagoras contrasts conjecture with an authority-based or prophetic knowledge-as-πίστις at 7.2; faith with opinion at 7.3; humanly constructed concepts of the unity of God with the more certain prophetic witness at 9.1; irrational opinion with truth at 11.1; the poetic with the prophetic wisdom and truth (knowledge) with plausibility (NOT probability) at 24.6; truth with opinion at 25.2; and reason and the knowledge of God with false opinion at 27.1. He would then seem to operate on this matter in a primarily Stoic rather than Epicurean or Platonist framework; for it would appear that for Athenagoras there can be no true opinion (or at least none which can have lasting or absolute value). How, then, can the Christian know with any certainty that which lies at the heart of his or her faith?

This theme, of a distinction between knowledge and opinion, is not an issue in the *De resurrectione*.

Key Framework for the Epistemology of Athenagoras

When Athenagoras criticizes the poets and philosophers, in whom he has only just looked for an affirmation of the oneness of God, he does it on the grounds that they would gain only a marginal understanding (περινοῆσαι) of the truth – one derived through speculation and through some 'affinity' (συμπάθειαν) between their own souls and the breath (or Spirit?) of God (τῆς παρὰ τοῦ Θεοῦ πνοῆς); and that they would be unable to find being because they do not 'humble themselves to learn about God from God, but each [relied] upon himself' (*Legatio* 7.2). With these arguments Athenagoras provides, albeit negatively, a key to his own understanding of where knowledge and apprehension of God is properly sourced: from the self-revelation of God. All that is left now is to discover how he thinks that this self-revelation of God might itself be accessed.

The structure of the *Legatio*, at least insofar as it pertains to the knowledge (or knowing) of God (for these two are by no means the same thing), is based most clearly on three blocks of writing which follow one another, although the subject is also discussed elsewhere, as we will see below. These blocks consist of:

a. chapters 4 to 7: there he considers, often negatively, various philosophical approaches to the knowledge and the knowing of God, and then demonstrates the superiority of the Christian approach, based as it is primarily on the Spirit-inspired prophetic witness;
b. chapters 8 to 9: there he demonstrates how a crucial attribute of God – his oneness – can be inferred logically, without any recourse to specifically Christian revelation; but in the end this is of no real value without the

witness of the prophets; and

c. chapters 10 to 12: there Athenagoras lays out his understanding of the Christian teaching on the Trinity and of the (only possible) grounding of a Christian ethics in that teaching.

The God known by mind and thought alone Athenagoras speaks at a number of places of knowing, contemplating or apprehending (grasping) God, and also of those who are not able to do so. He speaks at 4.1 of the divine (he employs the abstract τὸ θεῖον),[16] uncreated and eternal, being contemplated by thought and reason alone ʿνῷ μόνῳ καὶ λόγῳ θεωρούμενονʾ[17] and at 22.9 as being contemplated by reason ʿτοῦ λόγῳ θεωρητοῦ θεοῦ[18]); at 10.1, of God being apprehended (or grasped) by mind and reason aloneʿ νῷ μόνῳ καὶ λόγῳ καταλαμβανόμενον); and again, at 23.7, of the invisible God as apprehended (or grasped) by mind and reason (τὸν ἀΐδιον νῷ καὶ λόγῳ καταλαμβανόμενον θεὸν). At 27.2 Athenagoras speaks of souls, weak and docile, not directed by reason, ignorant and unacquainted with sound teachings, unable to contemplate (ἀθεώρητοι) the truth or unable to understand (ἀπερινόητοι) who the Father and Creator of the universe is, which is the same thing. This last attribute, although negative like the rest, still testifies to the notion of the necessary contemplation of God.

This notion of God being 'apprehended' or 'grasped' derives from a primarily Stoic epistemological concept (Cicero says 'like being "grasped" by the hand': *Academica* 1.40-41). The Greek verb καταλαμβάνειν carries with it this connotation of being 'seized' or 'grasped', and the Stoics in particular employed the adjective καταληπτικός to create the sense of an impression being either 'capable of grasping' or, more usually, 'capable of being grasped'. Thus we have their expression καταληπτικὴ φαντασία, 'cognitive impression'. There is also the derived noun, also epistemologically employed, κατάληψις, meaning 'certainty' – which reflects the notion that, for the Stoics, knowledge is certain. Diogenes Laertius declares that, for the Stoics, 'the cognitive impression is the criterion of truth, that is, the impression arising from what it is' (7.54). At *Timaeus* 27d Plato speaks of the absolute distinction between that which exists always and has no beginning and that which is becoming always and is never existent; at 28a, of the former as apprehensible (only) through thought aided by reason (τὸ μὲν δὴ νοήσει μετὰ λόγου περιληπτὸν) and of the latter as the object of opinion only aided by unreasoning sensation – something which perishes. (One could also look up *Timaeus* 52a, where the self-identical Form is said to be an object which it is the province of Reason to contemplate τοῦτο ὃ δὴ νόησις εἴληχεν ἐπισκοπεῖν). At *Phaedrus* 247c (and also at 247e), Plato speaks of the 'truly existent'[19] as being 'visible only to the mind (μόνῳ θεατὴ νῷ) – while Alcinous speaks of the

16 See Chapter 5 on first principles.

17 See on 'contemplation' chapter 2.2.153.3f. of Alcinous' *Didaskalikos*.

18 Here the personal and not the abstract for 'God' is employed.

19 Athenagoras speaks at 12.3 of him who is 'truly God' (τὸν ὄντως θεόν).

intelligible world being alone judged by thought aided by reason (τὸν μὲν νοητὸν κόσμον κρίνει νόησις μετὰ λόγου, 4.8.156.13).

At 12.3 Athenagoras says that Christians, in their choice of lifestyle and evaluation of this life and the next, are attended solely by the knowledge of him who is truly God and of the Word that issues from him: a knowledge as to what the unity of the Son with the Father is, what the communion is of the Father with the Son, what the Spirit is, what the unity of these three, the Spirit, the Son, and the Father is, and what their diversity is when they are united. And this is not mere knowledge – knowing *about* – but *knowing*. For εἰδέναι will signify more than knowing facts: knowing in the sense of being certain or seeing 'in the mind'.[20] But what does it mean, in a Christian context, for God to be known only through mind and reason? As we will see later when we consider the shape and flow of the three epistemological 'blocks' in chapters (4) 5 to 7, 8 to 9, and 10, it is not for nothing that Athenagoras describes the Son of God at 10.2 as the mind and reason (νοῦς καὶ λόγος) of the Father and at 24.2 as mind, reason and wisdom of the Father.

One possible difference between Plato and his second-century followers on the one hand, Athenagoras on the other is that, while the former speak for the most part of the truly existent being 'visible' or 'grasped' or 'apprehended' by mind and reason alone, Athenagoras speaks – at 4.1, 22.9 and (negatively) at 27.2 – of the divine being 'contemplated (θεωρούμενον)' by mind and reason (though at 10.1 and 23.7 he also speaks of God as being 'grasped' by them). Whence comes his use of the verb θεωρεῖν? At *Phaedrus* 247d Plato, having already said that the 'truly existing essence' is 'visible only to the mind', speaks of the divine mind as 'gazing upon truth' (θεωροῦσα τἀληθῆ). At 2.1.152.31 Alcinous speaks of the contemplative (theoretical) life lying in the knowledge of truth – and note that Athenagoras speaks at 7.2 of poets and philosophers seeking, through some affinity of their souls with the breath of God, to find and understand the truth; and at 2.2.153.3 Alcinous declares that 'contemplation is the activity of the mind when thinking upon the intelligibles' (ἡ θεωρία ἐνέργειά τοῦ νοῦ νοοῦντος τὰ νοητά). At 4.6.155.20f.. Alcinous says that thought is the activity of the mind when it contemplated (θεωροῦντος) the primary intelligibles; and at 4.7.156.7f. these primary intelligibles are said to be judged by νόησις, not without the aid of scientific reason (τοῦ ἐπιστημονικοῦ λόγου), through a kind of comprehension (περιλήψει τινι) (clearly a reflection of *Timaeus* 28a).

Thus Athenagoras employs: the Platonic idea of contemplating God (at 4.1, 22.9 and 27.2 where he contrasts God and matter); the Platonic formulation, found at *Phaedrus* 247d, that the divine mind contemplates the truth; Alcinous' notions, found at *Didaskalikos* 2.1.152.31, 2.2.153.3 and 4.6.155.20f respectively, that knowledge of faith is the contemplative life, that the process of mind thinking upon intelligibles is contemplation and that the activity of the mind is the contemplation

[20] The verb εἴδω can mean both 'to see' and 'to know'. The perfect οἶδα – 'I have seen' – can be employed in the present sense as 'I know'.

[21] Athenagoras uses this Aristotelian term elsewhere of the Word.

of the primary intelligibles; and the Stoic sense of 'grasping' one's God (at 10.1 and 23.7).

Athenagoras is at least equally concerned with those who cannot achieve a true and complete knowledge of God: at 10.1 he speaks of God as incomprehensible (ἀκατάληπτον) (to human thought on its own?, might one ask) before speaking of him as being apprehended (grasped) καταλαμβανόμενον by mind and reason alone; at 13.1, of those who are ignorant about the nature of God; at 22.12, of those who fail to see the greatness of God and are unable to rise up to it through reason (for they are not, he says, attuned to the heavenly realm[22]); and at 27.2 (as we saw earlier) of those who are unable to contemplate the truth and understand who the Father and Creator of all things is. Thus those who do not or cannot contemplate or grasp the nature of God through mind and reason – through the Son as Word, as mind and reason of the Father – will never do it. While Athenagoras is clearly happy to employ the Stoic idiom of 'grasping'[23] and the Platonic idiom of 'contemplating' the divine, we shall see below that the knowledge of the divine he has in mind under such descriptions is one achievable only through the agency of the divine itself.

These are not major concerns in the *De resurrectione* except at 13.2, 25.4 and 15.5. There our author speaks of humankind being made by God in part for the 'contemplation (θεωρὸν) of God's majesty and universal wisdom'; of God's majesty and universal wisdom being the object of humankind's contemplation (τῇ τούτων θεωρίᾳ); of the end (or goal) of human beings consisting in a life capable of prudence and rational discernment (ἔμφρονος καὶ λογικῆς κρίσεως) which should include unceasing rejoicing in the contemplation of God and of God's decrees; and of 'understanding and reason [being given] to humans to discern intelligibles' – these include the goodness, wisdom and justice of God – which the human being composed of body and soul receives from God.

Thus, for Athenagoras, certain knowledge of God is not only desirable but also possible. Such knowledge can be accessed. And that happens essentially – although Athenagoras does not always spell this out – through the Son–Word construed as mind, reason and wisdom of the Father and through the Holy Spirit regarded as an artist who inspires and 'plays' the prophets (9.1). For Athenagoras, the particular 'knowing about' and 'of' this God he worships is the primary, even the sole focus of the epistemological framework he works in. It is clear that, for him, this knowing of God is primarily about the self-revelation of God. This is the revelation of which the poets and philosophers, when they sought to find and understand the truth – that is, the divine being – managed to find no more than a peripheral understanding (περινοῆσαι), because they would not humble themselves to learn about God from God (that is, from God's self revelation), but

[22] Note 7.2, where the poets and philosophers are said to have a marginal grasp of a knowledge of God through συμπάθεια with the breath of God.

[23] We note, however, that Athenagoras speaks at 23.7 of Plato understanding the 'grasping' of the eternal God through mind and reason.

each one relied upon himself (7.3). For the Christians, the truth of and about God comes from God alone. And this truth is accessed by the faithful in two ways. It is accessed, first, through the ministry of the Word; at 4.1 (see also 10.1; 22.9 and 23.7) God is said to be contemplated or apprehended by thought and reason alone, at 10.2 and 24.2 the Son is named mind and reason of the Father, and it follows therefore that the Son is the primary means through which the Father is known. And, second, it is accessed through the ministry of the Spirit. This is seen particularly at 7.3, where the prophets are divinely inspired and their mouths are moved like musical instruments by the Spirit; at 9.1, where the prophets are in ecstasy at their thoughts being moved by the divine Spirit and being made to utter what they were inspired to say – the Spirit is making use of them like a flautist; and at 10.4, where the Holy Spirit is said to be active in those who speak prophetically.

Athenagoras also reinforces the notion of God's self-revelation – this primary and sole means of truly accessing knowledge of the divine – over against purely human attempts, which are fated to fail. At 11.1 he speaks of the Christians' doctrines as being ordained and taught by God, and not human-made, like most of those of the poets and philosophers (on this theme see also 7.2 and 7.3: in the latter he refers negatively to 'human opinions'). At 32.4 he says that 'our doctrine' is taught by God, which gives the Christians 'our' own law: in other words, he is making clear that Christian teaching is not put forth with an eye to particular human laws. The contrast is, again, between man-made teaching of the logical kind – teaching on the oneness of God of chapter 8, characterized there as 'thoughts of this kind' (τοιαύταις ἐννοίαις[24]) – and the knowledge which comes from God's own self, principally through the prophets.

The *De resurrectione*, when speaking of knowledge about God, employs the term γνῶσις (1.2, knowledge of truth as to the nature of God, knowledge of God and of God's activity; 11.4, knowledge of reality: τὴν τῶν πραγμάτων γνῶσιν).

God speaking through pagans Between chapters 4 and 7, Athenagoras explores the question of why the Christians are the subject of official persecution while those pagans who consider theological matters and who in some cases promote the notion of a single God are not. 'Poets and philosophers were not regarded as atheists', he says, 'for giving their attention to matters concerning God' (5.1). In chapters 5 and 6 Athenagoras identifies poets and philosophers who have spoken with some measure of truth about the divine, but this is qualified in chapter 7, where he identifies their 'truth' as at best partial. At 5.1 Athenagoras speaks of Euripides as being perplexed as he contemplated the fact that some, through ignorance and

---

[24] Ibid. Note that ἔννοια is a Stoic term: Aetius, 4.11.1–4, says that for the Stoics 'conceptions (ἔννοιαι) arise through our own instruction and attention'. Plutarch (*On common conceptions* 1084f–55a) says that for the Stoics 'conception is a kind of impression, a printing in the soul'.

the notion of 'common preconceptions' (see below), wrongly name particular entities as gods. Athenagoras then recognizes that this poet properly identifies the nature of God's existence 'through a knowledge of the intelligible' (τοῦ κατ' ἐπιστήμην νοητοῦ). Euripides questioned, says Athenagoras, those who claimed to find natures beneath certain realities which they wrongly named as divine, while he himself demarcated the existence of (another) God in his works, 'recognizing the invisible [*sc.* the 'intelligible'] from the things which appear' (5.2). This god, whose spirit guided these works, he discerned to be God (5.3). Athenagoras then quotes from pseudo-Sophocles (whose work he wrongly presumes to be authored by the famous Athenian poet, as did others in his time), whom he says recognized the unity of God who created heaven and earth. In chapter 6, Athenagoras suggests that the Pythagoreans Philolaus, Lysis and Opsimus were right to claim that God is one and above matter (he employs here the Pythagorean term μονάς). Likewise at 6.2, continuing his claim that Christians are not alone in proposing the oneness of God, he quotes from the *Timaeus* to show that Plato 'understands the uncreated and eternal God to be one' when he speaks of the Creator and Father of the universe at 28c3–4 and that the 'other gods' at 41a, the sun, the moon and the stars, are created entities. At 6.3 he says that Aristotle brought forth the concept of God as 'one' when he likened God to a composite living being consisting of body (the ether, the planets and the fixed stars) and soul (the reason which controls the movement of that body; although Athenagoras would not be comfortable with this particular claim). The Stoics, he suggests at 6.4, also got it right on the oneness of God; but he expresses a certain reservation that, notwithstanding their correctness on unity, they provide multiple names for the divine being.

At 7.1 Athenagoras acknowledges that, while these poets and philosophers do 'get it right' on the notion of God as one, they do so 'reluctantly'. We recall here, of course, that his primary purpose in this section of the treatise is to argue that, if the poets and philosophers speak of the divine as one and are not discriminated against, the Christians should not be either. At 7.2 he declares that, in the case of the poets and philosophers, each one is moved by his own soul, through some affinity with the 'breath of God', and gains no more than a peripheral understanding of true being; this is because they choose not to humble themselves to learn about God from God himself but each relies upon himself. The poets and philosophers are, it seems, able to connect with the Spirit of God, but they do not seem to know this and, not knowing it, they do not pursue it but apparently assume it is all their own work. While there is no suggestion here of a Justin-like *logos spermatikos* notion whereby all can speak some measure of truth in proportion to that portion of the divine *logos* within them, nor of Clement of Alexandria's notion that Greek philosophy is a part of the divine providence's plan to prepare the ground for the coming of the Gospel to the Greeks, there is a clear suggestion that non-Christians can access, no matter how, some portion of the truth through contact with the Spirit: some kind of 'brush' with the divine, presumably initiated by God himself. None of this is an issue in the *De resurrectione*.

Athenagoras' challenge to ancient epistemologies While Athenagoras in so many respects operates within a particular philosophical framework and, as we have seen, within a particular philosophical conversation, here, in the area of epistemology, he is quite clear that particular aspects of the epistemologies which sit at the heart of different philosophical schools of antiquity are simply unacceptable to him as a Christian whose belief system, his understanding of a knowledge of the divine, is grounded and sourced in the self-revelation of God. In his dealing with the sources for knowing of, or about, God he repudiates at least three ways familiar to contemporary philosophical traditions, two of them Epicurean–Stoic – the preconception (πρόληψις) and the impression (φαντασία) – and one Sceptical Academic – the plausible (πιθανός):

πρόληψις At 5.1 Athenagoras speaks of poets and philosophers who were not regarded as atheists for giving attention to matters concerning the knowledge of God (ἐπιστήσαντες περὶ θεοῦ); we are reminded here that the primary concern of Athenagoras was to argue that there was therefore no good reason why Christians should be so regarded. He speaks of the poet Euripides being perplexed by those who, through the notion of 'the common preconception' (κατὰ κοινὴν πρόληψιν) (Pouderon translates this, wrongly, as '*le sens péjoratif de "préjugé*"', and Crehan as 'common intelligence'), ignorantly (ἀνεπιστημόνως) name gods; and then of his setting out his own teaching on the existence of God through 'knowledge of the [divine] intelligible' (τοῦ κατ' ἐπιστήμην νοητοῦ). (Pouderon translates this as '*l'Etre intelligible par la connaisance*', and Crehan, as 'what is intelligible by pure reason'.) Athenagoras here contrasts 'knowledge' gained through κοινὴ πρόληψις and that achieved through ἐπιστήμη τοῦ νοητοῦ, a divinely sourced knowledge we might call it. He then quotes from Euripides (frg. 900), to the effect that Zeus ought not, if he inhabits the heavenly realm, subject humans to this unhappy misconception.

According to Diogenes Laertius (10.31), Epicurus regarded one of the criteria of truth to be the προλήψεις, alongside sensations and feelings – and later Epicureans added to this list 'the focussing of thought into an impression'. 'For the Epicureans', says Diogenes (10.33),

> a preconception (προλήψις) is a perception, a correct opinion, a conception (ἔννοιαν), or a universally stored notion (καθολικὴν νόησιν ἐναποκειμένην) of that which has frequently become evident externally … what primarily underlies each name is something self-evident. What we inquire about we would not have inquired about if we had not had prior knowledge of it, nor would we have named something if we had not previously learnt its delineation by means of preconception (προλήψις). Thus preconceptions are self-evident (ἐναργεῖς)

– and therefore, by implication, require neither proof nor definition.[25] Long and Sedley comment that 'a preconception is a generic notion of any type of object of experience, the concept naturally evoked by the name of that thing'.[26] Epicurus, in his *Letter to Menoecus*, speaks of the common notion (ἡ κοινὴ νόησις) of god as being 'imperishable and blessed' and says that nothing alien to these attributes should be attached to him (123–4). The knowledge of gods is self-evident. But, he continues, many of the attributes which some attach wrongly to the gods are not preconceptions, but false suppositions (οὐ γὰρ προλήψεις εἰσὶν ἀλλ' ὑπολή ψεις ψευδεῖς). The Epicurean Velleius in Cicero's *De natura deorum* asks:

> For what human nation or race does not have, without instruction, some preconception of the gods? Epicurus' word for this is *prolēpsis*, that is what we may call a delineation of a thing, preconceived by the mind, without which understanding, inquiry, and discussion are impossible. Preconceptions or prenotions [give us concepts] of the gods as eternal and blessed which nature has engraved on our minds. (1.43–9)

Diogenes also points to the Stoic Chrysippus, who said that sense perception and preconception are the criteria (of truth): preconception is a natural conception of universals (ἔννοια φυσικὴ τῶν καθόλου) (7.54). Plutarch wrote that the Soics regarded the common conceptions and preconceptions as the very seeds of their school and claimed them to be the source of its unique agreement with nature (*On Common Conceptions* 1060a). The Stoic Epictetus wrote that 'preconceptions are common to all men, and one preconception does not conflict with another' (*Discourses* 1.22.1–3.10). Sextus Empiricus – whose Scepticism was (unlike that of Carneades' New Academy), Pyrrhonian or derived from Pyrrho – said that 'it is agreed that a preconception and conception (ἔννοια) must precede every object of investigation, even if the multitude of such preconceptions and conceptions ultimately leads to a suspension of judgement (*Against the Professors* 8.331a–332a). Galen reports that Chrysippus' *On Reason* described reason as a collection of certain conceptions and preconceptions (*On the Doctrines of Hippocrates and Plato* 5.2.49). Plutarch on the other hand reports that the Stoics criticize Epicurus for 'ruining the preconception of the gods by abolishing providence … [they] say that god is preconceived and thought of not only as immortal and blessed but also as benevolent, caring and beneficent' (*On Common Conceptions* 1075e).

Long and Sedley note that 'throughout their history the Stoics did not budge from the thesis [first found in Zeno] ... that infallible knowledge of the world is possible and that all normal human beings have a natural faculty to make secure discrimination between discoverable truths and falsehoods'.[27] 'The gods' existence and providence, cited as examples of cognition established by rational

---

25 E. Asmis, 'Epicurean epistemology' (above, n1), p. 282.

26 Long and Sedley, *The Hellenistic Philosophers* (above, n6), I, p. 89.

27 Long and Sedley, *The Hellenistic Philosophers* (above, n6), I, p. 249.

argument, are standard cases of items the Stoics referred to as 'preconceptions and conceptions'.[28] Asmis says that 'what makes an Epicurean preconception natural is that it has been imposed on human minds by the external environment, whereas Stoic preconceptions, for example, are rooted in human nature. The Epicurean preconception of God is produced, like any other, by repeated sensory presentations.'[29]

'*Athénagore*', says Zeegers, '*comprend la* πρόληψις *dans un sens résolument opposé à celui que les philosophes grecs lui accordaient dans la formation des jugements*'[30] '*Il est inutile*', she adds, with respect to this matter at least, '*d'insister d'advantage sur le caractère philosophique du commentaire d'Athénagore.*'[31] I believe that Zeegers goes too far here, in that Athenagoras' apparent dismissal of κοινὴ προλήψις as a proper source for knowledge of God does not disqualify him from inclusion in the ranks of the philosophers. Where, then, does his understanding of the notion of προλήψις and of that of ἐπιστήμη τοῦ νοητοῦ come from, and what does he understand by them?

In the second century, only Justin Martyr (*First Apology* 2.3; 2A 4.4; *Dialogues* 17.1) and Athenagoras employed προλήψις. Philo has earlier spoken of how God 'in his prescience (προλήψει) foresaw all things' (*De confusione linguarum* 140); and at *De spectaculis* 2.46 he uses προλήψις in the sense of 'anticipation', as does Clement of Alexandria later (*Paedagogus.* 1.6 and *Stromateis*. 2.2). Origen uses it, later still, in the common sense of 'prejudice' (*Contra Celsum* 1.52). Yet it cannot be said that Athenagoras is influenced by Justin in this, given that the latter employs the term each time in the common, pejorative sense of 'prejudice' (and therefore not philosophically), whereas Athenagoras – pace Pouderon's translation of the term in the *Legatio* as '*préjugé*' – clearly recognizes its philosophical provenance (which, however, he rejects). In fact it is obvious that his rejection of the notion places him firmly within the philosophical–epistemological debate, simply because he feels the need to deal with it. It is clear that only some philosophical schools, primarily the Stoic and Epicurean, had the preconceptions at the centre of their epistemological framework; Athenagoras' implicit challenge to their usefulness simply puts him on one side of the philosophical debate, not beyond it. Athenagoras clearly contrasts here, in epistemological terms, (κοινή) προλήψις – which he understands to be the Epicurean–Stoic notion, though these two are distinct, of preconceptions of the existence of God which are common to all races – and ἐπιστήμη τοῦ νοητοῦ (knowledge of the intelligible). For Athenagoras, knowledge, not just of God's existence but of God's very being, comes only through revelation: namely the self-revelation of God (which, as we have seen above from 7.2, must be read as qualifying even the 'correct' readings of the poets and philosophers on knowledge

[28] Ibid, p. 253.

[29] Asmis, 'Epicurean epistemology' (above, n1), p. 279.

[30] N. Zeegers-Vander Vorst, 'La "prénotion commune" au chapitre 5 de la Legatio d'Athénagore', Vigiliae Christianae 25 (1971): 163.

[31] Ibid., p. 165.

of God) confirmed through reason (much in the sense that Alcinous speaks at 4.7.156.6f. of the primary intelligibles being judged by νόησις not without the aid of ἐπιστημονικοῦ λόγου, or at 4.8.156.13 of the intelligible world being judged by νόησις μετὰ λόγου). Self-revelation is not confirmed through the sort of natural intuition which the Epicurean–Stoic notions of a 'preconception' possibly represented for him; whereas true ἐπιστήμη – expressed as ἐπιστήμη νοητοῦ – represents a reliable and certain knowledge of the divine.[32] The sphere of ἐπιστήμη νοητοῦ is that of the perception, in Platonist terms, of the eternal, immutable Forms,[33] of the 'direct apprehension of intelligible reality'.[34] Thus ἐπιστήμη νοητοῦ provides an acceptable form in which the Christian may speak of knowledge of and about God, but only of course if this knowledge is sourced in God himself (see again 7.2 of the *Legatio*). In philosophical terms, Athenagoras is very much engaged in the contemporary conversation over what constitutes the source of true knowledge of God.

φαντασίαι Athenagoras also dismisses sources for the knowing of God the impressions–representations (φαντασίαι) (27.1f.) by which he believes that demons mislead humans about the truth of what is properly divine. Here Athenagoras is seeking to explain how demons can influence the choices and actions of human beings for the worse. For this purpose, his framework and language is primarily Stoic, though clear Platonic and biblical elements are also present. He explains that movements of the (human) soul which are not directed by reason but by fantasy, ἰνδαλματῶδες – and I should point out that this word is employed only by Athenagoras among Christian writers – in the realm of conjectures, δόξας (here he continues his diatribe against any reliance on opinions, clearly regarding all as false)– such movements derive certain images from matter, and they mould them independently and give birth to them. This happens for the most part when a soul attaches itself to the spirit of matter, blends with it and does not look up to heavenly things and to their creator, but down, to earthly things – that is, when it becomes mere flesh and blood and is no longer pure spirit. When such movements of the soul, irrational and fantastic (see also 27.1), give birth to illusory images (φαντασίας) in the form of a mad passion for idols (27.2), such a soul, weak and docile, ignorant and unacquainted with sound teachings, is unable to contemplate the truth or to understand who the Father and maker of all things is. Demons, being associated with matter and greedy for the savour of fat and the blood of sacrifices, and because their business is to delude human beings, make use of such delusions, which come from idols and from statues. The demons take credit for such movements of the soul, which, given its immortal nature, foretell the future or heal its present ills. The psychology, as indicated above, is primarily Stoic.

32 Though whether it actually does with Euripides himself in the final analysis will still be open to question.

33 Dillon, *The Middle Platonists* (above, n6), p. 92.

34 Ibid., pp. 273f.

Pouderon integrates it into '*la théorie stoïcienne de la perception*'.[35]

The Greek term φαντασία is one employed in both Epicurean and Stoic epistemology, although there it does not normally have the pejorative sense given it by Athenagoras. Although the word 'was sometimes applied to dreams and hallucinations',[36] it is more often value-neutral and simply designates an 'impression' on soul or mind (its presence in a particular person does not necessarily involve assent to its veracity). Epicurus spoke of φαντασία as something 'gained by focusing our thoughts and senses on some object', but he regarded φάντασμα as something which might come through sleep, for example (*To Herodotus* 46–53). Lucretius declared that 'whatever impression (*visum*) the senses get at any time is true' (4.469–521). But, says Diogenes Laertius, for the Epicureans even 'the figments (φαντάσματα) of madmen and of the dreaming are true, [because] they cause movement; [for] the non-existent moves nothing' (10.31–2). Epicurus also said that, 'while all φαντασίαι are true, opinions are not all true. Some are true, some false, given that opinions are merely judgements we make on the basis of our φαντασίαι' (*To Herodotus* 23). Every impression, for the Epicurean, is the product of something existent and therefore true (Sextus Empiricus, *Against the Professors* 8.6). The Stoics, for their part, employed φάντασμα more often negatively, to designate a 'figment' of the imagination (see Diogenes Laertius 7. 49–51 and Aetius, 4.12.1–5). Diogenes Laertius provides probably the most accessible and useful description of the Stoic understanding of an 'impression' (φαντασία):

> A presentation (or mental impression) (φαντασία) is an imprint (τύπωσιν) on the soul:[37] the name having been appropriately borrowed from the imprint made by the seal upon the wax. There are two species of impression, the one apprehending (τὴν καταληπτικήν) a real object, the other not (τὴν ἀκατά ληπτον). The former, which [the Stoics] take to be the test of reality (κριτήριον τῶν πραγμάτων), is defined as that which proceeds from a real object (ἀπὸ ὑπάρχοντος), agrees with the object itself, and has been imprinted seal-fashion and stamped upon the mind: the latter, or non-apprehending, is that which does not proceed from any real object (μὴ ἀπὸ ὑπάρχοντος), or, if it does, fails to agree with the reality itself, not being clear or distinct. (7.45–6)

Athenagoras may well have taken his understanding of φαντασία from the latter class of impressions. Crehan suggests that the verb ἐναποσφραγίζειν (to imprint: see ἐναποσφραγίσηται at 27.2) is Stoic, but Pouderon argues that the notion of the 'assimilation of the sensation to an imprint on the soul' belongs both to Platonism (*Theaetetus* 192a, Alcinous, 4.4.154.34f) and to Stoicism (Diogenes

---

35 *Athénagore: Supplique au sujet des chrétiens et sur la résurrection des morts*, translated by B. Pouderon, Sources Chrétiennes No. 379 (Paris, 1992), p. 174, note 1.

36 F.H. Sandbach, *The Stoics*, 2nd edn (Bristol, 1989), p. 86.

37 Some early Stoics took this notion quite literally.

Laertius 7.45). ἐναποσφραγίζειν and its derivatives are not employed by Philo or by any Christian writer in this or any other context before Athenagoras. Yet again, in the final analysis, given the primary and ultimate truth of *Legatio* 7.2 – Athenagoras' criterion–canon that true knowledge of and about God can come only from God himself –even true and existent impressions (if such exist for him) are unacceptable as sources of certain knowledge of the divine.

πιθανός At 24.6 Athenagoras, implicitly at least, repudiates the Scepticism of the New Academy when he contrasts truth with 'probability/plausibility' or what is 'probable/plausible' (πιθανός).[38] This debate, which concerned in part the interpretation of Plato's heritage and ranged between the so-called 'dogmatists, advocates of 'certain knowledge' (like Antioch of Ascalon), the modetate Sceptics of the New Academy (the so-called 'probabilists') and the hardcore Pyrrhonists, provides some background for Athenagoras' reflections. He sides with the 'dogmatists', but for reasons different from theirs. At 25.2 he also contrasts truth and conjecture/opinion concerning the particular providence of God. This is simply, in my view, a further repudiation of the probabilists. Although this is not a matter on which Athenagoras expends much energy, it is probably worth looking at the origins of the probabilist argument.

The moderate Sceptics of the New Academy, who believed that they were merely being faithful to the memory and example of Plato himself, felt that, if they were to reject the certainties claimed by Epicureans and Stoics and to accept the Sceptical notion of 'suspension of judgement', they needed a principle by which they could move forward in terms of behaviour and ethical life, if they were not to become captive to what seemed to be the only other alternative to certainty, that of 'opinion' – the one 'in which falsehood and deception are engendered' according to Plutarch (*Against Colotes* 1122a–f). The rationale of the suspension of judgement, he said, was not to deflect sensations; it removed opinions and made natural use of the rest. Sextus Empiricus spoke of the way in which Carneades himself had taken as his criterion –both the convincing impression (τὴν τε πιθανὴ ν φαντασίαν) and what is simultaneously convincing, undiverted and thoroughly explored (*Against the Professors* 7.166–75). He also spoke of 'convincingness' – plausibility – in the same piece. Cicero, in his defence of the Scepticism of the New Academy, said that its members were following the 'convincing' which he translated as *probabile* (*Academica* 2.59). But as Schofield properly points out, when Cicero translate τὸ πιθανὸν as *probabile*, we should not make the mistake of understanding this in the sense of the English word 'probable' or 'likely'[39] but rather in the sense of the Latin *probare*, 'to accept' or 'to approve'. For the New Academy saw τὸ πιθανὸν as something of which someone could be convinced or persuaded. It was conceived of as a rational procedure and not a mere probability,

---

[38] See Cicero, *Academica* 2.32f. and 2.104f., where he equates probabile with 'resembling the truth'.

[39] M. Schofield, 'Academic epistemology' (above, n3), p. 350.

which would be only a higher form of opinion about what was more likely than not. But for Athenagoras the πιθανόν probably was no more than a purely rational or logical argument and offered no more certainty than a mere opinion. It is not and cannot be truth. It is simply a form of conjecture.

ἀνάμνησις But there was also a fourth source of knowledge in antiquity: remembering. The notion of learning by way of 'remembering' pre-natal truths, as we see it presented in Plato's *Meno* (81d4–5: 'all inquiry and learning is but recollection') and *Phaedo* (72e3–8b3) and as Alcinous writes of it in his *Didaskalikos*, in the context of his own argument for the immortality of the soul (25.3.177.44f.: 'acts of learning are instances of remembering' (αἱ μαθήσεις ἀναμνήσεις) is not found in the *Legatio* even for the purpose of refutation – unless the notion of the πρόληψις has something to do with it. Alcinous says that learning cannot arise in any way other than by remembering what was formerly known: 'we derive our thoughts through recollection, on the basis of small sparks, under the stimulus of certain particular impressions, remembering what we knew long ago but forgot at the time of our embodiment' (25.3.178.8f., drawing on the *Phaedo*).

Summary

Thus Athenagoras repudiates any suggestion that an authentic or true or perfect knowledge of God – an imperfect or incomplete knowledge is certainly possible, even if unconscious of the influence of God (see chapters 4 to 7 of the *Legatio*) – can come through 'preconceptions' commonly held by humankind (to which the Epicureans and the Stoics attached some sense of certainty); or through 'impressions' or 'representations' which 'impress' themselves on human consciousness like seals on wax and can then be grasped in a second stage of cognition; or through a process of reflection which seeks the near-certainty (but not quite) of the 'plausible', the 'persuasive' or the 'convincing'. Such certain knowing about, or of, divine being is rather provided in the first instant and guaranteed by the witness of the prophetic Spirit (see 7.3; 9.1; 10.4) and by the Son–Word, who is described, as we saw above, as the mind and reason of the Father (see 10.2 and 24.2): a Father who is himself eternal mind and eternally rational (10.3) and can, in Platonist terms, be known by mind and by reason alone (see 4.1; 10.1; 22.9; 22.12; and 23.7[40]). This is true knowledge; all else is imperfect and unreliable opinion, conjecture, or even guesswork.

We see also here the juxtaposition of chapters 8 and 9 of the *Legatio*, where in the former proofs for the existence of only one God are provided by rational and routine logic, while in the latter it is made clear that the material in chapter

---

[40] See also *Timaeus* 28c and 52a; *Phaedrus* 247c; and Alcinous 10.4.165.5. We note, too, 4.7.156.6, where for Alcinous the primary thoughts are judged by thought with the aid of reason (νοῦς μετὰ λόγου).

8 is, on its own, merely a human construct – merely notions, ἔννοιαι – and that it is the voices of the Spirit-inspired prophets who provide the clinching, indeed (it would seem) the sole sufficient proof. The arguments of chapter 8, persuasive though they may be, are mere 'thoughts', which in Alcinous are styled as 'natural concepts' (φυσικαὶ ἔννοιαι). These Athenagoras has put through the metaphorical sword at 5.1. The primary (and, if necessary, sole) proof for the existence of the one and only God comes from the Spirit-inspired prophetic witness and from the Word as *idea* of the Father – that is, from God himself. It is in fact logic and reason which merely confirm what God, as the Spirit and the Word, has already told us or made accessible to us about Godself.

There may also be other ways in which things, including things about God, might be known, according to Athenagoras, even if imperfectly:

Physikos Logos

At 3.2, when introducing the three specific allegations brought against the Christians, Athenagoras speaks as follows. If these are but fabrications and slanders and can be explained through that 'natural principle (φυσικῷ λόγῳ) by which evil opposes virtue and through a divine law (θείῳ νόμῳ) [by which] opposites war against each other', and if the emperors themselves can witness to the Christians' innocence from the above allegations (by virtue of the fact that they merely command the Christians not to confess to their faith), then Athenagoras urges the emperors to examine the Christians' behaviour, their teaching and their faithfulness to emperors, family and empire (3.2). The phrase φυσικὸς λόγος is found also in Alcinous, where the author speaks of it – Dillon translates it 'reasoning faculty working on the physical level', and Louis, '*la raison naturelle*' –that by which we discern truth from falsehood (4.1.154.18), that is, the instrument by which we judge rather than the agent who judges. Later Alcinous speaks of 'that natural and scientific reasoning (ὁ φυσικὸς καὶ ἐπιστημονικὸς ... λόγος)' which is constituted of 'simple forms of knowledge and which arises in us by nature' (φύσει; Louis: *qui se trouve naturellement en nous*, 4.7.155.35). Dillon declares that '*logos physikos* here almost defies translation'.[41] Antiochus (*Academica Priora* 30) speaks of αἴσθησις (perception) as constituting the instrument of judgement, but also of the 'natural force of the mind' (δύναμις φυσική, 'which it directs to the things by which it is moved'. This, says Dillon, 'corresponds' to Albinus' (Alcinous') *logos physikos* which, he continues, one might render as 'an activity of the mind working through nature', the mind 'in act' receiving impressions from the outside world.[42] Athenagoras may well have borrowed the phrase from Alcinous – it appears nowhere else in early Christian literature – but he clearly employs it differently, not as an attribute or feature of the human mind but simply as a common law of nature which recognizes the inevitable conflict of

41 Dillon, *The Middle Platonists* (above, n6), p. 273.

42 Ibid.

opposites. Pouderon states that Athenagoras (here and at 31.1, where he speaks of evil habitually opposing virtue by 'some divine law or principle' (θεῖον νόμον καὶ λόγον)) identifies natural law and the divine power of providence, and that φυσικὸς λόγος '*est d'inspiration stoïcienne*'.[43] The phrase itself does not, to my knowledge, actually appear in any extant Stoic writing and, while it is possible that it is simply the equivalent of the Stoic concept of a divine natural law (according to Cicero, *De natura deorum* 1.14.36, Zeno would have asserted that the law of nature is divine; and at his *Republic* 3.33 the Stoic Laelius says that 'true law is right reason, in agreement with nature, diffused over everyone, consistent, and everlasting'), the fact is that it is not the φυσικὸς λόγος which is crucial here, but rather the notion of strife between opposites. In any case, φυσικὸς λόγος is not for Athenagoras a particular source or ground of knowing, and certainly not of knowing God.

At 25.4, the author of the *De resurrectione* speaks of the natural reason (ὁ φυσικὸς λόγος) given to human being to live in accord and harmony with itself. The phrase is therefore employed more with a meaning similar to that of Alcinous (see above) and not that of *Legatio* 3.2 – where it means 'natural principle'; but φυσικὸς λόγος is not intended in the *De resurrectione* as a means of knowing God.

A natural theology? At 5.2 and 5.3, Athenagoras continues the epistemological direction of this chapter by demonstrating, through Euripides, how something invisible (in this case God) can be shown to exist through the visibility of its works. Euripides, says Athenagoras, sees God across his works, discerning from the visible – air, ether and earth, elements of God's creation – a manifestation of the invisible. This one, whose works these are and by whose spirit they are guided, he takes to be God; and Athenagoras quotes what he thought to be from the hand of Sophocles (but in fact was not) to support this concept of knowing about something from its works (5.3). Thus Euripides can teach about this God both where he is and that he must be one. Thus God, or aspects of God, can be known through observations; observations which witness, through the goodness and the beauty and the majesty of God's creation, to those aspects of God himself.

Knowing Something of God through Logic

In chapters 8 and 9 of the *Legatio* Athenagoras provides yet another affirmation of his view that true and certain knowledge of and about God ultimately can come from God alone, that reliance on other sources, be they one's self-sourced knowledge, common preconceptions, impressions, even the argument from what is most plausible, cannot provide this certainty but (at best) only an imperfect and possibly flawed comprehension of the divine. In chapter 8 Athenagoras provides a logical argument for the oneness of God and his relationship with the world, and

---

[43] *Athénagore*, transl. Pouderon (above, n33), p. 226.

in chapter 9 he confirms these conclusions with reference to the unimpeachable witness of the prophets.

To understand the place of Athenagoras' argument of chapter 8 in the development and exposition of his epistemology, one needs to see it both in the context of his comments introducing chapter 9 – where he declares that, if the argument from chapter 8 was all that Christians had to rely upon in their proclamation of the oneness of God, then their doctrine could very well be regarded as no more than a human construct and hence, one presumes, opinion rather than knowledge – and in the context of his comments at 7.2, where he makes clear that the shortcomings of the poets and of the philosophers in their endeavours to discover the true God lie in their unwillingness to learn about God from God himself and in their persistence to conduct the process through their own efforts. True knowledge about God is sourced in God alone. The actual ordering of chapters 8 and 9 is not perhaps crucial; Athenagoras nowhere even implies that the prophets are not the first or primary resource of knowledge about God, but rather – and very clearly – that they are so. Indeed Athenagoras may well be simply demonstrating for the benefit of his readers, for whom such reasonings would be expected, that a logical proof for the oneness of God can be mounted; then and only then does he make it clear, however, that the proper proof actually lies elsewhere.

In chapter 8 Athenagoras offers a logical argument for the concept of God as one – what Pouderon calls a '*démonstration rationelle de l'existence d'un Dieu unique*'. Barnard calls it a *reduction ad absurdum* argument[44] and Malherbe suggests that the entire argument has to do with the τόπος of the gods[45] (a discussion of this claim will follow in due course). At 8.1 Athenagoras refers to God as the Creator of this universe, mirroring exactly the well-known phrase of Plato at *Timaeus* 28c3–4. He seeks to argue here that this God was 'one' from the very start; and he refers to the reasoning (λογισμὸν – a Stoic term according to Dillon[46]) which informs the Christians' faith. His argument is in two parts: one concerns the matter of *what* and the second of *where* God might be (this latter is known as the location argument). The first argument concludes at 8.3 with an answer of sorts to the major question: God is uncreated, impassible and indivisible; he does not consist of parts – and therefore he must be unitary. The second argument concludes at 8.8 with the following answer: God, the maker of the world, is from the beginning one and alone.

The arguments which Athenagoras employs are both Platonic and Stoic. Crehan maintains that 'the argument about God's location was a stock subject of debate

---

44 L.W. Barnard, Athenagoras: *A Study in Second Century Christian Apologetic* (Paris, 1972), p. 90.

45 A.J. Malherbe, 'The structure of Athenagoras, "Supplicatio pro Christianis"', *Vigiliae Christianae* 23 (1969), p. 15, note 77.

46 Dillon, *The Middle Platonists* (above, n6), p. 92.

in Stoic schools of philosophy'.[47] Grant argues that Athenagoras' argument on God's location may well come from pseudo-Xenophanes' *De Melisso Xenophane Gorgia*.[48] At 8.2, where Athenagoras says that two or more gods 'could not be in one and the same' (ἐν … ἑνὶ καὶ ταὐτῷ), Malherbe suggests that he means 'in one and the same place' and not 'in one and the same genus' (*contra* Ubaldi, Bardy, Crehan, Schoedel and Pouderon: '*ils ne pouvaient appartenir à un seul et même être*').[49] I would side with Ubaldi and the others, since Athenagoras has not yet spoken of 'place' or 'space' (though he has not spokenof 'genus' or 'category' at this point either). Yet it is clear that the first argument, as stated above, is about the *nature* of God (8.1–3), while only the second (8.4–8) addresses the matter of God's *location*. At 8.3 Athenagoras states that, unlike Socrates – who, being created and perishable, is indeed composite and divisible into parts – God, being one, is uncreated, impassible and indivisible; he does not consist of parts (οὐκ συνεστὼς ἐκ μερῶν). Alcinous too speaks of God as being 'without parts' (ἀμερή ς, 10.7.165.74). At 8.4, beginning the second part of his argument, Athenagoras declares that God in his capacity of maker of the world is above (ἀνωτέρω) the things which have been created. We are reminded of the Pythagorean Philolaus, referred to earlier, at 6.1, who also said that God is one and stands 'above' (ἀνωτέρω) matter. It is here that the notion of 'place' or 'space' is introduced by Athenagoras. Philo says that 'God is his own place' (*Legum allegoriae* 1.44), that God 'is himself the space which holds him' (*De somniis* 1.63), that God 'contains but is not contained' (1.185), andthat God 'contains all but is not contained' (*De sobrietate* 63 and *De confusione linguarum* 136) – although in the latter paragraph he goes on to say also that '[God] is nowhere, because he himself created space and place coincidently with material things, and it is against all right principle to say that the Maker is contained in anything that he has made'. Justin Martyr says in his *Dialogue* that 'the ineffable Father and Lord of all neither has come to any place, nor walks, nor sleeps, nor rises up, but remains in his own place' (127.2). Theophilus of Antioch says that God is 'his own τόπος' (*Autolycus* 2.10). The reference to the spherical shape of the world at 8.4 can also be found in Eudoxius.[50] In essence, Athenagoras' argument is that there is neither space nor place for more than one God. God is above all space and fills all space; there is no place or space for another! He concludes this argument with the observation that another God cannot be; for he could exercise providence, having created nothing. For Athenagoras, God's function as ποιητής of this world is essential to his being God. But this logical argument, as noted above, is not and cannot be, for

[47] *Athenagoras: Embassy for the Christians; The Resurrection of the Dead*, translated and annotated by J.H. Crehan, Ancient Christian Writers 32 (New York, 1956), p. 131, note 51.

[48] R.M. Grant, *The Early Christian Doctrines of God* (Charlottesville 1966), pp. 107f.

[49] Malherbe, 'Structure of "Supplicatio"' (above, n43), p. 15, note 77.

[50] *Athénagore*, transl. Pouderon (above, n33), p. 288.

Athenagoras, the primary basis for the Christian belief in the oneness of God. It merely provides affirmation, as 9.1 tells us, of what the Christians already 'know' through the prophets directed by the Spirit of God.

At 9.1 Athenagoras makes clear that the preceding argument – the logical argument for the necessary unity of God – is not by itself sufficient for the Christian; if it were, the Christian argument would be a mere human construct. Athenagoras' choice of language here is very instructive. The argument moves from ἔννοια to λογισμός when the divinely inspired prophets give their confirmation to it. Thus the primary and essental foundation for Christian belief is not logical argument – although the Christians can demonstrate (but not ultimately 'prove') the truth of what they believe– but the revelation of God through the inspired words of the prophets. These represent true and certain 'knowledge' because they are, essentially, the self-revelation of God (learning of God from God, as 7.2 has it);logical argument, by itself, is no better than 'opinion'. But the prophets do affirm the λογμισμός, the concept to which reason has been applied, of the Christians. Athenagoras speaks of them being moved in their ecstasy by the divine Spirit, who employs them as a flautist would a flute.[51] Parallel imagery can be found in Philo, at *Quis rerum divinarum heres* 259 and *Quod deus sit immutabilis* 24 and in Plutarch, at *De defectu oraculorum* 436f., though Crehan does point out that the image of the flute and flute-player can be found independently of Philo (132, n. 53).[52] The notion of the ecstasy of the prophets' thoughts is also found in Philo (*De specialibus legibus* IV.49; (and one can see again how the λογισμός in chapter 8 now attains a higher status as confirmed by the witness of the prophets). This is now a λογισμός, but one to which not human reason but the reason of God has been applied. Athenagoras then quotes Baruch and Isaiah (three times) as examples of the prophets' confirmatory witness to the effect that God is one (9.2). The logical argument confirms, but cannot itself prove, what the self-revelation of God through the Spirit-inspired prophets has already given to the believers. Athenagoras then urges the emperors to read the prophets and on that basis to end the abuse visited upon the Christians (9.3). In doing this they are to work μετὰ τοῦ προσήκοντος λογισμοῦ – 'with fitting discernment' (in Schoedel's translation), which highlights again the elevated status of the Christian argument that God is one.

Conclusions

Athenagoras' primary theology, on the being and nature of God, is both biblically and divinely sourced (5.2; 9.2; 10.2*; 10.4; 13.2; 13.4*; and 18.2: primarily Old Testament; the witness of the New is mainly to the Christian ethics) and Platonist and Stoic (God and matter (4.1; 6.1; 7.2; 15.1; 15.2; 15.3; 15.4; 16.3; 16.4; 19.4;

[51] Ibid., p. 140.

[52] *Athenagoras*, transl. Crehan (above, n45), p. 132, note 53.

20.5; 22.12; 24.1; 24.2; 25.1; and 27.2: see Alcinous, chapters 8 and 10); being and becoming (4.2 and 15.1: see *Timaeus* 27d–8a); the contrast between active (God) and passive (matter) causes: Stoic; the contrast of the world of thought and that of sense-perception, the intelligible and perceptible worlds (15.1; 19.2; and 36.3: *Timaeus* 27d–8a; Alcinous 4.7.155.35ff.); and a God accessible only to mind and reason – similarity of language and thought can also be seen particularly with the Middle Platonist Alcinous (at 3.2; 4.1; 5.1; 7.2; 10.1; 10.2; 10.3; 11.2; 13.1; 15.1; 15.4; 16.1; 19.2; 19.4; and 22.4), while that of the Spirit, particularly in terms of its providential, cohering, and unifying role, its task of pervading and giving form to matter, is, at least in the language employed, profoundly Stoic (6.2; 5.3; 6.4; 10.4; and 22.5). Athenagoras relates himself explicitly to the contemporary philosophical conversations about the relation between Creator and Supreme Being, about the relation between creation and Providence, Ideas and Forms, the temporal or atemporal nature of creation itself – as he does to any contemporary intra-Christian conversation.

Athenagoras argues for God's essential goodness and providence on the basis of a natural observation of the orderliness of the creation (4.2; 5.3; 7.1; 10.5; 13.2; 15.2; 15.3; 16.1; 16.3; 24.3; 34.2). He does this by making a clear and demonstrable connection between the goodness and the fairness of the creation and the goodness and fairness of the divine. And the Word of the divine is the *idea* and *energeia* of the Father and, in Platonist terms perhaps, the paradigm on which the creation itself is modeled. This truth of the goodness and fairness of God will be known, then, from the contemplation of the divine (chapter 3), from logic, from contemplation confirmed by reason (see Alcinous, 4.8.156.11f.), from the biblical and prophetic witness and from Christian teaching as λόγος. But it is the self-revelation of God – the self-revelation of God through the Son–Word and through the Spirit – that provides the only sufficient ground for such knowledge and teaching. All else may confirm the truth about God, but cannot, of itself, prove.

As I have indicated earlier, the basic epistemological framework of the arguments found in the *Legatio*, both positively and negatively, is to be found in the three blocks: chapters 4 to 7, chapters 8 and 9, and then chapters 10 to 12. At 4.1 Athenagoras introduces the Platonist notion of the God contemplated solely by mind and thought. He then, at 4.2, makes clear that in the good, perhaps even perfect ordering and arrangement of the world, there exists evidence of the goodness and perfection of its creator. These, he says, are signs conducive to piety, and this piety, taken as the worship and fear of God, is the clearest sign of our knowing of God. In chapter 5 Athenagoras introduces the testimony of the poets, principally Euripides, and employs him to demolish any suggestion that the knowledge of God might come, apart from divine revelation, through some sort of communally stored memory. Yet again he points to the signs of the creation as witnessing the existence and the oneness of its creator. In chapter 6 he employs the major philosophical schools – though he will not accord the Epicurean a place there – as witnesses to the concept of God as one. He lists them in order of value perhaps, starting with the Pythagorean (he may have accepted the common wisdom of the day, which claimed that Plato himself was a disciple of Pythagoras); then followed Plato (who was certainly most important to him), Aristotle, and finally the Stoics (of whose language he makes extensive use, but by the thought of whom he is rather less taken). He then qualifies, at 7.2, any endorsement of poetic or philosophical grasp, or apprehension, of the truth of God by making clear that the very marginal and incomplete knowledge which the claimants have of truth, true being and God is peripheral, and what they do have comes to them only because of some linkage between their souls and the breath of God. Christians, on the other hand, have the wisdom and divinely inspired testimonial of the prophets to rely on, so that they know and not simply opine (7.3). We have already looked in detail at chapters 8 and 9, where Athenagoras has demonstrated that he can show the essential unity of God through logical argument but, having done so, concludes that this, on its own, is mere human teaching and ultimately unreliable, or at least imperfect. Christians, nevertheless, have the prophetic witness, the witness of God himself through the Word and Spirit, and that is all that is needed.

In chapter 10 Athenagoras begins to bring this particular set of arguments to a close by outlining the Christian witness to the Trinity. Here the Son is the *idea* or image of God, and his unity with the Father is sourced in the Spirit. He is the mind and reason of the Father and thus the agency through which the Father can be known, contemplated, grasped, apprehended. There is also the Spirit, active in those who speak prophetically. Here it is unclear how the Son and the Spirit are the agencies which make God the Father known. For they, as agents, are at one with the Father. With the Father, they *are* God, and therefore what they inspire or mediate is from God. And then, at 11.1, we are reminded yet again that the emperors can access the truth through doctrines which are not human constructs, but ordained and taught by God. This epistemological framework surfaces again and again in the work, most notably one chapter later, where Athenagoras explores the Christian-lived ethics with the observation that in their living Christians are attended only by the knowledge of this ‘one’ who is truly God, of his Word, and of his communion with both Son and Spirit (12.3).

We know, then, what we know primarily from the biblical witness, from the prophetic witness (through the inspiration of the Holy Spirit who ‘plays’ the prophets like instruments), and from the Son–Word as Mind and Reason and as *idea* and *energeia* of the Father. Logic and reason merely confirm the human mind in what God has already revealed of Godself. Athenagoras’ thought, then, has no place for universal preconceptions, for impressions left on the mind like seals on wax by natural causes, for moderate Scepticism or ‘probabilism’ and its criterion of plausibility. He does not even bother to repudiate the hardcore Pyrrhonists. He would probably applaud the certainties of Stoicism, but not their claimed sources. Here Athenagoras is the biblical philosopher who knows where truth is to be found; the poets and other philosophers can only grasp the truth dimly when they are touched by the breath (the Spirit) of God. They rely ultimately on themselves, for they do not know the touch of God even when it rests upon them – which is even the fate of some Christians: those who think they need only the logical cleverness of chapter 8. Athenagoras participates without doubt in the Middle Platonist conversation of the second century, but he brings to that conversation the particular insights of the faith community from which he comes.

At 12.2, 15.5 and 25.4, the author of the *De resurrectione* speaks of a 'rational judgement (ἡ λογικὴ κρίσις) given to a human being, whereby this being might live in accordance with its own given nature and in contemplation of God. At 13.1 and 24.4 he speaks of the 'innate law' (νόμον ἔμφυτον) given to human beings for the safeguarding and protection of the things suitable for intelligent beings with a rational life. This is no suggestion, however, that such a law will allow anyone access to a particular and certain knowledge of God. At 14.1, 14.2 and 24.2 he speaks of a 'universal and natural axiom (τῆς κοινῆς καὶ φυσικῆς ἐννοίας); but this is never, as was condemned in the *Legatio* (5.1), an inadequate means of knowing of God, but simply as a series of natural rules and observations from human experience which human being might find useful to consider.

Chapter Five
What do we know about God? First principles

> Plato thought that … that alone truly exists which is always such as it is, which he called *idea*.
>
> (Cicero, *Tusculan Disputations*1.58; see also *Academica* 1.30)

> The judge of things was [for Antiochus of Ascalon] the mind. It alone perceives that which is eternally simple and uniform and true to its own quality. This thing they call the *idea*, a name given it by Plato; we correctly call it form (*species*).
>
> (Cicero, *Academica* 1.30)

Background

The presenting issue in the *Legatio* is the claim of unjust and unfair treatment of Christians by the Roman authorities. Against this background, Athenagoras, like Socrates in his trial some 600 years earlier, acknowledges the prejudice of the crowds – the 'mob' (1.3) – and the slanders directed against the defendants. Against the background, then, of what he regards as the most serious of the three specific allegations made against Christians by pagans – atheism, incest and cannibalism (3.1) – Athenagoras sets out to prove that the Christians are not atheists, some twenty-seven out of the thirty-seven chapters in the treatise being given over to the refutation of this particular charge.

A doctrine of God independent from the need to establish God's capacity and willingness, qua Creator, to reconstruct human beings from their decomposed *post mortem* state to new life (and his worthiness in so doing) is not central to the *de Resurrectione*.

Defence against the Charge of Atheism

To regard Christians as atheists, Athenagoras begins, is irrational (ἀλόγως) (4.1 and 4.2); it is so obvious that we are not atheists, he says, that it seems madness even to take the time to refute those who suggest this. It may be appropriate that a Diagoras of Melos be charged with atheism, for activities on his part which are consistent with atheism are widely documented. Yet Christians are theists who believe in the one, good, providential Father and Creator – the one who is truly God - and do it in a way which is consistent with what contemporary philosophers understand of the divine being. And Athenagoras begins his refutation of this particular charge in a manner which perhaps may seem odd for a Christian theologian and –apologist – although Tertullian himself later on committed an entire treatise, the *Adversus Hermogenem*, to the refutation of the Platonic notion that matter is a primary principle, along with God (*hylē* is not, of course, the term employed by Plato – it probably comes from Aristotle). Athenagoras declares that it is precisely on the ground of the Christians' differentiating God from matter – the one as uncreated, eternal and able to be contemplated by thought and reason alone; the other as created and perishable – that they must be recognized and acknowledged as theists. And yet it is here, where the Christian and the Platonic views on what constitute primary principles diverge, that Athenagoras chooses to stake his ground (see chapter 15 for a fuller discussion of the gulf between God and matter; and also 6.1; 16.2f.; 19.3f.; and 24.1). He then argues at 4.2 that, if Christians had clear evidence in the order, perfect harmony, magnitude, and arrangement (*inter alia*) of the world, and yet, like Diagoras, still did not believe in the existence of God, then they would deserve condemnation as atheists. But this is not the case; Christians teach that there is but one God, the Creator of the all, uncreated as true being, and that all things have been created by that Word which issues from him. Thus it is indeed *alogos* to condemn the Christians for atheism. From the very beginning, then, Athenagoras lays out the rule of the Christian belief in God: that he is very much other than matter, that he is One, that he is uncreated, that he can be contemplated by mind and reason alone, that he is Creator of the All, that he is true being. From chapter 5 onwards, Athenagoras focuses on the oneness of God (the word 'unity' is best left for Trinitarian contexts), which would appear, notwithstanding the opening salvo by way of God's differentiation from matter, to be the primary divine attribute for Athenagoras. Perhaps it was because many of the poets and philosophers could be brought as witnesses to the oneness of God that Athenagoras thought it critical first to differentiate the Christian position from the philosophical one, particularly the Stoic, and only then to move on to discuss those positions held in common.

First Principles

Athenagoras' presentation of a doctrine of God is, in part at least, set against a framework informed and shaped by contemporary metaphysics. Diodorus Cronus (d. *c.*284 BCE), leader of the dialectical school, said that the ultimate constituents of the world were 'minimal and partless bodies', existents irreducibly small and thereby ultimately indivisible. For Epicurus, the first principles (and he identifies them with the elements, στοιχεῖα), or 'ultimate indivisibles',[1] are 'bodies' and 'space (or void)' (*To Herodotus* 39–40). These two are the only components of the 'all'; for they alone have independent existence. They are not reducible to something more fundamental. The 'all' itself does not change, for there is no space or void beyond the 'all' into which change can occur. Other existents might appear to be such 'indivisibles', but they are actually only properties of body and space/void and include inseparable properties and accidental properties, time, and facts about the past.

For the Stoic, there are two ultimate and indestructible principles, both 'ungenerated and indestructible' (or 'incorruptible') (ἀγενήτους καὶ ἀφθάρτους) – unlike the elements themselves, which have been endowed with form and are destroyed when all things are resolved into fire, becoming 'incorporeal and destitute of form' (Diogenes Laertius 7.134). Both are bodies, of course, as everything else in the Stoic world. The first is that which acts upon or the active principle; the other is that which is acted upon or the passive principle. For a body – and only bodies 'exist' – must be capable either of acting or of being acted upon. Sextus Empiricus says that for the Stoics there is a power which in itself is self-moving and must be divine and eternal (*Against the Professors* 9.75–6).[2] For the Stoics, says Diogenes Laertius, god is 'the individual entity whose quality is derived from the whole of substance', who is 'indestructible and ungenerated' (ἄφθαρτος καὶ ἀγένητος) (7.137). According to Diogenes again (7.134), the passive principle is a substance without quality, that is, matter, while the active principle is the *logos* inherent in this substance, that is, god. God is everlasting and the *dēmiourgos* of each thing throughout the whole extent of matter. Principles and elements are to be distinguished from each other, as we have seen. But this apparently dualistic system is in fact monistic, for god and matter are always conjoined and it is their conjunction that creates the four elements – fire, air, water and earth – and it is the divine *logos* that makes matter take the form now of fire, now of water, and now of earth;[3] God and matter 'are never found in dissociation from one another'.[4] Matter and god are 'never found in actual separation' but rather are separated in thought in order for us to understand their causal relations.[5] The immanent principle, god, acts upon the principle matter (Seneca, *Letters* 65.2) and is never identified with the form present in matter. God is immanent in the matter but not *qua* form. But God is immanent and not transcendent because bodily contact is necessary for causal capacity.

[1] K. Algra et al. (eds), *The Cambridge History of Hellenistic Philosophy* (Cambridge, 2005), p. 362.

[2] Plato, in the *Phaedrus*, speaks of 'that which moves itself [and] must be the beginning of all motion' (245c–e). This entity is also ungenerated and indestructible (ἀγένητον καὶ ἀδιάφθορον).

[3] F.H. Sandbach, *The Stoics*, 2nd edn (London, 1989), p. 73.

[4] A.A. Long, *Stoic Studies* (Cambridge, 1996), p. 228.

[5] D. Sedley, 'Hellenistic physics and metaphysics', in Algra et al. (eds), *Hellenistic Philosophy* (above, n1), p. 384.

Even in Plato himself there are clear lines of demarcation between the principles, though he does not employ terms like ἀρχή or ὕλη. At *Timaeus* 27d–8a he differentiates between the intelligible – that which always exists and has no becoming, the ever uniformly existent, self-identical and uniform (as at 28c–9a); – and the perceptible – that which is always becoming and never exists, being that which becomes and then perishes. At 48e f. Plato recognizes that previously (at 28a) he had distinguished two forms (εἴδη) – which was both suitable and sufficient for his purpose: a paradigmatic form, the intelligible and ever uniformly existent, and a copy, one subject to becoming and visible; but now he needs to declare a third form, one which is baffling and obscure: the receptacle and nurse of all becoming. By way of an explanation and illustration of this point, Plato uses first the example of fire and the other primary elements and, second, of figures made from gold. With respect to the first he says that none of the elements – fire, water, earth or air – remains identical in appearance; they all lack stability and therefore one can never call them 'this' or 'that', but only 'suchlike' (49b f.). But that 'wherein' the elements always are in appearance, coming severally into existence, and that 'wherefrom' they perish, that and that alone can be properly described as a 'this' or a 'that', or as having stability (49e–50a). With respect to the second illustration, Plato says that when one asks 'What is it?' concerning figures made out of gold and then reshaped and remade into other figures from the same material, the proper answer is not that is the name of the particular figure but rather 'gold'; for the figure itself is simply 'suchlike' (50b). From this Plato deduces that the same account must be given of the substance which receives all bodies (50b f.). It must always be called by the same name, for it never departs from its own quality (50c). For, while it is always receiving all things, nowhere and never does it assume any shape similar to any of the things that enter into it. It is laid down by nature as a moulding-stuff for everything, being moved and marked by the entering figures, and because of them it appears different at different times. The figures that enter and depart, on the other hand, are copies of those that are always existent.

Thus, for now, three 'kinds', γένη, are to be conceived: that of becoming, that of the 'wherein' it becomes, and that of the source 'wherefrom' the becoming is copied and produced. It is appropriate to liken the recipient to a mother, the source to a father, and that which is engendered between them to an offspring. And the substance 'wherein' must be devoid of all those forms which it is about to receive from any quarter (50d). Therefore the substance, which is fitted to receive, frequently and over its whole extent, the copies of all things intelligible and eternal should itself, of its own nature, be void of all forms (51a). The mother and receptacle of this generated world – which is perceptible through sight and the senses – should not be called by the name of earth, air, fire, or water, but rather invisible, unshaped (unformed), all-receptive (πανδεχές), as it partakes of the intelligible in a perplexing and baffling way. Are there, then, 'self-subsisting realities' like 'fire' (51b)? Or is for example the 'fire'we see, which is perceived by our bodily senses, the only existent fire, the only fire possessing sensible reality? And is and the intelligible form of every object nothing more than a verbal expression? Plato then declares that, if reason and true opinion are two distinct γένη, then most certainly these self-subsisting forms exist, being imperceptible to our senses and being objects of reason alone (51d). At 52a Plato then describes and differentiates not only the self-identical form, ungenerated and indestructible, the object which it is the part of reason to contemplate and the object perceptible by sense, generated, becoming in a place and out of it again perishing, and apprehensible by opinion with the aid of sensation – this was the two-fold distinction of *Timaeus* 27d–8a; but also a third kind (γένος), namely ever-existing place. Place admits of no destruction and which provides space for all things which have birth, an entity apprehensible by a kind of bastard reasoning aided by non-sensation, an entity which is barely an object of belief.

Thus Plato postulates here three distinct things: being, becoming and place. It seems to me (and this is certainly the view of Alcinous, 8.2.162.30f., and of other Platonists) that, although Plato does not himself employ the language of matter (ὕλη), that to which he refers as the 'third' kind (or genus) at 52a is what others, including his own followers, identified as matter. Such an entity does not appear at 27d–8a, where the distinction is made solely between the intelligible as model and the perceptible as copy. It would seem acceptable therefore to suggest that, for Plato himself (as for the Stoics after him), both God and matter belong to the category of the eternal, the ungenerated and the indestructible, and the copies, which are made from the intelligible forms and received and moulded in matter, to that of the generated and the perishable.

Among Plato's successors, the first principles were normally held to be g/God, the Forms and matter. Apuleius deals with them in the order God–matter–Forms (*de Platone* 190–93) and Alcinous, matter–Forms–God (*Didaskalikos* 8–10). Although Plato himself never employs the word ὕλη, it is clear from the *Timaeus* that he would have endorsed this trilogy and that (as we saw above) the 'receptacle' of 51a is for him that substance at *Timaeus* 51a which is 'devoid of all forms' – what others term 'matter', as Aristotle and Plato's other disciples believed.

Athenagoras and First Principles

From the very opening of the refutation in the *Legatio* of the charge of atheism leveled against Christians, Athenagoras' approach, even if only negatively, is informed and shaped largely by contemporary metaphysics, particularly by a contrast between the standard philosophical *archai*, God and matter. At 4.1 he claims that the charge of atheism against Christians is groundless and even ridiculous. It is not rational, he contends, to apply the term 'atheist' to those who distinguish God from matter and who demonstrate that matter – created and perishable, and therefore not a first principle according to most standard systems – and God – uncreated, eternal and able to be contemplated by mind and reason alone – have an immense gulf between them. Here it would seem that Athenagoras probably has the de facto monism of the Stoics – that notion of God and matter as being conjoined and actually inseparable – more in the firing line than a Platonist ontology, for it is clear that he wishes to separate God and matter before concluding that the latter is unqualified to be regarded as a first principle. It is also true, as I will note below, that Athenagoras clearly chooses to interpret Plato – against the clear intention of Plato himself and against the interpretations of his later followers like Alcinous – as including matter in the 'always becoming/never existent/object of opinion/perishable' element of *Timaeus* 27d–8a and not identifying it, as Plato clearly did, with the third γένος of *Timaeus* 51a (which 'partakes of the intelligible' 'in a most perplexing and baffling way'). In the following section (4.2), although he does not name 'matter' as such, Athenagoras confirms that the one God and Creator of the universe is not created, since what is created is non-being (τὸ μὴ ὄν) – and he clearly means here matter qua that which is always coming into existence; whereas not being (τὸ ὄν) is uncreated.

Here, then, Athenagoras firmly places matter in the class of that which is 'becoming always and never existent' and therefore is not a first principle. Why would he apparently misrepresent Plato on this topic? It may be that he was working from a doxography, as he claims at 6.2 to be doing in his work on Plato's *Timaeus*, and did not have access to the later passages from the original work. In this case he simply assumed that Plato included matter when he referred to the generated, sensible and perishable nature of the becoming – because this would not be, by itself, an unreasonable reading of 27d–28a. Or he was well aware of the later passages in the work but simply chose to portray Plato's position as consistent with his own.

At 6.1 he appeals, with or rather without historical accuracy, to the witness of the Pythagorean Philolaus, who, he claims, declared that God is one and 'above matter' rather than co-existent with it. Even at 6.2, where he is not dealing with matter at all, Athenagoras makes clear that Plato, at *Timaeus* 41a, speaks of the one God–Creator as alone uncreated; even the lesser gods are the creatures of this one only God. At 6.3 Athenagoras declares that Aristotle and his school have said that God is a composite living being, namely one composed of body and soul. This body is the ether, the planets and the sphere of the fixed stars, all moving in a circular path, while the soul is the reason which controls the motion of the body. This soul is itself unmoved, yet it is the cause of the motion of the body. At 6.4 Athenagoras speaks of the Stoic notion of the Spirit of God moving through the permutations of matter – the names of the 'gods' corresponding to elements of matter such as 'fire' (Zeus), 'air' (Hera), and so on. Athenagoras does not himself endorse this view; his purpose here is solely to enlist the somewhat imperfect testimony of the Stoics to the oneness of God. At 7.1 he maintains that all the poets and philosophers – or at least those discussed previously by him – point to the oneness of the divine (τὸ θεῖον) –here he employs the abstract term for divinity – when they get down to the matter of 'the first principles of the All'. He says here nothing more about 'first principles', given that (again) his primary purpose is to enlist support for his claim for the oneness of God. At 7.2 he develops this further when he declares that the poets and philosophers – essentially because they have relied upon their own resources, upon guesswork and speculation, and not upon God in seeking to know of God – have gained no more than a peripheral or marginal understanding of God and have come up with a variety of doctrines concerning the world and the first principles (?) (this is a clear reference back to his speaking of ἀρχαί at 7.1) of God, matter and the Forms (for the last, Athenagoras employs εἶδος and not ἰδέα, which usually designated the forms immanent in matter rather the forms as transcendent –for Plato (see *Timaeus* 51a), for Alcinous and for himself earlier on). While the world is not normally included in any Platonist list of first principles, its relationship to the God–Creator and its relationship – qua ordered matter – to matter qua something pre-existing, unformed and unqualified were important metaphysical issues in contemporary thought, particularly among Middle Platonists like Plutarch, Calvenus Taurus, Atticus, Alcinous and Apuleius. It is crucial that Athenagoras introduces the concept of first principles here, for from now until at least the end of chapter 16 his discussion of these, both explicit and implicit, is central to his whole argument about the nature of divine being.

In chapter 8 Athenagoras offers an argument based on reason and logic for there being only one God.[6] This is the reasoning which supports 'our faith'; but, as chapter 9 makes clear, it is not the source for that faith but rather confirms what the Spirit-driven prophetic witness of the scriptures has already provided. At 8.3 Athenagoas declares that God – unlike Socrates, who is created and perishable like matter itself – is uncreated, impassible, and indivisible. God is partless. This last is surely a standard description of first principles – what Epicurus called the 'ultimate indivisibles': that which cannot be further reduced to more fundamental elements, and that which alone can thereby have independent existence. Yet for Athenagoras it belongs to God alone. He confirms this at 8.4, where he speaks of the notional two or more gods being independent and assumes, like Philolaus at 6.1, that God is above the things created. At 8.6 Athenagoras speaks of all things being 'filled' by God; there is nothing, there can be nothing beyond a primary principle. At 8.7 it is claimed that God 'fills' that which is above the world. It is said, both here and elsewhere in chapter 8, that there is no place (τόπος) for a notional second god. God alone fills the void; there is no void beyond the being and extent of God. God alone, therefore – as Athenagoras' reasoning would imply – is a first principle. God, the Creator of the world, is from the beginning one, and alone as a first principle.

At 10.1 God is declared to be uncreated, eternal, infinite (with a host of other attributes), and ruler of the universe. There is no talk here of God as indestructible, and this may be because in this particular context there is no explicit contrast with matter. At 10.2 – and at 10.3 – Athenagoras speaks for the first time of the notion of *idea* (ἰδέα) – as opposed to speaking of the form (εἶδος). For Athenagoras, the Son of God is the Word of the Father in *idea* (ἐν ἰδέᾳ), and only Athenagoras describes him this way. He refers elsewhere to forms-in-matter, or rather 'forms of the matter' (τὰ εἴδη τῆς ὕλης; see 15.4; 22.5,9; and 24.2), as matter given form and quality (compare *Timaeus* 51a and Alcinous); but only here does he refer to the notion of the *idea*. But, lest anyone might think that here Athenagoras has in mind a derived form or a lesser form – lesser, that is, than the divine being – he

6 See also Chapter 4 above for my discussion of ch. 8 as an epistemological issue.

makes clear that this Son–Word through whom everything comes into existence is one with the Father, is in the Father and the Father is in him by the power and unity of the Spirit, is the mind and reason of the Father, and did not come into existence but was with the Father from the beginning, coming forth only to serve as *idea* and *energeia* to give form to unqualified matter (10.3). This notion of matter as something unqualified is Stoic in origin [rather Aristotelian?] and carries with it the suggestion that matter is not so much created as eternally unformed. At 12.3 this Son is again proclaimed the Word who comes forth from the entity who is truly God, as the Son who shares a oneness with the Father, a communion with the Father, and a oneness with Father and Spirit. At 13.2 the Creator and Father of the universe is pronounced utterly self-sufficient, as thereby utterly independent and self-reliant.

At 15.1, picking up again his starting theme of chapter 4, he abuses the crowd for their inability to distinguish matter –created, not-being, perceptible – from God – uncreated, being, intelligible – something the Christian can do. Here is a reflection of *Timaeus* 27d – the intelligible differentiated from the sensible – and of the notion that Christians can name entities for what they actually and properly are. At 15.2f., Athenagoras employs the image of the artisan and his materials, of the potter and his clay and of the craftsman and his vessel in order to illustrate further the huge gulf which exists between God and matter – matter which does not, which indeed cannot receive articulation, form and order without God the Creator. Even if there be something to admire in the finished product, it is surely, Athenagoras says, the creator and not the creation that deserves praise and honour. The material forms – the τὰ εἴδη τῆς ὕλης – are not the same as he who is truly God, and are perishable and corruptible against the eternal nature of God (15.4), the one who cannot perish. Here God alone is the primary, indestructible first principle.

In chapter 16 Athenagoras continues this argument, but now it is not unformed, unqualified matter which is contrasted with God but rather matter formed and qualified as the *kosmos*. The world as arranged by God, formed as a perfect sphere, should not be worshipped whatever its beauty; its creator alone should be (16.1). As an illustration, Athenagoras employs the idea that people admire the imperial residences which the emperors have built, but it is the emperors themselves whom they honour above all (16.2). The world, he says, did not come into being because God needed it, for God is self-sufficient and dependent on nothing external to himself (16.3) – that is, God is the independent first principle. He is all things to himself, himself a complete *kosmos*. If the world were a harmonious instrument, one would not worship it but the player. Even Plato and the school of Aristotle, he says, in speaking of the beauty of the world, revere the creator alone. One does not worship the beggarly and weak elements, or passable matter, but their Creator and ruler alone. Matter and the elements may be beautiful, but they are perishable and thereby not first principles, even by the criteria of the Stoics and Platonists. Even Plato testifies (at *Politicus* 269d) to the mutability of matter and of the elements constructed from it (16.4). This is Athenagoras' proof that Plato himself included matter within the category of the sensible.

In chapter 17 Athenagoras seeks to demonstrate that the pagan gods are not gods or, more particularly, that their images are not gods. They were not gods from the beginning, they are the handiwork of men (and therefore younger than their craftsmen); they are earth, stones and matter (17.5). At 19.1 Athenagoras declares that each of the entities divinized by the poets must have a beginning and thereby be perishable, hence it cannot be classed as a first principle. For these entities are either, as *Timaeus* 27d requires, something uncreated and eternal or something created and therefore perishable. At 19.2 he then quotes from *Timaeus* 27d directly on the uncreatedness of the intelligible, that which always is, and the createdness of the sensible, that which is not, that which has a beginning to its existence and therefore an end. He then makes clear that he is speaking metaphysically when at 19.3 he describes the way the Stoics speak of two causes – the one active and efficacious insofar as it is providence, the other passive and mutable in so far as it is matter. The world, he continues, is subject to becoming and mutable. The gods derive their substance from matter. Matter is not more ancient than God, for the active cause (God) necessarily precedes those things that come into being (19.4). At 20.1 Athenagoras reaffirms that there is nothing created which is not also subject to dissolution. At 20.5 he restates his position that 'the divine must differ somewhat from earthly things and things derived from matter'. At 21.5 he speaks of the 'god' who is created, perishable, with nothing of a god about him. Such a god, being 'perishable', cannot be classified as a first principle.

At 22.3 Athenagoras continues his diatribe against equating matter with God when he introduces Empedocles' theory, according to which Love is the ruling principle and the composite entities the ruled, the ruling principle being the master of the other. If this is so, says Athenagoras, how can one attribute one and the same power to the ruled and to the ruling principle, making perishable, unstable and changeable matter equal in rank to the uncreated, eternal and ever self-same God? We are reminded of *Timaeus* 52a, where the first γένος is described as the 'self-identical Form' (τὸ κατὰ ταὐτὰ ε̂ἶδος). Matter, therefore, cannot be a first principle, while God surely is. At 22.5 Athenagoras continues in this vein and draws again on a Stoic element, comparing the uncreated and eternal God to these composite entities resulting from the mutation of matter and, through the spirit of God, pervading matter to produce 'material forms' – entities which perish at the cosmic conflagration. At 22.6 he refutes any suggestion that even Cronus is a god – given that Cronus, qua time, changes, while the divine is immortal, immovable and unchangeable (the last property being a necessary prerequisite for something's being a first principle). If his offspring, Zeus, is air, he changes too; but and the divine neither changes nor decays. At 22.9 Athenagoras refers to the twists and turns by which his opponents divinize the elements, while they don't see the God who is alone contemplated by reason. At 22.12 he says that they are fixated on the material forms and divinize the elements, without realizing that, even if the elements were beautifully ordered, they are of no value without the providence of God and cannot move without their creator. At 24.1 he again characterizes Christians as those who in their teaching distinguish God and matter and their respective substances, echoing again the key themes of chapters 4, 15 and 16. At 24.2ff. he continues this theme, beginning with a re-articulation of the Christian doctrine of the Trinity, speaks of the spirit opposed to God – created along with the rest of the angels by God, and entrusted particularly with the administration of matter and material forms – and then, with an eye yet again to *Timaeus* 41a, he speaks of the angels brought into being by God to exercise a particular providence over the things set in order by him (over against God's general or universal providence over everything). Among those angels who violated the trust and the charge given them by God was the prince of matter and material forms. At 25.1 he again refers to the prince of matter, who directs and administers things in a manner opposed to God's goodness, and at 25.3 he suggests that our inclination to move, with respect to the appointment of God, either faithfully or faithlessly depends very much on the one hand on our affinity with the divine and, on the other, on our kinship with matter. For Athenagoras, the gulf between matter and God could not be greater.

At 27.1 Athenagoras, dealing with human psychology and particularly with how humans are exploited through their own delusions and led astray by demons, shows how such deluded souls derive false images from matter, attaching themselves to the spirit of matter and blending with it rather than looking to heavenly things and to their Creator. He speaks further at 27.2 of evil demons associated with matter. At 29.3 he reiterates that the divine needs nothing. At 30.3 we are again reminded that the uncreated God is alone eternal; this rules out matter as a first principle. Thus for Athenagoras God, and possibly his inseparable Word as the *idea* of the Father, is alone a primary principle, while matter, created, perishable, changeable and dependent cannot be so.

The Attributes (Qualities) of the Christian God

One For Athenagoras, and for early Christian theologians generally, it is crucial, as it was indeed for many philosophical school traditions, that God should be one (see 4.2; 5.3; 6.1; 6.2; 6.3; 6.4; 7.1; 8.1f.; 8.8; 10.1; 10.2 (the sole Trinitarian reference made in this particular language[7]); 23.5; 23.7 and 24.1) – primarily one as the only god. To support this claim and to link the Christian claim to the broader philosophical one, Athenagoras draws on the witness of the poets and philosophers in chapters 5 (Euripides and pseudo-Sophocles), 6 (the Pythagoreans, Plato, Aristotle and the Stoics) and 7 (where he points to the weakness of the poetic–philosophical argument over against the strength of the prophetic). He draws on logic in chapter 8 to demonstrate that there can be only one God and that this God must be providential; and on the prophetic witness in chapter 9 to provide the

[7] See below, the discussion of Athenagoras' presentation of the Trinity in Chapter 6.

primary and sufficient basis for this position.

At 4.2 Athenagoras gives the one God as the sole first principle, repudiating any suggestion that matter – and especially matter as conceived by the Stoics; for in that tradition the two principles, being active and passive,[8] were regarded as in fact conjoined and inseparable – exists as a first principle alongside God. At 5.3 he quotes from pseudo-Sophocles to support the notion that God exists and must be one. In chapter 6 he draws on the main philosophical traditions, with a decreasing measure of warmth, as witnesses to God's unity. At 6.1 he cites the famous Pythagorean Philolaus on the fact that God is one and above matter (the language is almost certainly not that of Philolaus himself; but Athenagoras' point is nevertheless well made).[9] Then he cites the less known Pythagoreans Lysis, who defined God as ineffable number, and Opsimus, who defined God as the excess of the greatest number over that nearest to it. God therefore, for the Pythagoreans, is one – a monad (μονάς). While μονάς is a Pythagorean term, it is clear that Athenagoras is happy to own it for himself, for it makes his point rather well. While Plato spoke of the active one and of the infinite dyad as forming the substrate of the physical world (Aristotle, *Metaphysics* I.6.987a29f.), and his successor Speusippus (at the head of the Academy between 407 and339 BCE) spoke of the one being without qualities and thus presented an extreme form of divine transcendence, Xenocrates (396–14 BCE) advanced two supreme principles: the monad (whom he identified with *nous* (fr. 16)) and the dyad. This monad, he declared, was Father, Zeus, Odd, Intellect and supreme God (Aetius, fr. 15).[10] In the late second century BCE, however, a Platonist from Alexandria, Eudorus, pushed to the extremes of monism by positing a supreme 'one', an utterly transcendent God who was above the monad (conceived of as Form and limit) and above the dyad (conceived of as matter and limitlessness). After him, around the turn of the new era, the great Philo of Alexandria described the 'one', the monad, as the truly existent in his treatise *Quis rerum divinarum heres* 187. Here Philo says that the μονάς is the image of God, who is alone in his unity. Plutarch (*c.*45–*c.*125 CE) speaks of the 'one' as God; and the Pythagorean Alexander Polyhistor says that the principle of all things is

---

[8] R.M. Berchman, *From Philo to Origen: Middle Platonism in Transition* (Chico, 1984), p. 27, says that '[w]ith Antiochus the Platonic distinction between Being and Becoming is reduced to the Stoic distinction between that which is active, and that which is passive'.

[9] C.A.Huffmann, *Philolaus of Croton: Pythagorean and Presocratic* (Cambridge, 1993), pp. 406ff, argues that this quotation is likely to be spurious and probably Athenagoras' own language. Philo, in *On the Creation*, quotes Philolaus – although Huffmann challenges this attribution as well – to the effect that 'There is a supreme ruler of all things, God, ever one, abiding, without motion, alone like unto himself, different from all things (e1sti ga/r h9gemw_n kai_ a1rxwn a9pa/ntwn qeo_j ei9=j a0ei_ w1n, mo/nimoj, a0ki/nhtoj, au0to_j au9tw=| o3moioj, e3teroj tw=n a1llwn)' (p. 100).

[10] See J. Dillon, *The Middle Platonists 80 BC to AD 220*, rev. edn (London, 1996), passim.

the monad. Athenagoras, then, employs Pythagorean–Platonist language happily, although he does not assume that his audience understand it – as he feels the need to explain that μονάς means (or derives from) 'one' (εἷς, μία, ἕν). It is important that, although it is possible that Athenagoras deals first with the Pythagoreans for chronological reasons, this order may also indicate his acceptance of the quite common assumption, even among the Platonists, that Plato was himself a disciple of Pythagoras and therefore that the latter stood at the beginning of the Platonist tradition.

At 6.2, having assured the emperors that he makes no claim to a superior or even complete knowledge of the teachings of the philosophers and would not, in any case, presume to instruct those whose learning in such matters is well established, he brings in the testimony of *Timaeus* 28c3–4, quoting it from a doxography (as he himself acknowledges) together with the less known passage at 41a, to demonstrate that Plato clearly understood that the uncreated and eternal God are one. And, he adds (reminding us that his primary purpose in the work is to demonstrate that Christians are not atheists), if Plato is not regarded as an atheist when he understands the Creator of all things to be the one and uncreated God, neither can Christians be regarded as atheists when they acknowledge him as the God by whose Word all things are created and by whose Spirit all things are given coherence. At 6.3 he brings as witness Aristotle, who asserted the existence of a single deity consisting of soul and body (the former being the ether, the planets and the sphere of the fixed stars; the latter being the reason which controls the motion of the body). Thus the Aristotle' unmoved mover of is one. Athenagoras by no means reclaims the alleged position of Aristotle, that God consists of body and soul – how could he? – but the Stagirite's witness to the oneness of God is all that Athenagoras needs from him. And then at 6.4 Athenagoras presents the evidence of the Stoics. While he is clearly not greatly impressed by, for example, the multiplication of names for the divine being (a standard Stoic procedure), it is clear to him that the natural conclusion of their thinking is that God is one. It is evident, however, that their failure to differentiate this one divine being from matter is something which he cannot accept (and indeed much of the *Legatio*, as we have seen earlier, is devoted to refuting this very position). The same would appear to apply to his consideration of the Aristotelian school.

At 7.1 he summarizes how the poets and philosophers confess (though reluctantly), on the matter of first principles, that the divine being is one. He goes on, however, with a timely reminder that his primary reason for arguing that the Christian belief in the oneness of God is consistent with the views of the poets and philosophers is that this will demonstrate that Christians are not atheists and therefore should be free from official and public condemnation; and he proceeds to complain that, while these same poets and philosophers are by all accounts free to speculate on the divine being, Christians are subject to judicial action for so doing. Notwithstanding this, however, Athenagoras' point is that the testimony of poets and philosophers points to the sole occupancy by God of the status of first principle. In chapter 8 of the *Legatio* Athenagoras offers a logical argument for the concept of God as one, what Pouderon calls a '*démonstration rationelle de l'existence d'un Dieu unique*'.[11] Barnard calls it a *reductio ad absurdum* argument[12] and Malherbe suggests that the entire argument has to do with the τόπος of the gods.[13] At 8.1 Athenagoras refers to God as the Creator of this universe, mirroring exactly the language of Plato at *Timaeus* 28c3–4. His argument that God is 'one' from the beginning is in two parts: one concerns the matter of *what* God is and the second *where* God might be (the location argument). The first argument concludes at 8.3 with an answer of sorts to the major question: God is uncreated, impassible and indivisible; he does not consist of parts. The second concludes at 8.8 (and indeed for the whole two-phase argument) with the answer: God the maker of the world is from the beginning one and alone. The arguments which he employs are both Platonic and Stoic.[14] As I have already pointed out in the previous chapter, in chapter 9 of the *Legatio* Athenagoras makes clear that, if all that the Christians possessed were a logical argument, then their teaching would be something man-made and thus not of lasting value. But the Christians, of course, have more. They have the voices of the prophets confirming these arguments from chapter 8, prophets moved and 'played like musical instruments' by the Holy Spirit (9.1). Athenagoras then proceeds to quote from *Baruch* (3.36) and (three times) from *Isaiah* (44.6; 43.10–111; and 66.1) to highlight the Christian contention that God is one (9.2). He then leaves on the bar table, as it were, these instruments of evidence for the consideration of the emperors. In chapter 10 he describes God initially as uncreated, eternal, invisible, impassible, incomprehensible and infinite, able to be apprehended by mind and reason alone, encompassed by light, beauty, spirit and indescribable power, the one who, through his Word he created, adorned and now rules the universe. He then declares that he has already provided sufficient evidence (chapters 4–9) that the Christians are not atheists and that God is one. Now, from 10.2 on, as he speaks in more detail of the Word–Son and of the Holy Spirit whom he has already introduced, he begins to speak, with respect to the divine being, of a different sort of oneness, one which measures a particular class of persons: the divine persons.

At 10.2 Athenagoras moves to make some Trinitarian reflections (see Chapter 6 below for a more detailed discussion) and to a different, though related sense of oneness, this time as unity between otherwise distinct entities. Here he describes the Father and the Son, the latter as the Word of the Father in *idea* and *energeia*, as one based on the fact that all things have come into existence in the likeness of the Son and through him. Is this then a oneness of being, of activity, or of operation? While the second named might seem immediately apparent from the

---

11 B. Pouderon, *Athénagore d'Athènes: Philosophe chrétien* (Paris, 1989), pp. 125f.

12 L. W. Barnard, *Athenagoras: A Study in Second Century Christian Apologetic* (Paris, 1972), p. 90.

13 A.J. Malherbe, 'The structure of Athenagoras, "Supplicatio pro Christianis"', *Vigiliae Christianae* 23 (1969): 15, note 77.

14 On the discussion of this part of the *Legatio*, see above, Ch 4, pp. 93–6.

context (for someone not wishing unnecessarily to read fourth-century notions back into the second century), in the next sentence the Son is described as being in the Father and the Father as being in the Son by the power and unity (ἑνότητι) of the (Holy) Spirit. This suggests a more intimate relationship than simply one between co-workers. At 10.5 we return to this theme when Athenagoras speaks of the power in unity (τὴν ἐν τῇ ἑνώσει δύναμιν) and yet diversity in rank of God the Father, God the Son, and the Holy Spirit. This reference to a diversity which acts as a counterpoint to the unity of the three persons suggests again that the unity goes beyond mere co-working and assumes intimacy and fully integrated being. Athenagoras' problem here – which he addresses with some sophistication – is how to maintain his earlier affirmation of the oneness, the soleness, the singleness, the uniqueness of the Christian deity alongside a clear profession of its threeness. For Christians, apologetically, the oneness of God was never really a major problem in a philosophical context; the multiple nature of the Christian God (as we will see in Chapter 6) was (and is). At 12.3, within a discussion of Christian ethics and its reliance on the belief in a God who watches all, Athenagoras points out that Christians are attended solely by a knowledge of that one who is truly God and of the Word which comes forth from him, a knowledge indeed (for Athenagoras wishes to make clear that the precise nature of the one Christian God lies in his threeness) of what constitutes the unity (ἑνότης) of the Son with the Father, the communion of the Father with the Son, of the Spirit, and of the unification or fusion (ἕνωσις) of Father, Son and Spirit, and of their diversity when united. Again he points to the oneness of God reflected in the unity of the three persons, and in the following words there is even the hint (but only implicitly) that Christian affection for others (and not only for friends) may well be modeled and grounded in the affection of the three persons, for each other. Later, at 15.4, as Athenagoras dismisses again any suggestion that matter may stand with the deity as a first principle, he refers to God as he who is 'truly God'. At 23.5 God is referred to as 'the uncreated One', but this is actually a reference to Plato's language where, Athenagoras says, Plato, who is a Sceptic, one who suspends judgement on other matters (such as the knowledge of God?), makes a clear division between, on the one hand, the uncreated God and those created by the uncreated One to beautify the heavens (*Timaeus* 40a–b) and, on the other, the daemons. At 23.7, again with reference to Plato, he includes among the attributes of the eternal God apprehended by mind and reason that of 'oneness of nature' (τὸ μονοφυές), a word which is only employed by Athenagoras among Christian writers before the fourth century, and not at all by Philo. At 24.1 he again implicitly refers to God as 'one' and asks whether it would make sense, even if poets and philosophers did not support his position on the oneness of God (and on other matters), to condemn the likes of the Christians, who in their teaching distinguish God and matter (here he is returning to this primary point in his overall argument). At 24.2 he speaks of God, the Son his Word, and the Holy Spirit as being united in power yet distinguished in rank as the Father, the Son, and the Spirit (see Chapter 6 for a fuller discussion of the details of this Trinitarian reflection). Again, he clearly feels the need to affirm the oneness of God in the threeness of his essential being. At 30.3 he says that the uncreated God is 'alone eternal'. This underscores the fact that God's oneness points to his exclusive possession of first principle status. The oneness of God – one as God and one as three persons – is critical to Athenagoras' apologetic purposes and to his proof that Christians are not atheists. But this is not an issue in the *De resurrectione*.

Uncreated It is equally important for Athenagoras' apologetic purposes that God is uncreated. At 4.1 he speaks of God as uncreated and eternal in order to distinguish him from matter which, he says, is for its part created and perishable. He has begun here, though by implication only at this stage, to associate the Platonic notions of being and becoming with the categories of created and uncreated and thus of God and matter. At *Timaeus* 27d Plato speaks of the absolute distinction between that which exists always and has no beginning and that which is becoming always and is never existent. We noted above, however, that, while it is clear that for Plato and his later followers like Alcinous matter is not included in the uncreated, perishable and perceptible of 28a but rather as the third γένος of *Timaeus* 52a, Athenagoras has apparently chosen to read Plato so as to include matter at the former point. Again, while later on Athenagoras is at pains to associate Christian positions with their philosophical counterpart, here he wants to begin by showing clearly where the fundamental differences also lie. At 4.2 Athenagoras makes now explicit the relationship between uncreatedness and the category of being[15] when he declares that the one God, Creator of this universe, is uncreated; for, while not-being is created, being is not. Here Athenagoras draws directly from *Timaeus* 28a to speak of the essential nature of God. At 6.2 he says that Plato understands the 'uncreated and eternal God to be one'. If Plato recognizes other gods such as the sun, moon and the stars (see *Timaeus* 41a), then he recognizes that these are created. Athenagoras' primary concern here is to emphasize the oneness of God; but it is becoming commonplace with him to describe God as 'uncreated and eternal'. At 8.3, within his reasoned argument for the oneness of God, he speaks of God as uncreated, impassible and indivisible (as he does not consists of parts). His argument from 8.2 on is that, if there were two Gods, they would be dissimilar (and therefore not Gods), given that uncreated entities are dissimilar [*sic*], deriving their very existence from no one and without reference to models. Therefore there cannot be more than one uncreated entity; therefore there cannot be two Gods but only one. At 10.1 he summarizes his previous arguments by confirming that Christians bring before the emperors a God who is uncreated, eternal, invisible, impassible, incomprehensible and infinite, who can be contemplated only by mind and reason, who is encompassed by light, beauty, spirit and indescribable power, and who created, adorned and now rules the universe through his Word.

[15] W. R. Schoedel, *Athenagoras* (Oxford, 1972), p. xxi, says that here Athenagoras shows little awareness of the difficulties involved in this connection of God, rather than of the Ideas, with Being. I believe that Schoedel fails to give Athenagoras sufficient credit.

Athenagoras begins his descriptors for God with one which sets the Christian God apart from the Middle Platonist one. While both are understood as 'uncreated', this, for the Christian God, is peculiar to him. For the Platonist – see Alcinous 14.3.169.32f. – even the 'generated' world is actually uncreated and thus 'God' is not (normally) explicitly described as 'uncreated'. At 15.1, as Athenagoras continues to draw a clear distinction between God and matter and mentions the inability of Christians to worship statues, he speaks of Christians as those who distinguish and divide the uncreated from the created, being from non-being, and the intelligible from the perceptible. At 19.2 Athenagoras says that he has no disagreement with Plato when the latter (at *Timaeus* 27d, which he quotes) claims that that which always is, the intelligible, is uncreated, while that which is not, the perceptible, is created, having a beginning to its existence and an end (which God does not). Here Athenagoras very much places his understanding and his profession of God within a Platonist framework (though almost certainly misinterpreted at points). At 22.3, when he speaks of Empedocles and his notion that Love is the ruling principle and composite entities the ruled, Athenagoras declares that if one attributes one and the same power to the ruled and the ruling, one will then make the perishable, unstable and changeable matter equal in rank to the uncreated, eternal and ever self-same God. (Here he is again concerned to challenge contemporary notions of God and matter as being equal, qua first principles.) At 23.5 he says that Plato makes a division between, on the one hand, the uncreated God and those gods created by him and, on the other, daemons (*Timaeus* 40a–b; see above, p. 114). Here God is distinguished not only from daemons but also from other entities described as 'gods', whom God himself created. Pouderon calls this use of Plato by Athenagoras, and also that at 23.9 (see below), as 'improper'.[16] This may indeed by historically true; but it still enabled Athenagoras, who clearly believed that his reading of Plato is accurate, to make his point. At 23.9f., Athenagoras says that Plato, at *Phaedrus* 246e, distinguishes Zeus, the son of Cronus, from Zeus, the great Prince in heaven, charioteer and Creator of the universe, calling the latter 'great' because he might separate the heavenly from the earthly Zeus, the uncreated from the created. Here again, it is an essential attribute of the true God that he is uncreated, unlike all other entities. At 30.3 Athenagoras again distinguishes God from the lesser Zeus: the latter is one who knows birth, since the uncreated God is alone eternal.

Again, this is not an issue for the *De resurrectione*.

Eternal The concept of God as an eternal being is equally important to Athenagoras' presentation of God. And for him it clearly does not involve eternity in time, for God is above and beyond time, but eternity as an always existing being, or as a being which is present in all times. Athenagoras almost invariably uses 'eternal' in company with the descriptor 'uncreated'. This would be appropriate, given the standard philosophical concept of first principles as essentially 'ungenerated and

[16] Pouderon, *Athénagore d'Athènes* (above, n11), p. 268.

imperishable'. At 4.1 Athenagoras describes God as uncreated and eternal, while matter is created and perishable. The eternity of God therefore speaks to the fact that God has neither beginning nor end. It is also one of the leading attributes applied by Alcinous to God in the *Didaskalikos* (10.3.164.3). Dillon comments that this notion of God's eternal nature probably derives from *Timaeus* 29a, where the Demiurge is said to contemplate the eternal.[17] In the *Didaskalikos* passage, Dillon further comments that this attribute, along with others on a list, is not to be taken literally, given that God is there described as 'ineffable' in order for Alcinous to 'characterize his relations to his creation'. At 6.2 Athenagoras declares that Plato at *Timaeus* 28c3–4 has recognized that the uncreated and eternal God – these attributes are what truly separate God from matter, for example, and therefore are at the centre of God's essential being – is one. At 10.1 'eternal' comes second again – after 'uncreated' – on the list of attributes applied to God. At 10.3 God is described by Athenagoras as 'eternal mind' and 'eternally rational', in that he had his Word in himself from the beginning, though this is not to be understood, even by a Christian theologian, in a temporal sense. 'Always', for God, does not mean always in time but always non-temporally. At 22.3, in his discussion of Empedocles' notion of Love as the ruling principle, Athenagoras describes God as the uncreated, eternal and ever self-same God. At 23.7 God is described as the 'eternal God apprehended by mind and reason'. At 30.3, when speaking of the births and deaths of the 'gods', Athenagoras declares that the 'uncreated God is alone eternal'. Thus again, God's eternity is a distinguishing mark of his being, for it belongs to him alone. And again this is to be understood non-temporally. 'Beginning' can, for example, refer only to God's creation of things in time, including his creation of time itself. With respect to God's nature, 'beginning' can have no real meaning. The eternity of God therefore is a hallmark of his existence, given that God is, in Plato's terms, the 'always existing' – but an existence beyond and outside of time, which is itself a created entity.

This is not an issue for the *De resurrectione*.

Imperishable/indestructible We have seen above, particularly in the discussion of first principles, that Athenagoras regularly describes God as having the attribute of imperishability and indestructibility alongside that of being ungenerated. This is what, for the philosophers, makes God one of the first principles and, for Athenagoras, the sole first principle.

Able to be contemplated by thought/mind and reason alone In Athenagoras, the concept of God being able to be contemplated or apprehended solely by thought and reason is critical to his understanding of God and clearly betrays a Platonist provenance. At 4.1 Athenagoras describes God, in the context of his assertion that God is to be distinguished from matter, as an uncreated and eternal entity, able to be contemplated by thought and reason (νῷ μόνῳ καὶ λόγῳ θεωρούμενον).

[17] J. Dillon, *Alcinous: The Handbook of Platonism* (Oxford, 1993), p. 103.

Plato describes the 'always existent' of *Timaeus* 27d and 28a as apprehensible only though thought aided by reason, and that 'which is becoming always' (also of *Timaeus* 27d) as an object of opinion aided by unreasoning sensation and as perishable (see also, 52a where the self-identical Form is said to be the object which it is the province of reason to contemplate). At *Phaedrus* 247c (and e) Plato speaks of the 'truly existent' which is 'visible only to the mind'; while Alcinous speaks of the intelligible world being alone judged through thought aided by reason (4.8.156.13). At *Phaedrus* 247d Plato, having already described the 'truly existing essence' as something 'visible only to the mind', talks now of the divine mind as 'gazing upon truth'. At 2.1.152.31 Alcinous says that the contemplative (theoretical) life consists in knowledge of truth, and at 2.2.153.3 he declares that 'contemplation is the activity of the mind when thinking upon the intelligibles'. At 4.6.155.20f. Alcinous speaks of thought being the *energeia* of the mind in contemplation of the primary intelligibles and at 4.7.156.7f. of these primary intelligibles being judged by νόησις, not without the aid of scientific reason, by a kind of comprehension. At 4.7.155.35f. Alcinous had spoken of a 'natural and scientific reasoning' constituted by 'natural concepts' found in the soul once it has come into the body; to this one might compare Athenagoras' own 'scientific and theological doctrine' (τοῦ φυσικοῦ καὶ τοῦ θεολογικοῦ λόγου) at 13.1.[18] At 10.1, as Athenagoras presents his Trinitarian reflections, he describes God as uncreated, eternal, invisible, impassible, incomprehensible and infinite, able to be apprehended by mind and reason alone. The verb employed – καταλαμβανεῖν – is that found in the philosophers, where the notion of knowing as 'grasping' first principles is commonplace. What is more significant here, however, is that shortly thereafter, at 10.2, the Son of God is described as the mind and reason of the Father. Thus it would appear that Athenagoras is suggesting, albeit indirectly, that the Father can be known only through his Son. In chapter 22 Athenagoras is challenging those (including the Stoics) who identify the gods with the elements – Zeus with fire, Hera with earth and so on. He accuses them of making the gods out to be material entities and of divinizing the elements. At 22.9 Athenagoras says that these people 'twist and turn themselves in every direction' and miss the true God, who is contemplated by reason. At 22.10 he claims that those who divinize the myths about gods do anything but approach God. At 22.12 he declares that they fail to see the greatness of God and are simply unable to rise up to it through reason, because they have no συμπάθεια with the heavenly realm (a case analogous to that of the poets and philosophers at 7.2, who gain a peripheral and imperfect understanding of God through some measure of συμπάθεια with the breath of God). At 23.4 and 23.5–6 he looks at the attitude of Thales, the first to distinguish between God, daemons and heroes, and Plato himself; he even quotes from the

[18] No other Christian writer before the fourth century employs θεολογικός. Philo employs θεολογεῖν for 'to speak about God' (*De opificio mundi* 12, his only extant use of the term). He also refers to Moses twice as ὁ θεολόγος (*Moses* 2.115 and *De praemiis et poenis* 53).

Timaeus at some length (40d–e) on the topic of matter. At 23.7 he asks rhetorically whether Plato, who came to understand the eternal God apprehended by mind and reason and who singled out his attributes – true being, oneness of nature and goodness, which is truth flowing from him – thought it beyond his powers to learn the truth concerning those beings, the daemons, who are said to have come into existence from the perceptible realms of earth and heaven. (Athenagoras actually uses here the verbal form περινοήσας, which at 7.2 he employed to describe, in Schoedel's translation, a 'peripheral' or less-than-perfect 'understanding' of the truth about God.) Surely not, Athenagoras replies. In his characterization of Plato as one who has come to understand the eternal God apprehended by mind and reason (and there are plenty of passages in the *Timaeus* and elsewhere to support this), Athenagoras simply brings in Plato as someone on the side of the Christians, who argue for just such a God.

This is only an issue in the *De resurrectione* to the extent that the declared end of human being includes the contemplation of God's majesty and of God's decrees (13.2 and 25.4).

Father Athenagoras' characterization of God as Father – either alongside the epithet of 'Creator' or on its own – designates primarily the Father to the Son (four of the eight references in the *Legatio*), but also the Creator of this universe (a constant theme drawn from the *Timaeus* and part of the Athenian conversation; see above, Chapter 3). This descriptor is of course found among the philosophers, but it is also biblical. The first time when God is called just 'Father' in the *Legatio* (though he is also called 'Creator' in the same sentence) is in a quotation from the *Timaeus* 41a; so this usage cannot be classified strictly as Athenagoras' own. At 10.2 Athenagoras refers to God as 'Father', but as the first person of the Godhead, as Father to the Son. It is said there that the Son is the Word of God in *idea* and *energeia*, that Father and Son are one, and that the Father is in the Son and the Son in the Father by a powerful unity of the Spirit. The Son, says Athenagoras, is the mind and reason of the Father (and I believe, by implication, the (sole?) means by which the Father might properly be known; see Chapter 6 on the Trinity). At 10.3 the Son is the first-begotten of the Father; the Father, as eternal mind, had his Word–reason with him from the beginning; and the Son came forth from the Father, to serve as *idea* and as *energeia*. At 10.5 it is said that Christians cannot be atheists when they come up with a conception God the Father, God the Son, and the Holy Spirit; again, the Father is Father to the Son. At 12.3 Athenagoras speaks of the unity of the Son with the Father, the communion of the Father with the Son, and the unity and diversity of the Spirit, the Son and the Father. The Father here is again Father to the Son. At 16.4 God is again referred to as Father in no particular relation, but this is a quotation from the *Politicus* (269d) where Plato speaks about heaven and earth receiving many fine qualities from god but not being worthy of the same worship as he is, since they are subject to change. At 24.2, after he has once more affirmed to the emperors that Christians distinguish God and matter, he offers more Trinitarian reflection and says that there is God and the Son, his Word, and the Holy Spirit, united in power yet distinguished in rank as the Father, the Son and the Spirit; and he declares again that the Son is the mind, reason and wisdom of the Father. It is clear here, as others have observed, that for Athenagoras (and for most of his contemporaries) God is primarily the Father and the Father is primarily God. What is clear from this consideration of Athenagoras' presentation of God as Father is that, when he employs this designation on its own, he normally means God as Father to the Son, his Word, alone.

God is never described as Father in the *De resurrectione*.

Father and Creator When Athenagoras refers to God as Father and Creator of the universe, it is clear that he has *Timaeus* 28c3–4 in mind. At 6.2, as he seeks philosophical support for his assertion that God is one – and that the Christians' share in this common belief means that they are not atheists (and therefore their persecution is misguided) – he quotes (accurately) *Timaeus* 28c from a doxography describing God as 'the Creator and Father of this universe (ποιητὴν καὶ πατέρα τοῦδε τοῦ παντός). Here Athenagoras simply wishes to suggest that the God of whom Plato speaks is the one whom Christians worship. At 13.2 he speaks again of God as the Creator and Father of this universe, but this time he substitutes δημιουργός for ποιητής. He does so, in my view, notwithstanding that ποιητής is his preferred word in this context, because he then goes on to speak of God's actual ordering of heavens and earth; hence he must have *Timaeus* 41a in mind. In any case, he normally employs δημιουργός when he is thinking of God as being so engaged. In this passage he attacks those who have no real knowledge or theological skill in talking of God (13.1) and believe that the worship of God is primarily about offering sacrifices, when God has no need of such things. The best sacrifice for the Christian is, he suggests, simply to know God. At 27.2 he again refers to God as Father and Creator of the universe, this time reversing the order of descriptors (but retaining ποιητής), substituting τῶν ὅλων for τοῦ παντός (this is a regular substitution in Athenagoras and for him means the same thing) and omitting τοῦδε (the inclusion of which is normally, though not invariably, an indication that *Timaeus* 28c is foremost in his mind). Here, where Athenagoras is speaking of the delusionary nature of φαντασίαι as indicators of truth, he says that when the soul is weak and docile, ignorant and unacquainted with sounding teaching – that is, unable to contemplate the truth – it is simply unable to understand who the Father and maker of the universe is. Again, in his presentation of God as Father and Creator, Athenagoras shows to what extent he has taken on board Platonist language.

God is never described this way in the *De resurrectione*.

Creator Athenagoras' favourite epithet for God is undoubtedly 'Creator' (usually occurring on its own, that is, without 'Father') and his preference for the non-biblical ποιητής – which even Plato employs once, at *Timaeus* 28c – over the more biblical δημιουργός is clear. At 4.2 God is ποιητής of this universe, and at 6.2 (bis) δημιουργός (there Athenagoras quotes from and interprets *Timaeus*

41a). At 7.1 God is he who ordered our universe; and throughout chapter 8, where Athenagoras attempts a reasoned argument for the oneness of God, God is ὁ τοῦδε τοῦ παντὸς ποιητής (at 8.1 and 8.8, though the latter has τοῦ κόσμου), as well as πεποιηκότος (one who makes) (8.4) and ὁ τοῦ κόσμου ποιητής (8.4 and 8.6). In this chapter Athenagoras prefers κόσμος to τὸ πᾶν. At 10.5 Athenagoras, following his Trinitarian reflections, speaks, with obvious reference to *Timaeus* 41a (and *Timaeus* 28c?), of God as maker and builder of the world – an unusual combination of words, which he probably employs to make clear that for him the ποιητής and the δημιουργός are the same entity – one who appoints a band of angels and other ministers to govern the visible world on his behalf. The use of both terms for 'Creator' also highlights – as we have seen in the *Republic* (for instance in Plato's reflections on the 'form' of the couch) – that God as Creator creates both from nothing (ποιητής) and by way of putting in order that which he has already been brought into being (δημιουργός). At 12.1 God is represented as he who made both us and the world – Athenagoras employs the word previously encountered in chapter 8 as an obvious alternative for ποιητής – and to whom all will give an account of their life. At 13.3 the Creator and Father is the δημιουργός who preserves and governs all things and whom Christians worship. This Creator God, then, is the Father and Creator who continues to care for his creation as he governs it with knowledge and skill. At 15.2f., God as Creator is compared with the artisan who gives order and form to the materials he works with and thus, like God, is worthy of praise and honour – which the worked materials are not. Here God is characterized as a τεχνίτης, which is unusual in Athenagoras and elsewhere. However, here it simply fits the context of the analogy of the artisan and his materials. Athenagoras simply wishes to confirm that matter – God's working material – is not a first principle, alongside God. This is a basic contention in the *Legatio*, one from which Athenagoras began his defence of Christian theism. At 16.1 he continues this theme, declaring that God as τεχνίτης is worthy of a worship which the world, his creation, is not (16.2f.). The world created by God is beautiful and harmonious, but it is its Creator (now ποιητής) and ruler that must be served and not the created elements (16.3) At 16.4 Athenagoras continues this theme (God is now δημιουργός and the elements are his skilled work) and supports his argument with a quotation from Plato's *Politicus* 269d – referring to God as Father – whereby the elements receive wonderful qualities from god but, being corporeal, cannot be free from change and therefore are not godlike. At 19.4 Athenagoras resumes this same theme to challenge the Stoic view of matter as a first principle, and speaks of matter needing a craftsman and, oddly enough (for God needs nothing), of the craftsman needing matter. God is represented here, like in Stoicism (notwithstanding his reservations on other aspects of the Stoics' argument), as the active cause which necessarily precedes those things which come into being. Philo speaks of God as the ἡ ποιητικὴ δύναμις (*De mutatione nominum* 29), and Alcinous of the 'active cause' (11.2.166.34). At 22.12 Athenagoras returns to his theme of chapters 15 and 16 declaring, against the background of a challenge to those who divinize the elements and cannot contemplate God by reason, that the elements, no matter how beautifully ordered, cannot be of any use and cannot move without their Creator (see also Plato, *Politicus* 269d). At 23.9, in a chapter in which he continues his discussion of daemons, Athenagoras comments that, when Plato, at *Phaedrus* 246e, writes of Zeus, the great prince of heaven, driving his winged chariot, by 'Zeus' he means not the son of Cronus but rather the Creator of the universe. He does so, says Athenagoras, for the sake of clarity, calling this entity the 'great' so that he might separate the heavenly from the earthly Zeus, the uncreated from the created (Seneca makes the same distinction at *Qaestiones naturales* 2.45). In this way Athenagoras re-affirms that the 'gods' of the pagans are created, and therefore not truly gods, and that Plato supports the Christian view that the God of the Christians is alone uncreated. At 25.4, where he speaks of the Christian ethics, Athenagoras says that each person is a well-ordered creature to the extent that they depend on the one who made them. Here again he employs the word for creator that was used at 8.4 and 12.1. At 27.1 Athenagoras declares that the soul not directed by reason, but by conjecture and fantasy, produces illusions; and this is particularly so when it attaches itself to the spirit of matter and blends with it. Here Athenagoras presents the concept of seeing God through that which he has made. At 30.6, at the conclusion of his argument that Christians are not atheists, Athenagoras repeats that they cannot be atheists when they recognize the Creator of this Universe – a clear allusion again to *Timaeus* 28c. The descriptor 'Creator' (of the universe, of all things, or on its own) is therefore Athenagoras' favourite title for God. He employs it either in association with that of 'Father' (when he provides a direct reference (sometimes by quotation) to *Timaeus* 28c) or on its own, in chapters 4, 6, 7, 8, 10, 12, 13, 15, 16, 19, 22, 23, 25, 27 and 30. In this he not only wants to bring Plato along in support of his overall position but he wishes above all to make clear that it is a non-negotiable tenet of Christian belief and teaching that the Christian God is also the Creator God and that the relative confusion within philosophical circles about the identification (or not) of the supreme entity with the Demiurge is not an issue for Christians. The ποιητής for the Christian is also the δημιουργός. For only then can the Christian God also care for, and redeem, what he has created in the first place.

In the *De resurrectione*, God is described as Creator of the universe at 5.1, 13.2 and 18.2 ('universe' is always τὸ πᾶν); as Creator of human beings at 11.7, 12.1, 12.3, 12.5 (bis), 12.6 (bis) and 19.4; and simply as Creator at 8.1, 10.4, 11.1, 13.2, 13.3, 14.4, 14.6, 18.2, 18.3 and 19.3. For 'Creator', our author employs ποιητής or associated terms seventeen times, and δημιουργός seven times. At 3.2 he speaks of the power of God

> which can give shape to substance regarded by these thinkers as shapeless, can arrange in many different patterns that which is unstructured and disordered, can gather into one the parts of the elements, can divide seed which is one and simple into many, can make an articulated organism of that which is undifferentiated, and can give life to that which is not alive – such a power can also unite what

> has been dissolved, can raise up what has fallen, can restore the dead to life, and can change the corruptible into incorruption

and at 8.4 he speaks of the 'wisdom and power of him [God] who links every kind of animal with its appropriate properties'.

True being Athenagoras also represents God as true being. At 4.2 he speaks of God, the 'one' and the Creator of the universe, as being himself uncreated – on the grounds that being (τὸ ὄν) is not created, only non-being (τὸ μὴ ὄν) is. Here, for the first time in Christian thought, God is equated with being in the sense of the Platonic 'always existent', over against that which is never existent, the 'always coming to be'. At *Timaeus* 27d Plato speaks of the absolute distinction between that which exists always and has no beginning and that which is becoming always and is never existent. This notion of God as τὸ ὄν can be also found in Philo, *Quod Deus immutabilis sit* 11; *Quis rerum divinarum heres* 187; *De legatione ad Gaium* 6; and *Quaestiones et qolutiones in Exodum* 2.68, Plutarch 392e ff., and Seneca, *Letters* 58.16f., where it is employed to denote being par excellence: what Seneca calls the *quod est*, which cannot be grasped by sight or touch nor by any of the senses, but by thought alone. *Timaeus* 52c also refers to the supreme entity as the 'really existent'. At 8.7, in his logical argument for the oneness of God, Athenagoras asks whether it would be possible for a second God, pitted against being, to find a place to stand. It cannot be, for there is only one God and one being. Again, the identification of God with true being is clear. At 15.1, making a counterfactual linkage with the previous chapter, Athenagoras hypothesizes that, even if pagans did in fact recognize the same gods (which they do not), it would not matter. For they, the 'crowd', in their inability to distinguish matter and God and the gulf between them, and in their inconsequential worship of statues, cannot be compared to the Christians, who, in their belief system, do distinguish and divide the uncreated from the created, being from non-being, the intelligible from the perceptible, and who give each of them their proper name. The language Athenagoras employs for the opposites comes primarily from the *Timaeus*, and again God is identified as the uncreated, the intelligible and true being. Here again, in this presentation of God, Athenagoras employs language which clearly demonstrates that he wishes to be known as operating within a primarily Platonist framework.

This is not a phrase employed in the *De resurrectione*.

Good It is likewise crucial to Athenagoras' presentation that God should be represented as essentially good. At 23.7 the attributes of God (according to Plato) are said to be true being, oneness of nature, with the good (τὸ ἀγαθὸν) which is truth flowing from him. At 24.2 Athenagoras says that the Christians recognize powers concerned with matter which operate through it. One in particular, says Athenagoras, is opposed to God.[19] But this is not because there is a counterpart to God as Strife is to Love in Empedocles (again: see 22.3) or as Night is to Day in nature; for if anything stood opposed to God, his power and might would have caused it to cease to exist. Rather, this is because the spirit concerned with matter – who is clearly to be identified with Satan – is opposed to God's goodness. This goodness, Athenagoras says, belongs to God as an attribute and is co-existent with him, just as colour co-exists with corporeal substance: without it he would not exist. It is not a part of him – for Athenagoras has made clear elsewhere that God has no parts – but it is a quality necessarily associated with him. This does not mean that God, for Athenagoras, is, in Platonist terms, the Good; for God is even beyond such attributes as attach necessarily to him. Barnard says that here Athenagoras avoids the Platonic identification of the Form of the Good with the highest soul, that is, God.[20] '*La Bonté*' of God, says Pouderon, is '*disctincte de lui*'.[21] At 25.1 Athenagoras declares that the prince of matter acts in a manner opposed to God's goodness, which may be seen from what happens in the direction and administration of what has been entrusted to him. At 26.2 we are told that God, different from the pagan deities, is perfectly good and eternally does what is good.

At 12.5 in the *De resurrectione*, our author speaks of the goodness and wisdom reflected through creation and out of which God created human being.

Qualities of God Discernible from the Creation

While Athenagoras demonstrates that it is possible to understand the nature of God from his creation, his theology is not thereby primarily (if at all) a natural one. His first source of knowledge about God is scripture (and the Son–Word and the Spirit), but what we know from it can be confirmed by our observation of what God has made, much as it can be confirmed by logic and reason. But, while God may be discovered from his creation – his good order, beauty, and so on – he cannot be truly known as Godself. For Athenagoras, God is known from the pledges to piety – which is itself a form of knowledge – pledges evident in the order, perfect harmony, magnitude, colours, shapes and the arrangement of the world (4.2). Even the poet Euripides discerned Another from his works, understanding the invisible apart from the visible (5.2). God gives order to the universe (7.1) and thus he is seen in the perfection of that ordering. God created and adorned the universe through his Word (10.1), which is the *idea* and *energeia*

[19] The word ἀντίθεον is used 6 times by Philo, but never for Satan; and once by Irenaeus in the sense 'hostile to God'. The Fathers (Justin, Ignatius, Origen and Clement of Alexandria) prefer *Satanas* and *diabolos*.

[20] Barnard, *Athenagoras* (above, n12), p. 86.

[21] Pouderon, *Athénagore d'Athènes* (above, n11), p. 120.

of the Father (10.2 and 10.3) – that is, both the model of the perfect world and the activity of God in giving form to that world. God is concerned with the elements, the world with all that is in it, and its good order; and he sets in place angels and other ministers who will oversee this creation on his behalf (10.5). God stretched out the heavens and gave them their perfect spherical form, and he established the earth as a centre, brought together water into seas and divided the light from the darkness, adorned the sky with stars and caused the earth to make the seeds sprout, made animals and formed man (13.2). God gives articulation, form and order to matter (15.2). God provides the arrangement and good order of all things (15.3). God is responsible as Creator for the beauty of the world (see *Timaeus* 29a), for its size and arrangement of things in the elliptic and around the pole, and for its spherical shape (16.1). The sky and the elements are admired as the craftsmanship of God, yet it is the latter who should alone be worshipped (16.5). Athenagoras attests to the greatness of God (22.12). The elements do not move without God as their Creator (22.12). The God who is one, good, Creator–Father and providential can be discerned through what he has created (because what he has created is a copy, an image perhaps, of his own self). Perhaps it is that the Word rather than the Father is the paradigm (*idea*) for the creation. God is, after all, the perfect order, the *teleios kosmos*.

Providential In chapter 8 Athenagoras draws a very clear linkage between God as creator and God as provident being. The context of Athenagoras' comments or reflections on providence would seem, however, to be situated within a broader conversation, in which the notion of divine providence (fate, free will and so on) divides the Platonists, the Stoics, the Aristotelians and the Epicureans. For Athenagoras, free will is gifted both to angels and to humans, and many choose wrongly. The Creator governs the world by exercising his providence over it (8.4). The exercise of this providence [like goodness, perhaps?] is essential to the true God (8.8).

The concept of providence is linked here to that of creation. God governs the world through his providence. God preserves and governs all things with the knowledge and skill by which he guides them (13.3). The elements are of no use, no matter how beautifully ordered they may be, without the providence of God (22.12). God has universal and general providence over all things (24.3). God set all things in order and gave the angels a particular providence over them (24.3). The eternal providence of God rests equally on all (*contra* Aristotle, although it is not certain that Aristotle actually restricted divine providence to the heavenly realm, as Athenagoras suggests (25.2)). The particular providence of God is concerned with truth, not with conjecture or opinion (25.2). Thus Athenagoras builds a clear picture of God as the one who creates, gives order, shape and form, and provides ongoing care and nurture. This presentation is of course biblically consistent, but here he offers a particular challenge to those within the philosophical community who might question whether the supreme entity is the creator and former and/or whether God continues to provide for that which he has created.

In the *De resurrectione* the providence of God is associated, in a manner which does not contradict with the *Legatio*, with the judgement of God upon human being (regarded as a being composed both of an immortal soul and of a mortal (and resurrected) body. As part of this providence and in a manner which is just, God 'endowed human being with intelligence and an innate law to safeguard and protect the things which God gave that are suitable for intelligent being with a rational life' (13.1). The Creator's care extends to everything, the invisible as well as the visible, the small and the great (18.2). At 18.3 our author speaks again of the 'care of God' for his creation, and at 19.3 he declares that 'the Creator stands over his creatures as a guardian over all that is or will be and a judge of both our deeds and schemes'.

Other Attributes of God

God is encompassed by light, beauty, spirit and indescribable power (10.1). God is perfect fragrance and is in need of nothing. God does not need even his creation (13.2). God is all things to himself; self-sufficient and in need of nothing – God and world are not identifiable: inaccessible light, complete or perfect order, spirit, power and reason (16.3). God is the player who gives the instrument (the world) its harmony and rhythm, who creates the beauty of the world (16.3). The elements are beautiful because of God's craftsmanship (16.4; see *Politicus* 269d. There is no self-made beauty on earth; it comes from the hand and the mind of God alone (34.2).

Conclusions

The God whom Athenagoras puts forth has oneness and goodness and is Creator–Father (Father both as Creator – though for Athenagoras God as Father alone is not designated as Creator – and (always) as Father to the Son); he provides for what he has created. God's goodness and beauty are evident to all in his creation, and this includes human beings. This tells us something about God's own goodness and beauty (though Athenagoras does not qualify him, like Plato, as 'the Good'). The one God is the Creator God whose care encompasses all of creation. This is essential to God's very being (but not a part of it, because God has no parts).

God is other than matter; there is indeed an unbridgeable chasm between them as to their respective natures. This is the starting point for Athenagoras in his presentation of the Christian God. God is one both by being the only God – there is no other god, and the poets and the philosophers, even despite themselves, but touched somehow by the breath of God, attest to this – and by virtue of being one with the Son and the Spirit, in community with them. God is uncreated and alone so. It is, for Athenagoras, this uncreatedness which distinguishes God from all else and particularly from matter God is eternal, but in the sense of being above and beyond time; indeed he alone is eternal. This can be said of no other (and especially not of perishable matter – not even of the beautiful world which God has created and continues to provide for and to govern). God can be contemplated (or apprehended) by mind and reason alone – this is where true knowledge of God comes from – and the Son is the mind and reason of the Father; thus God is known through him and through the Spirit-inspired prophetic wisdom.

This is the God whom Christian teaching and the scriptures present and which Athenagoras offers to the Greeks. The God of the Christians is, like that of the philosophers (certainly the Platonists and the Stoics), a God whose transcendence cannot be questioned. Neither can the fact, also important to the major philosophical traditions, that he alone is God. But he is a God who is not only the Creator of all there is, and alone uncreated; he is also a God who maintains his interest in and care for that which he has created – unlike the Epicurean God – and a God who touches, especially through his Word, that which he has created. Yet Athenagoras, notwithstanding his allegiance to the Platonist school and to the Middle Platonist conversation, and despite his failure to make much of the fact of the Incarnation (which he acknowledges but briefly), makes clear that he holds to the particular Christian understanding of God as One and Three: as One God, Father, Son and Holy Spirit. The Son and the Spirit are united to the Father through an indivisible bond and they are, like the Father, also God.

Chapter Six
Subordinate topics

Topics in the *Legatio* other than that of God's essential nature – those to do with ethics, anthropology–psychology, the soul, and so on (the theme of resurrection is dealt with only secondarily in the *Legatio*, while in the *re Resurrectione* it is, naturally, the major topic) – are largely subordinate to that of divine being, though they are not thereby unimportant in and of themselves. In the *De resurrectione*, the themes of the human being, with its nature and psychology, and of the soul in particular, loom large in Athenagoras' dealing with the question of resurrection; they will also receive treatment in the *Legatio*. His dealing with a doctrine of the Trinity, of the Word–Son and of the (Holy) Spirit, which are exclusive to the *Legatio,* are subordinated to his primary focus on the nature of divine being but are intimately tied up with it – the Word primarily (but not solely) in relation to creation, and the Spirit in relation to Providence and knowledge – being integral to that principal topic. As in other chapters, here too the *De desurrectione* will be discussed briefly at the end of sections, given the 'not proven' status of the authorship of that work.

The primary theme of the *Legatio* is Athenagoras' defence of Christians against the charge of atheism. In this *apologia* for the Christian faith Athenagoras argues that the Christians cannot be atheists since they teach about God in a manner which is consistent with the mainstream of Greco-Roman philosophical thinking on divine being. Their God is distinguished from matter (the starting point for Athenagoras' argument, and one to which he returns throughout the work); he is one; he is uncreated and eternal; he can be contemplated or apprehended by mind and reason alone (and his Son–Word is the mind and reason of the Father); he is the Creator and Father of his creation; he is eternal mind. He is good, he is beautiful, and above all he is providential (for detailed treatments of the above see Chapter 5). What, then, of the lesser topics? What contribution does Athenagoras make to the development of Christian thought in those areas?

The Word–Son–Jesus

Unlike Athenagoras' doctrine of God, that of the Word–Son is not particularly shaped by contemporary philosophical thought, though its presentation certainly is so in part. Athenagoras does not have a highly developed doctrine of the Word–Son in the *Legatio* – such as will emerge in later Christian thought – but he does clearly help to pave the way for its development. His doctrine of the Word–Son, such as it is, is not at all concerned with the person or work of the incarnate Jesus (see below), but rather with the role of the divine Word, primarily in the work of creation but also in God's ruling of the universe (see, for example, his notion of the Son as *idea* and *energeia* of the Father at 10.2 and 10.3). We also find in Athenagoras' discourse the Son depicted as the mind and reason of the Father (at 10.2) and as the mind, reason and wisdom of the Father (at 24.2), which suggests perhaps that he is the primary means by which the unknowable Father may be known, contemplated or grasped. Thus the presentation of the Word–Son in the *Legatio* is informed, at least in part, by a need to maintain the absolute transcendence of the Father Creator – a key concept, consistent with contemporary Middle Platonist thought – while at the same time offering the distinctive Christian understanding of a God who nevertheless engages (even if only indirectly) with his creation. The concept of the Son as the agent of creation is both biblical and patristic but, to be sure, far less 'personal' in the modern (not philosophical) sense of that term.

At 4.2 Athenagoras has been speaking of the Christian teaching about the one God, Creator of the universe, who is himself uncreated qua being – and he begins his defence of the Christians with the opening statement that the charge of atheism cannot be substantiated for those who distinguish between God and matter as clearly as they do. Then he declares that 'all things' were made through the Word which issues from God (διὰ τοῦ παρ' αὐτοῦ λόγου). This is, of course (as indicated earlier), both biblical and patristic language; but it can also be seen within the context of a philosophicalhandling of the figure of the Logos, particularly by Middle Platonists like Plutarch and Atticus, who identified the Demiurge with the supreme divine entity, and also more generally by second-century philosophers who, in their concern at the increasing distancing of the supreme divine entity from the physical world, looked keenly for a mediating figure to provide a linkage between the world of pure thought and the world of the senses. This provision of a mediating entity also, of course, plays in the hand of those contemporary philosophers who might find more acceptable a God who, while being the Creator, creates, in a sense, at arm's length, through the agency of his Word. Athenagoras' primary point here of course is that God is not only the sole uncreated entity but also the cause of that which is created, and one which establishes that this creative act is carried out through the agency of the Word.

At 6.2, Athenagoras quotes Plato's statement at *Timaeus* 28c3–4 that 'it is a task indeed to find the creator and father of the universe' and the only slightly less frequently cited one at 41a, where the Demiurge of 28c describes himself to the lesser gods as their creator and as the father of those works which are indestructible save where he wills it. Then Athenagoras –complaining that the Christians are considered atheists when Plato, who understands that the Creator of all things is the uncreated God, is not – says that the Christians acknowledge as God him by whose Word all things were created and upheld by his Spirit. The inclusion of this passage in a section dealing with claims (whether accurate or not) concerning Plato's position adds some weight to the suggestion made earlier that these references, while biblically and patristically sourced, relate also to particular philosophical concerns of the period. It is clear that from the outset Athenagoras, in his participation in this principally Middle Platonist conversation, wishes to establish what he makes more explicit in chapter 10 (see below), namely that the one Creator, the God whom Christians proclaim and worship, engages with what he has created through the agency both of his Word and of his Spirit.

At 10.1, where he concludes his initial set of arguments (chapters 4 to 9) on the oneness of God and on the fundamental distinction between God and matter and begins to introduce his first formal and explicit Trinitarian reflection (10.2–5), Athenagoras speaks of God as having created and adorned the universe which he now rules through the Word issued from him. For our present purposes it is important to note once more that, while Athenagoras' primary intention in these first few chapters (4 to 9) has been to witness to the oneness of God, here (at 10.1), in his summary of the argument so far, it is important for him to put it on record that, in God's creation and ongoing rule of the universe, the Word of God is the agent. This both maintains the absolute transcendence of God and the consistency of Athengaoras' position within contemporary philosophical thought and defends this essential element of Christian proclamation. It is also noticeable here that Athenagoras speaks for the third time of a creation through the Word (which is quite properly biblical) and not through the Son. That the next section of the chapter begins with the words 'For we think there is also a Son of God' raises the question of whether Athenagoras draws an occasional notional distinction, consciously or otherwise, between the Word of God and the Son of God (though clearly elsewhere he very much identifies them), or whether he is here deliberately linking them for those who might not so easily or readily make such a connection.

At 10.2 Athenagoras states the central Christian belief that there is a Son of God and dismisses any suggestion that this talk of a Son is 'ridiculous'. While the notion that a god might have a son (or daughter) would not seem, of course, ridiculous to pagans, it might appear so to philosophers with respect to a supreme entity for whom the title 'Father' does not suggest the 'begetting' of actual individual 'children' (except cosmically understood) and for whom the notion of an 'offspring' might be seen to compromise fatally the absolute transcendence of God. Athenagoras argues that Christians have not come to their understanding of the existence of God's Son by the same route as that taken by the pagan poets to reach their deities (who are presented in mythical form, as experiencing the baser passions, much as mortal men do at their worst). He then describes the Son of God as Word of the Father, in Form and Activity (ἐν ἰδέᾳ καὶ ἐνεργείᾳ),[1] for in

---

[1] See Justin, *1A* 32.10, where the Word–Son is named as the first power after God; *2A* 6.10, where Christ is called the δύναμις of the ineffable Father; and *Dialogue* 128, where Christ is the power sent from the Father. This power is indivisible and inseparable from the Father. The Father causes his power to spring forth and then makes it return to himself. E. Schwartz, *Athenagoras libellus pro Christianis. Oratio de resurrectione* (Leipzig, 1891), p. 107, says this employment of ἐνέργεια comes '*ex usu Peripateticorum*' ('from Aristotelian usage'). His view is shared by Schoedel in his translation, *Athenagoras. Legatio and De Resurrectione*, ranslated by W.R. Schoedel (Oxford, 1972), p. 21, whereas B. Pouderon,

his likeness and through him all things came into existence (ἐγένετο) (this picks up the theme of God creating through the Word from 4.2, 6.2 and 10.1 and clearly identifies the Son with the Word, thereby removing any lingering doubts on this point at least). He also thereby explains the description of the Son as *idea* and *energeia*, for the first is clearly a variation on the notion of the Son as the image of God, in whose image creation takes place, while the second captures the sense of the Son as the activity of the divine in the creative process itself. In the *Didaskalikos* Alcinous speaks of the Primary Mind (Intellect) being everlastingly engaged in thinking itself and its own thoughts, and this activity is Form (αὕτη ἡ ἐνέργεια αὐτοῦ ἰδέα ὑπάχει, 10.3.164.27f.). This is clearly an influence on the language chosen by Athenagoras, whereby he reflects a biblical and patristic understanding of the exemplary and creating–mediating role of the Word but couches it, given his immediate audience, in the language of contemporary Platonism. This is a significant descriptor for the Son, for nowhere else in the pre-Nicene Fathers is the Son so described; and it is repeated at 10.3. It clearly reflects a philosophical framework and suggests the willingness of Athenagoras to accept the concept of a realm of Forms, but one in which there is in fact only one *idea* – and that is the Son–Word. Thus the Son–Word is not only the mediator of the creative activity and power of God (qua *energeia*), but also the model and exemplar for his creative act (qua *idea*). Hence not only humankind but the whole of creation is made 'in the image of God', that image being the Son. Athenagoras later says that the Son is the first begotten of the Father (10.3), not because he came into existence (for God, who is eternal mind, had in himself his Word from the beginning, since he is eternally rational), but because the Word came forth to serve as *idea* and *energeia* for all matter which was without qualities. Thus, for Athenagoras, the Word is the means or agent by which God gives form to (unformed) matter; and this is clearly set *within* a Platonist framework. Here again, as at 10.2, the Son serves, in the context of the creative activity of God, as both model–exemplar and point of focus of that activity. What is important here – and this is what clearly sets Athenagoras apart on this matter, at least from near-contemporaries like Justin – is that his presentation of the Trinity is set within his primary defence of the theistic nature of Christian belief and reflects a perceived need to place this theme very much within a conceptual framework broadly acceptable to contemporary philosophical notions of divine being.

Athenagoras, also at 10.2, says that the Son is in the Father and the Father in the Son through the power and unity of the (Holy) Spirit (see the doctrine of the Trinity in the *Legatio*). And then he concludes the section by declaring that the Son of God – God being himself described at 10.3 as eternal mind and as eternally rational – is the mind and reason of the Father. The connection with the

Athénagore d'Athènes (Paris, 1989), p. 217, thinks that the usage is both Aristotelian and Stoic. Athenagoras himself employs the term at 18.1, 23.2 and 26.2 for activities associated with statues and at 25.3 and 25.4 for the activity of hostile spirits and of the prince of matter.

notions expressed in the *Didaskalikos* of Alcinous is unmistakeable. Given that Athenagoras is clear elsewhere (4.1; 10.1; 23.7) that God can only be apprehended through mind and reason, it would appear, again in this Platonist framework, that the Son–Word is the sole means by which the Father might be known. The Father remains 'other', transcendent, above the realm of the sensible. What Athenagoras does not do, and possibly could not do in the context of his present discourse, is to demonstrate how the Christian doctrine of the incarnation might fit within the philosophical framework.

At 10.5 Athenagoras speaks of God as both creator (ποιητής) and constructor (δημιουργός) of the world; of him setting a host of angels and other ministers (the influence is undoubtedly *Timaeus* 41a) in their places through the Word which issues from him and commanding them to be concerned with the elements, the heavens and the world and the good order of all that is. Again, as at 4.2, 6.2 and 10.1, it is the Word (Athenagoras does not speak here of the Son) that acts as the mediator–agent of God in his creative and world-governing activity.

At 12.3, in the midst of a presentation of a Christian ethics, Athenagoras (by way of a summary of his more extended treatment from 10.2 to 10.5) says that, in their attitude of giving priority to the next world rather than to this one, the Christians are accompanied solely by the knowledge of him who is truly God and of the Word which issues from him. This knowledge, he continues, is of the unity of the Son with the Father, of the communion of the Father with the Son, of the Spirit, of the unity between the Spirit, the Son and the Father, and of their diversity when thus united (the Trinity will be discussed below). What draws the Christians, he implies, is a life lived in the company of this fellowship of divine persons. Again, Athenagoras makes clear that conversation about God must, for the Christian, include or presume conversation about God's Word – for they are, as he explains elsewhere, inseparable (18.2) – and indeed about the Spirit.

At 18.2, where he also speaks of the joint rule of emperor and son given from above (that is, from God), Athenagoras declares that all things are subordinated to the one God and to the Word that issues from him and whom Christians consider to be his inseparable Son (υἱῷ ἀμερίστῳ). Here again Athenagoras identifies clearly the Word and Son of God. The subordination implied in this characterization of the divine Father and Son is unmistakeable but quite normal, standard even, in this period (however unacceptable it may become later, when all suggestion of subordinationism was removed from Trinitarian formulations). Yet there is also an equally unmistakeable desire on the part of Athenagoras to make clear to his imperial readers that the Son is inextricably linked to the Godhead, that he is more than a mere attribute or activity but is rather a 'person' in his own right as well as an integral part of the divine person and activity. Thus Athenagoras maintains the oneness and transcendence of God, both despite and because of his inseparable Word–Son.

At 24.2, again in a Trinitarian context in which God, the Son, his Word and the Holy Spirit are united in power yet distinguished in rank as Father, Son and Spirit, Athenagoras declares that the Son is the mind, reason and wisdom of the Father (see 10.2) and the Spirit is an effluence (ἀπόρροια), like light from fire. In this Athenagoras clearly seeks, as he did at 18.2 with respect to the Son, to indicate the distinct identities of the persons of the Son and (Holy) Spirit, distinct from, yet also unutterably one with, the person of the Father. Here is an obvious effort from Athenagoras to reconcile the monotheism of the Christians – in itself quite acceptable to the leading philosophical traditions of the day – with a multiplicity of 'divine persons' – not as acceptable to those same traditions. Pouderon also points out that here, contrary to the practice among the Fathers of the time, Athenagoras identifies the biblical figure of Wisdom with the Logos–Son rather than with the Holy Spirit.[2]

At 30.6, concluding his defence against the allegation of atheism and his argument that Christians are in fact essentially theistic, Athenagoras, according to Schoedel's translation, states that the maker of the universe and the Word proceeding from him are, both of them, God. There is, however, no basis for this in the received text, although Athenagoras has elsewhere (10.5) referred to the Son (but not the Holy Spirit) as 'God'. One ought not, however, get too excited about this, given the relative freedom and flexibility with which that word, unlike today, was applied in Athenagoras' time! The point here is that Athenagoras makes clear once again that the Christian belief in the one, uncreated, Creator God includes an acknowledgement of the Word which issues from the Father.

Athenagoras only alludes to incarnation once, at 21.4, when he asks whether, if a god assumes flesh by divine dispensation (κἂν σάρκα θεὸς κατὰ θεῖαν οἰκονομίαν), he is forthwith a slave of lust. The name Jesus never appears in the *Legatio*, although this is not unusual among second-century Fathers, and Athenagoras never once refers to the earthly existence of the Son – not even as an ethical exemplar. Neither does he make anything of Christ as the teacher of creation, as Justin does. It is worth asking the question – though I am not sure I have any sort of answer to it myself – whether Athenagoras' own particular (and apparent) reluctance to engage with the concept of the incarnation – given that he was not necessarily unusual in this, even if his influential predecessor Justin Martyr was not so reluctant – had anything to do with the primary focus he gives in his theologizing to the distinction, to be made from the outset (and Athenagoras begins his refutation from this point and returns to it again and again) between God as one, uncreated and eternal and matter as created and perishable – one belonging to the world of being and the intelligible, the other belonging to the world of becoming and the perceptible. What Athenagoras does with his doctrine of the Word–Son is to maintain his insistence on the oneness, uncreatedness, eternity, goodness, creatorship and providence of God – to maintain God as transcendent, as belonging exclusively to the world of the intelligible, and as having no immediate, direct contact with the created, perishable realm of the sensible, of matter – while still allowing the Creator–God to engage with that which he has created, arranged

[2] Pouderon, *Athénagore d'Athènes* (above, n1), p. 139.

and ordered through the agency and mediation of his Son–Word and of the Spirit (which provide the cohesion creation requires).

The *De resurrectione* does not deal at all either with the entity of the Word–Son–Christ or with the incarnation.

The Spirit

Athenagoras does not have a highly developed doctrine of the Spirit but nevertheless offers some interesting insights. What he does offer is both biblically authentic and philosophically nuanced. At 5.3, having had just spoken (at 5.2) of how the invisible Other can be discerned through the visible medium of his works, he refers to these works of God as being guided by his own Spirit. The Spirit is here the active manifestation of God's providential concern for his creation. Through the work of the Spirit, God never leaves or abandons his creation. He remains present, through the Spirit, in the constant care and provisioning of his creation.

At 6.2 Athenagoras speaks of the Word of God by whom all things are created and of the Spirit of God which upholds (συνέχεται)[3] those created things. This is Athenagoras' first Trinitarian exploration. Pouderon is right to see here a measure of Stoic influence, at least in the choice of language.[4] Spanneut comments: '*A côté du Logos créateur le Pneuma joue un rôle de cohésion dans la matière, qui est exactement stoïcien. Il joue le role jusqu'en Dieu même.*'[5] Galen (*On Bodily Mass* 7.525.9–14) says that, for the Stoics, it is 'the breathy [= pneumatic] substance which sustains [the material substance]'. Both Galen (*Synopsis of the Books on Pulses* 9.458.8–14) and Clement of Alexandria (*Stromateis* 8.9.33.1–9) speak of the Stoic account of a 'sustaining cause' (αἴτιον συνεκτικόν) in life. Long and Sedley explain that 'breath', for the Stoics, was 'the vehicle of god, the active principle or *logos*'.[6] According to Anthony Long, 'viewed macroscopically, tension is that property of the divine *pneuma* or *logos* which makes it, in its interaction with

---

3 Crehan translates συνέχεται by 'held in being' and Pouderon by '*donne cohérence à*'. While Clement, Origen and Gregory Nazianzus will all employ συνέχω, before Anaxagoras Philo had spoken of the world being 'held together by the life-breath' (πνεύ μα)' (*Opif.* 131), of the Logos 'holding' all things together (*Fug.* 112; *Mos.* 2.133) and of God 'holding' things together (*Sacr.* 40; *Migr.* 181; *Her.* 23; *Abr.* 74; *Mos.* 2.133; 238; *Spec.* 3.190). We note also *Legatio* 13.3, where Athenagoras says that Christians 'regard the demiurge as a God who upholds (συνέχοντα) and governs (ἐποπτεύοντα) all things with the knowledge and skill by which he guides them'. This is not inconsistent with 6.2; in the latter, Athenagoras merely places this in a explicitly Trinitarian context (unlike at 13.3).

4 Pouderon, *Athénagore d'Athènes* (above, n1), p. 224.

5 M. Spanneut, *Le Stoïcisme des pères de l'église* (Paris, 1957), p. 332.

6 A.A. Long and D.N. Sedley, *The Hellenistic Philosophers*, Vols 1–2 (Cambridge, 1987), I: 292.

matter, the universal principle of causation and dynamic coherence'.[7] Sandbach describes the Stoic view of a '"breath" passing through all things and not merely maintaining them, but also giving them their characteristics'[8] and adds that 'in the macrocosm God was conceived as a breath penetrating and controlling and unifying the whole of the world'.[9] Thus we have here the Stoic view of a breath or spirit which sustains the material and the universe, reflected in Athenagoras' act of assigning to the Spirit, within the Trinity, the function of sustaining or giving coherence to the whole of creation.

At 6.4, with reference to the Stoics who claim that the Spirit of God moves through all the permutations of matter, Athenagoras speaks of the Spirit of God penetrating the whole world (τὸ δὲ πνεῦμα αὐτοῦ διήκει διὰ τοῦ κόσμου).[10] Alexander (*On Mixture* 225.1–2) reports that the Stoics said that god is mixed with matter, pervading all of it and thus shaping it, structuring it and making it into the world. Yet Athenagoras took most of this section from Aetius, *Placita* 1.7.33, which he reproduced almost word for word. Aetius says that

> the Stoics made god out to be intelligent, a designing fire which methodically proceeds towards the creation of the world, and encompasses all the seminal principles according to which everything comes about according to fate, and a breath pervading the whole world, which takes on different names owing to the alteration of the matter through which it passes.
>
> οἱ Στωικοὶ νοερὸν θεὸν ἀποφαίνονται, πῦρ τεχνικὸν ὁδῷ βαδίζον ἐπὶ γενέσει κόσμου, ἐμπεριειληφός τε πάντας τοὺς σπερματικοὺς λόγους καθ' οὓς ἅπαντα καθ' εἱμαρμένην γίνεται. Καὶ πνεῦμα μὲν ἐνδιῆκον δι' ὅλου τοῦ κόσμου, τὰς δὲ προσηγορίας μεταλαμβάνον κατὰ τῆς ὕλης, δι' ἧς κεχώρηκε, παραλλάξεις.

Pouderon comments that at 6.4 Athenagoras '*n'est pas loin de faire sienne la conception stoicienne d'un Dieu "pénétrant" la matière*' (from Aetius, *Placita* 1.7.33). but he suggests also that we take a look at Wisdom 7.24, where Wisdom is also said to impregnate, traverse or penetrate (χωρεῖν) all things.[11] The latter passage may have been at the back of Athenagoras' mind, but the word for word reproduction of the text in the *Placita* is simply too close to ignore. It does, however, also need to be said that Athenagoras does not actually endorse the Stoic account of the Spirit's pervasion of matter but simply argues that this Stoic

---

7 A.A. Long, *Stoic Studies* (Cambridge, 1996), p. 213.

8 F.H. Sandbach, *The Stoics* (London, 1989), p. 71.

9 Ibid., p. 75.

10 At 22.8 Athenagoras speaks of those who say that Athena pervades (διήκουσαν) all things.

11 Pouderon, *Athénagore d'Athènes* (above, n1), p. 122.

position implies the oneness of God – which is what Athenagoras has actually set out to demonstrate.

At 7.2 Athenagoras speaks of poets and philosophers gaining only a peripheral understanding of God (as we have seen, they rely on their own insights rather than seeking to learn of God from God himself). To the extent that they get it right, this is because there is some affinity (συμπάθειαν) between their own souls and the breath (πνοῆς) of God. Why Athenagoras employs πνοή here and not πνεῦμα is not clear – although chapter LXX at Genesis 2.7 speaks of the breathing of life into humankind by God as the πνοὴ θεοῦ; but he obviously means the Spirit by this description. It is clear, however, that here Athenagoras is suggesting that the Spirit is at work in seeking to bring knowledge of God – certainly knowledge about God, if not of God – as part of the outworking of God's purposes for his creation. Thus the Word is not the only means by which God might be made known; the Spirit has also a part to play in this process.

At 7.3 Athenagoras says of the prophets that they speak through a divine, inspired Spirit about God and the things of God; the Spirit moves the very mouths of the prophets like musical instruments. At 9.1 the same prophets are portrayed in the ecstasy of their thoughts, as the divine Spirit moved them and they uttered what they had been inspired to say: the Spirit made use of them as a flautist might blow into a flute. At 10.4 the Spirit is active in those who speak prophetically. Here Athenagoras does not describe the Spirit as the direct medium for the transmission of the things of God to the creature – in the sense that the Word–Son might be such a medium, qua mind and reason of the Father – but rather as the activity of God which inspires and equips the prophets. (Perhaps the Spirit is as much an *energeia* of the Father in this context as the Son is?) It is the Spirit who enlivens the creation and gives it a voice. Justin Martyr has some references to Spirit as the 'prophetic Spirit'; hence this is a notion which Athenagoras has almost certainly taken from the Christian tradition itself.[12]

At 10.4 Athenagoras speaks of the Spirit as an effluence (ἀπόρροιαν) of God, which flows forth from him and returns like a ray of the sun; and at 24.2 the Spirit is an effluence from the Father, just like light is from fire. Pouderon translates ἀπόρροια as '*émanation*'.[13] Malherbe suggests the possibility of the primary influence of Wisdom 7.25 on Athenagoras' use of ἀπόρροια as 'emanation',[14] but he believes that a Platonic influence from *Phaedrus* 245c and 246c must also be taken into consideration (the basis of this claim is not clear to me, since the word itself is used in neither place).[15] Barnard also suggests that a development

---

[12] *1A* 6; 13; 31.1; 32; 33.1; 35; 39.1; 40.1; 41.1; 42.1; 44.1; 48; 51.1; 53 (*bis*); 59; 60.8; 63.1; 63.11; 63.14. Note that at 36.1 and 38.1 it is the divine word that moves the prophets.

[13] Pouderon, *Athénagore d'Athènes* (abov, n1), p. 133.

[14] A.J. Malherbe, 'The Holy Spirit in Athenagoras', *Journal of Theological Studies* 20 (1969): 538.

[15] Ibid., p. 541.

based on Wisdom 7.25 is more likely than a Middle Platonist influence.[16] The use of the image of the ray of the sun with respect to the doctrine of the Trinity was fast becoming a commonplace in Christian reflection. Ἀπόρροια or its variant ἀπορροή are employed a number of times by Philo: at *Legum allegoriarum* 1.63 (twice) of the effluxes of a river, at *De specialibus legibus.* 1.27 of an effluence of a liquid and at 1.40 in the image of the rays of the run, at *De migratione Abrahami* 71 (twice) of the outflow of a spring and of speech, at *De congressu eruditionis gratia* 33 of the outflow of speech and at *De Mutatione Nominum* 100 of the flowing of memory. At *De opificio mundi* 146 Philo says that each person, in respect of mind, is allied to the divine reason, having come into being as a copy or fragment or ray (effulgence) of that blessed nature. For 'ray' (or 'effulgence'), however, he employs ἀπαύγασμα (compare Hebrews 1.3, where the Son is described as the ἀπαύγασμα of the glory of God, and not as its ἀπόρροια). At *De gigantibus* 25 Philo speaks, with reference to Numbers 1.17, of the divine Spirit being bestowed on numerous persons but without there being any sense of its cutting away or a diminution; and by way of an example of this he employs the image of fire making fire without diminishing . However, Philo does not employ ἀπόρροια here. Among the Christian theologians before Athenagoras, Justin speaks of the Word being put forth and not being diminished thereby, much as a fire kindling another fire does not diminish itself (*Dialogue* 61.2); of the power of the Word going forth from the Father, like the sun from the heavens, and being indivisible and inseparable from the Father (128.3); and of the begetting of the Word from the Father, which does not entail a division of its essence (128.4). Later on, Tertullian develops the image of the sun and its rays to help in the understanding of divine persons (*Apologeticum* 21.12 and *Adversus Praxean* 8). The general images, then, are not original to Athenagoras, but the employment of ἀπόρροια in this context would appear to be so.

At 31.4 Athenagoras speaks of the heavenly Spirit as the one who assists us in remaining changeless and impassible in soul as though we were not body, so that we might achieve that better life beyond this one. Athenagoras presents the Holy Spirit in a way which is, at least in part, shaped by a Middle Platonist framework – but one entirely acceptable to, and consistent with, the biblical testimonial concerning the Spirit. The Spirit gives coherence to the creation, enlivens it and gives it a voice, and inspires and energizes the prophets, through whom God speaks. He is also the breath of God, through contact with which both the poets and the philosophers are able to give at least a partial, if peripheral, account of the nature of God. Thus Athenagoras witnesses both to a well established Judaeo-Christian tradition on the role of the Spirit as inspirer of the prophets and to an equally well established philosophical tradition on the function of spirit as the pervader of matter, as that which gives form and shape and coherence to otherwise unformed and incoherent matter. Athenagoras could employ both sets of traditions,

[16] Barnard, *Athenagoras: A Study in Second Century Apologetic* (Paris, 1972), p. 108.

given that they do not stand against each other. He never, however, employs them in tandem.

The *de Resurrectione* does not deal at all with the entity of the Holy Spirit.

The Trinity

Athenagoras presents a doctrine of the Trinity which demonstrates some sophistication in that it shows an awareness of the challenges facing Christian apologists whereby they must explain, to a world comfortable with monotheism but not with a seeming plurality of supreme gods, the paradox of the one God manifested in three distinct entities. It is worthy of comment, however, that even before Athenagoras begins his more formal articulation of the doctrine – even as early as chapter 4, where he starts his defence of the Christians with a presentation in their belief in the oneness of God – he makes clear that this one God has with him his Word through whom he works his creative will (4.2). At 6.2 Athenagoras shows that the Christians acknowledge as God him by whose Word all were created and by whose Spirit all were upheld (that is, given coherence). There is no suggestion here, of course, that either Word or Spirit are themselves identical with God, but there is, especially in the case of the Spirit, a clear reflection of a Trinitarian view of a God who works through other entities which are not, however, external to or separate from him.

Athenagoras offers his first explicit reflection on the doctrine of the Trinity in chapter 10 of the *Legatio*. From chapter 4 down to 9 he has hinted at a Trinitarian doctrine, although his immediate apologetic task has seen him focus on the oneness of God. But now, having established to his own satisfaction at least the latter, he can move to this fuller understanding and exposition of the Christian understanding of the nature and being of the divine. At 10.1 he concludes, for the time being at least (for he returns again and again, especially to the topic of oneness), his assertion of the essential and unique oneness of God and of the necessary distinction between God and matter, and then speaks of God as creating, adorning and now ruling the universe through the Word that issues from him. Thus this opening Trinitarian thrust has to do primarily with the engagement of the 'other' divine entities in the activity of creation strictly understood, in the ordering of that creation and in God's ongoing providential concern for the creation, ordered or arranged through these entities which are inseparable from him. At 10.2 Athenagoras presents the Word as the Son of God, as the Word of the Father in *idea* and *energeia*; as he in whose likeness and through whom all things have been brought into existence, presupposing that Father and Son are one. Thus at least these two divine entities – Father and Son – are distinct but yet one. Moreover, it is said here that this Son is in the Father and the Father is in the Son by the power and unity of the Spirit. Thus the Holy Spirit is introduced as the cohesive element which binds Father and Son as one (one nature, and certainly not as one 'thing').

At 10.5 Athenagoras speaks of the Christian belief in God the Father, God the Son and the Holy Spirit (not acknowledged here, unlike the Son, as 'God') and of the Christian proclamation of their (that is, the three persons') power in unity and diversity in rank. Schoedel comments that, for Athenagoras, 'Father' is still primarily the title for God as author of all that is.[17] Pouderon comments in the same vein that Athenagoras '*manifeste une tendance nettement subordinationiste*', '*le Père ayant droit plus que tout autre au titre de Dieu*'.[18] Barnard notes that here (and elsewhere) Athenagoras 'made a distinctive contribution to Christian thought [*sc.* on the Trinity] at a time when much doctrinal fluidity and vagueness still prevailed'.[19] He was, Barnard says, the first to make something of the internal relations of the holy triad with the employment of terms like ἑνότης (10.2 and 12.3); ἕνωσις (10.5); διαίρεσις (10.5; 12.3; and 24.2); and κοινωνία (12.3).[20] Schoedel's comment that Athenagoras may well have been arguing that Christians cannot be atheists when their theology bears witness to 'a plural conception of deity'[21] fails properly to acknowledge Athenagoras' primary focus and the emphasis in the *Legatio* on the unity (oneness) of God. Pouderon comments that both here at 10.5 and later at 24.2 we may well be seeing '*une tentative originale*' to reconcile divine monarchy with the trinity.[22] This, of course, sits at the very heart of the Christians' apologetic endeavour. Athenagoras, also in this section – before he goes on to speak of God setting in place, through his Word, a host of angels and other ministers concerned with the elements, the heavens and the world –describes his language about the power of the unity of Father, Son and Holy Spirit and of their diversity in rank as 'our teaching on the Godhead (τὸ θεολογικὸν ἡμῶν), thus establishing a formal creedal statement. No matter how one translates τὸ θεολογικόν, it is clear that Athenagoras understands that he is dealing with these matters in a manner consistent with Platonic method, as exemplified in Alcinous' exposition. His later reference to 'scientific or theological doctrine' (τοῦ φυσικοῦ καὶ θεολογικοῦ λόγου) at 13.1 confirms this. He knows – and he wants his readers to understand – that his methodology is consistent with contemporary philosophical practice. Thus in chapter 10 Athenagoras lays out a reasonably sophisticated doctrine of the Trinity, which recognizes the inter-relatedness of the three persons, their authentic unity as one God and their clear distinctiveness as three discrete entities. He only refers explicitly to the Father and to the Son as 'God', but he clearly implies as much for the Spirit.

At 12.3, having spoken about the encouragement given to Christians to lead the righteous and virtuous life through the knowledge that God will require an account; having acknowledged that the Christians are accompanied in their earthly

---

17 *Athenagoras*, translated by Schoedel (above, n1), p. xviii.

18 Pouderon, *Athénagore d'Athènes* (above, n1), p. 136.

19 Barnard, *Athenagoras* (above, n16), p. 107.

20 Ibid., p. 110.

21 *Athenagoras*, translated by Schoedel (above, n1), p. xviii.

22 Ibid., p. 131.

life by their knowledge of him who is truly God and of his Word; and having then spoken of the unity (ἑνότης) of the Son with the Father, he asks: What is the communion (κοινωνία) of the Father with the Son, what is the Spirit, what is the unity (ἕνωσις) of these three – the Spirit, the Son and the Father – and what is their diversity when united? Here again is a reasonably sophisticated expression of the doctrine of the Trinity, one which recognizes the paradox of the Three and of the One but does not seek to explain it away. The life to come is looked forward to, but in this life the Christian loves both his enemy and his friend. Is it implicit here that the Christian ethics of love, moderation and grace towards the other emerges from the reality which is the reciprocal unity and fellowship of the Holy Trinity? This knowledge of God informs both the Christians' life here and now and their hope for the life to come. And, above all, for Athenagoras it is a knowledge of God as three diverse persons in their community and in their oneness. It is perhaps that fellowship and communion into which the Christian hopes to enter in the next life, a possibility which in this present life exists perhaps only as hope?

At 24.2 – having established to his own satisfaction and (hopefully) to that of the emperors that, if not even the poets and the philosophers acknowledged the oneness of God or were critical of pagan gods, then persons such as the Christians, who distinguish between God and matter in terms of their respective substances, cannot be regarded as atheists – he speaks again of God and his Son, his Word and the Holy Spirit, united as they are in power yet distinguished in rank as the Father, the Son and the Spirit. This is so, he says, because the Son is mind, reason and wisdom of the Father and the Spirit is an effluence like light from fire. In these passages Athenagoras has begun to develop a doctrine of the Trinity which is as sophisticated as any other doctrine of its time or rather, in my view, more sophisticated than any (Tertullian will come half a generation later). While his language is still quite primitive and even subordinationist (but whose language was not so before Nicaea?) – and only twice, at 10.5 and 30.6, is the Son styled as 'God', while the Spirit never is – in reconciling the oneness of God with the three-ness of the divine persons he appears to have a good grasp of the problems confronting the church and its theologians. He has introduced a language of both unity and diversity in order to begin to deal with these issues, and he does it by keeping at least one eye on the philosophical conversation in which he is so clearly engaged. But he will not compromise, and his faithfulness to the Gospel is evident. He maintains the transcendence of God, in faithfulness to Platonist doctrine, but he introduces into the contemporary philosophical conversation the particular Christian take on how this unity and oneness may be differently understood and articulated.

The *De resurrectione* does not deal with a doctrine of the Trinity.

A Christian Ethics

Rist says of Augustine's understanding of Christian ethics that 'the basis of moral norms is the existence of God himself. Without him, they would not exist. Conversely, since they exist, they imply his existence'.[23] This could be said, equally, in my view, of Athenagoras' understanding of Christian morality.

The overall impression given in the *Legatio* is that, while a Christian ethics is important for Athenagoras (as ethics was important for all theologians and philosophers of the period), here it is subordinate to the primary concern of the treatise: to demonstrate beyond doubt that it is irrational and indeed foolish to regard as atheists persons who believe, and live, the way Christians do. One needs, in my view, to read chapters 11 and 12 together – for each closely informs and explains the sense of the other – and then to see them as pointing back, to chapter 10 and its detailed articulation of the Christian doctrine of God and the Trinity, and also forward, to chapter 13 and beyond and to the challenge there to pagan concepts of the divine.

At 11.1 Athenagoras informs the emperors that he is going through Christian teaching in great detail, so that they might be less likely to succumb to low and irrational opinion and be better placed to know the truth. While it is possible, as I have indicated above, that Athenagoras is here contrasting certain knowledge (or truth) such as the Christians have with uncertain opinion such as is commonly held (see Chapter 3 on Athenagoras' epistemology), it is equally possible that he is merely contrasting common prejudice (as our translators seem to suggest) with the considered judgement of educated philosophers such as the emperors or himself. For in any case he believes that he can persuade the emperors that Christians are not atheists (which is, after all, the primary theme of this work) because the doctrines held by Christians are not 'man-made' but ordained and taught by God.

In line with Alcinous' move in the *Disaskalikos* to introduce a section on ethics (chapters 27–36), Athenagoras now moves at 11.2 to do the same, although, as was noted above, he does so not in order to focus primarily on a Christian ethics but rather to demonstrate that such an ethics can only be attended by a belief in the one God.[24] He does this by introducing, by way of a conflation of Matthew 5.44–5 and Luke 6.28, the notion that 'love' is the centerpiece of Christian ethics: a love manifested in blessing and praying for the other, which will transform its adherents into children of the Father and may suggest something of the Plato's injunction of 'making oneself like God' (*Theaetetus* 176c; this holds centre stage in Alcinous' treatment of the Platonist ethics). We note, too, that Alcinous places what is good for us in the knowledge and contemplation of the primal good which is God and the primal thought (*Didaskalos* 27.1.179.40f.). All those things, he says, which are considered as good among men, Plato assumed to be acquired from participation

---

23 J.M. Rist, *Augustine: Ancient Thought Baptised* (Cambridge, 1994), p. 243.

24 A.J. Malherbe, 'The structure of Athenagoras, "Supplicatio pro Christianis"', *Vigiliae Christianae* 23 (1969): 17.

in this primal and most valuable good (which Alcinous has already linked with the reference to the father and maker at *Timaeus* 28c3–4: *Didaskalos* 27.1.179.36f.).

At 11.3 Athenagoras asks for full liberty of speech in his defence; the Socratic allusion is unmistakeable. Malherbe suggests here – with the use of παρρησία – a classic Cynic *topos*.[25] Athenagoras then claims that those who use syllogisms, etymologies, homonyms and synonyms, predicates and propositions, subjects and predicates – as noted above, Athenagoras is simply engaging here in a standard rhetorical criticism of 'logic-chopping' and is not for a moment suggesting that such endeavours are of themselves intrinsically bad (Malherbe insists, and quite rightly too, that Athenagoras is not being anti-philosophical here but rather engages in the old endeavour of bashing the sophists[26] – all those people cannot claim to make their followers blessed or bring them happiness (εὐδαιμονία), the standard goal of the philosophic quest ('happiness' being counted by Alcinous as one among the divine 'goods'). Christians, on the other hand, are concerned with loving rather than hating their enemies, with preferring to bless rather than speak evil of others, with praying for those who seek to do them injury. These are the Christian virtues which spring from the contemplation of and participation in the divine, whereby the faithful become 'offspring of the Father'. Others, however, prefer abuse and evil-seeking – the vices – and the artistry of words to the doing of good deeds.

At 11.4 Athenagoras concludes by claiming that among the Christians – even among the ones most despised by the cultured of the day – one can find common folk, artisans and old women who cannot judge the appropriateness of a doctrine by reasoned discourse, but who can establish through deeds the value of their principles (this was for some Christians a matter of pride, while for their enemies it was a matter of contempt; see 1 Corinthians 1.26; Tatian, *Oratio ad Graecos* 32.1; Origen, *Contra Celsum* 3.44 and 6.14). They work not words, but rather deeds. They may be unable to articulate Christian teaching verbally, but they do so in their actions. When struck they do not strike back; when robbed they do not prosecute. They give to those who ask; and they love their neighbours as they love themselves. Love, moderation and grace are the virtues at the centre of the Christian ethics. But this ethics, as we have and shall see, is not articulated here for its own sake, but rather to demonstrate how it proves the Christian belief in God.

At 12.1 Athenagoras continues his reflections on the Christian ethics, but now he proceeds to make it clear, as we saw above, that the very existence of this lived ethics provides clear proof of the Christian belief in God; thus the Christian is not an atheist. This ethics of love, moderation and grace towards the other could not be maintained without the ever-present watching of God over human affairs. It is only because Christians will one day be required to give an account of their lives to the God who created both them and the world that they choose a life of

---

[25] A.J. Malherbe, 'Athenagoras on Christian ethics', *Journal of Ecclesiastical History* 20 (1969): 3.

[26] Ibid., p. 1.

moderation and of care for others, and a carelessness for their own comfort and reputation. Suffering in this life, if that is their lot, is nothing compared to the glory to come.

At 12.2 Athenagoras demonstrates that this notion of a righteous life motivated by the threat of penalty can be found even in the writings of Plato (he alludes particularly to *Gorgias* 523c–4a). But not even Minos or Rhadamanthys, or their father, Zeus, will escape the wrath of God. At 12.3 Athenagoras attacks the ethics of the Epicureans, who attach value only to this life, as well as Homer's conception that death is only a form of sleep (*Illiad* 16.672) – a concept dismissed by Plato (*Apology* 40c) – and he declares that, unlike them, the Christian actually regards this life as of being little account. For the Christians, the only matter of importance – and it is this that informs both their ethics and their dismissal of this life – is the knowledge of him who truly is and of the Word–Son which issues from him: a knowledge of what constitutes the unity of the Son with the Father, the communion of the Father with the Son, the unity of Spirit, Son and Father, and the diversity between them, which remains even when they are united. As I have already noted, he life to come is looked forward to but in this life the Christian loves both enemy and friend.

Is it implicit that the Christian ethics of love, moderation and grace towards the other emerges from the reality which is the reciprocal unity and fellowship of the Holy Trinity? This knowledge of God informs both their life here and now, and, what is more, their hope for the life to come. These matters, concludes our author at 12.4, are, as we noted above, only a partial taste of the beliefs of the Christians, but provide the means by which one might evaluate the whole. The Christian ethics, then, is one of love, moderation and grace towards the other founded ultimately on the unity and fellowship of the 'three-in-one'. Malherbe argues that, while earlier on Athenagoras had seen scripture as that which simply confirmed his reasoning, here scripture becomes the very basis of the argument.[27] I am not sure that it is so simple. Christians are not atheists. Their very manner of living testifies to their belief in the one God who watches all.

At 13.1 Athenagoras begins an attack on his opponents which leas him into a foray against pagan religion. He first suggests that most of those who accuse Christians of atheism have little idea of theology (οὐδ' ὄναρ: have come across it'not even in their dreams') – that is, know little of what God is, are unlearned and have no mind for scientific (natural, φυσική) and theological doctrine and measure piety in terms of sacrifices. Athenagoras' reference to ὁ φυσικός λόγος καὶ ὁ θεολογικὸς λόγος finds some echoes in Alcinous. At 4.7.155.35 Alcinous refers to ὁ φυσικὸς καὶ ἐπιστημονικὸς λόγος constituted by 'natural concepts'. Diogenes Laertius says that Cleanthes makes φυσικόν and θεολογικόν the fifth and sixth parts of philosophy respectively (7.41). Thus Athenagoras is clearly working within an accepted contemporary philosophical framework. Here he effectively

[27] Malherbe, 'Structure of "Supplicatio"' (above, n24), p. 18.

accuses his opponents of being philosophically incompetent, something which he and the emperors to whom he appeals are not.

At 13.2 he picks up his earlier claim that his opponents 'measure piety in terms of sacrifice' and explains that the Christians do not sacrifice because the maker and Father of this universe (*Timaeus* 28c) needs no blood (see Justin, *1A* 10.1 and 13.1); neither does he need fat or the fragrance of flowers. For he is himself the perfect fragrance (see Irenaeus, *Adversus haereses* 4.14.3) and needs nothing from within or without Godself. The appropriate sacrifice for the Christian to offer is to recognize the one who ordered the heavens and gave them their spherical form, who established the earth as a centre, who brought water into seas and divided the light from the darkness, who adorned the sky with stars and caused the earth to make every seed spring up, who made animals and shaped man. All then that is needed from the faithful is to know the God of the Bible; for this description is that of Genesis. What is also particularly interesting here (as elsewhere in the *Legatio*) is Athenagoras' apparent acceptance of the pre-existence of (unformed) matter (see also Justin, *1A* 10.2). If, he continues at 13.3, Christians regard (know) the constructor as a God who conserves and governs all things, what sacrifice is needed? The verb συνεχεῖν was used previously, at 6.2, of the Spirit upholding or giving coherence to all things. Thus, says Athenagoras, what need is there of bloody sacrifice when the faithful offer up their knowledge of God as God and their worship of him? At 13.4 Athenagoras quotes from the *Illiad* (9.499–501), a passage employed by Plato at *Republic* 364d to illustrate the attempt by humans to beguile the gods through sacrifices. But, says Athenagoras, I will not do that of which God has no need. All that God requires is the unbloody sacrifice of our reasonable worship.

At 24.4 Athenagoras speaks of the choice for virtue or vice which is given both to angels and to men, and this is because, without the power of choice, punishment for wickedness and the honouring of the good would make no sense. And then at 25.3 he talks of how spirits hostile to God cause people to act in improper ways. Each person, however, is by nature a well-ordered creature to the extent that he/she depends on the 'one' who made them; for each nature has in its origin a reason common to all humankind; its body can do what it was set to do; and there is a common end for all. But where they depend (presumably by choice) on the activity of the ruling prince and his attending demons, their living will be determined by this dependence. Athenagoras' point here is that all persons have the same reasonableness (λογισμόν) within them; how they choose to live, however, is their own call.

Chapters 11 to 13 were intended to speak of a Christian ethics in order to demonstrate the nature of the God who inspires it. Chapters 24 to 25 were intended to speak of human choice for good or evil, virtue or vice, in order to demonstrate the working of the prince of matter and his demons.

The purpose of the *De resurrectione* does not require much reflection upon a Christian ethics apart from its consideration of the purpose of human life. At 12.5 Athenagoras says that

> God made man for his own sake and out of the goodness and wisdom which is reflected throughout creation … God made man simply for the survival of such creatures themselves that they should not be kindled for a short time, then entirely extinguished.

At 12.7 he continues:

> [W]hat is without purpose can have no place among the things created by God. As to that which was created simply for the sake of existing and living in accordance with its own nature, there can be no reason for it ever to perish entirely since the very reason for its existence is comprehended by its nature and is seen to be simply and solely this – to exist.

At 12.8 he says that,

> [s]ince, then, the reason is to seen to be this, to exist for ever, the living being with its natural active and passive functions must by all means be preserved; each of the two parts of which it consists makes its contribution: the soul … rul[es] the bodily impulses and judg[es] and assess[es] by proper standards and measures what constantly impinges on a man … the body is moved by nature to what is suitable for it and is receptive to the changes decreed for it, including, along with the other changes affecting age, appearance, or size, also the resurrection.

At 25.4 he concludes that

> the end of a life capable of prudence and rational discernment is to live eternally without being torn away from those things which natural reason has found first and foremost in harmony with itself, and to rejoice unceasingly in the contemplation of their giver and decrees.

The Human Person and the Soul

As with the subject of a Christian ethics, Athenagoras' presentation of a theology of the human person, and particularly of the soul, is intended in the *Legatio* primarily to demonstrate the nature of God, to advance his argument against the charge of atheism and to offer a proof that those who worship this God are not atheists. At 25.1, when he is speaking of angels who have fallen from heaven and can no longer rise to the realms above the heavens (as part of his discussion on demons), Athenagoras says that the demons which wander the world are souls of the giants. At 27.1 he begins a longer treatment of the human soul, placed again in the context of his discussion of the way in which demons influence humans for the worse. He speaks of how movements of the soul, not directed by reason but by fantasy and conjecture, derive particular images, now this now that, from matter or by simply moulding them independently and giving birth to them. This happens particularly when a soul attaches itself to the spirit of matter and blends with it, not looking up to heavenly things and their Creator but rather down to earthly things, or, to put it another way, when it becomes mere blood and flesh and is no longer pure spirit. Thus Athenagoras would seem to suggest here that souls in their original form are pure spirit. These soul movements, not directed by reason but by fantasy, give birth to illusory images which bring in their train a mad passion for idols. When such a soul is weak and docile, ignorant and unacquainted with sound teachings, unable to contemplate the truth, unable to understand who is the Father and Creator of the universe, when this happens, when a soul has impressed upon itself false opinions concerning itself, the demons associated with matter, greedy and eager to delude, take hold of these deceitful movements in the soul, invade the thoughts of those who possess the souls in question, and flood them with illusory images, which give the impression of movements coming from idols and statues. In this way the demons gain the credit even where these souls bring about their own outcomes in a rational way, just by themselves, on account of their immortal nature.

The psychology reflected here is primarily Stoic and based on the very original theory of perception of the Stoics.[28] The Greek term φαντασία is very much one employed in Stoic psychology, although it does not normally have the pejorative sense given it here. The word 'was sometimes applied to dreams and hallucinations',[29] but it is more often value neutral and simply means 'impression' – on the soul or mind; besides, its presence in a particular person does not trigger that person's assent. The Stoics more often employed φάντασμα for a 'figment' of the imagination, as we know from Diogenes Laertius' *Lives* (7. 49–51) and from Aetius' *Opinions* (4.12.1–5). Diogenes Laertius also provides probably the most accessible and useful description of the Stoic understanding of an 'impression' (φαντασία):

> A presentation (or mental impression) [φαντασία] is an imprint on the soul: the name having been appropriately borrowed from the imprint made by the seal upon the wax. There are two species of impression, the one apprehending a real object, the other not. The former, which [the Stoics] take to be the test of reality, is defined as that which proceeds from a real object, agrees with the object itself, and has been imprinted seal-fashion and stamped upon the mind: the latter, or non-apprehending, [is]that which does not proceed from any real object, or, if it does, fails to agree with the reality itself, not being clear or distinct. (7.45–6)

[28] On Athenagoras' indebtedness to Stoicism here, see Pouderon, *Athénagore*, p. 174, note 1 (quoted earlier in this book). On the Stoic theory of perception, a good introductory survey is that of Julia Annas, *Hellenistic Philosophy of Mind* (California, 1992), esp. 'Perceiving and thinking', pp. 71–87 (with further references).

[29] F.H. Sandbach, *The Stoics*, 2nd edn (London, 1989), p. 86.

Athenagoras may well have borrowed his sense of φαντασία from the latter class of Stoic impressions. As for his other terminology, we have seen earlier that there is some controversy as to its Stoic or non-Stoic origins: the term for 'imprinting', for instance (ἐναποσφραγίζειν, 27.2), is considered Stoic by Crehan,[30] whereas Pouderon argues that the notion of the 'assimilation of the sensation to an imprint on the soul' belongs both to Platonism (through *Theaetetus* 192a and Alcinous, 4.4) and to Stoicism (as corroborated by Diogenes Laertius 7.45).[31] The word itself is a rare and late compound; neither it nor its derivatives are employed by Philo or by any Christian writer before Athenagoras.

At 31.4 Athenagoras speaks again of the Christian desire to live a virtuous life on earth so as to secure a good after-life with a God who knows everything we say and do. The Christian hopes to live this better life by abiding with God and by remaining, with his help, changeless and impassible 'in soul', as though we were not body at all. Thus for Athenagoras, it is the soul that is preserved in the after-life. At 33.1 he speaks of the Christian hope for eternal life and contempt for the things of this life, which extends even to the pleasures of the soul. At 36.2 he suggests that those who commit evil deeds are those who do not believe that they will render an account of their lives and that there will be a resurrection; they believe instead that the soul perishes along with the body – which Christians apparently do not. But those who believe otherwise know that nothing will remain unexamined by God and that the body which promotes the irrational impulses and lusts of the soul will be punished. At 37.1 he wishes to put aside his brief excursus on resurrection and trusts that the emperors, having heard his defence, will believe that he has destroyed the accusations made against the Christians and has demonstrated that they are godly, mild and chaste in soul.

The *De resurrectione*, naturally, has much more to say on the matter of the human person and the soul.

Why the Human Being Was Created

At 12.3 Athenagoras claims that God did not make the human being for his own use; for God does not need anything. Neither did God make the human being for the sake of any other of his created works. Indeed reason can find nothing which is the cause of the creation of human beings (12.4). God, he concludes, made such beings for their own sake; and he made them out of his goodness and wisdom, which is reflected throughout the whole creation. God made the human beings simply in order for them to survive; they should not be kindled for a short time, then entirely extinguished (12.5). At 12.6 Athenagoras argues that the Creator has decreed an unending existence to those who bear his image in themselves, are

30 Crehan, *Athenagoras* (New York, 1995), p. 158, note 140.

31 B. Pouderon, *Athénagore. Supplique au sujet des chrétiens et Sur la résurrection des morts*, Introduction, texte et traduction (Sources Chrétiennes 379) (Paris, 1992), p. 175, note 4.

gifted with intelligence, and share the faculty for rational discernment, so that, knowing their Creator and his power and wisdom and complying with law and justice, they might live without distress, eternally, with the powers by which they governed their former life, even though they inhabited corruptible and earthly bodies.

At 15.5 Athenagoras says that 'understanding and reason have been given to people to discern intelligibles, not only substances but also the goodness, wisdom and justice of him who endowed men with these gifts'. At 24.4 he says that we must distinguish 'creatures who have no share in rational discernment and those who act in accordance with an innate rational law and can exercise prudence and justice'. And he concludes at 25.4 that

> the *telos* of a life capable of prudence and rational discernment is to live eternally without being torn away from those things which natural reason has found first and foremost in harmony with itself, and to rejoice unceasingly in the contemplation of their giver and of his decrees.

The Human Being as a Composite Creature

At 10.5 Athenagoras says that the human being consists of body and soul. The soul dwells now in a corruptible and passible body, while it is itself incorruptible. 'God made man of an immortal soul and a body and endowed him with intelligence and an innate law to safeguard and protect the things which he gave that are suitable for intelligent beings with a rational life' (13.1). 'It is universally considered that human nature is constituted by an immortal soul and a body which has been united with it at its creation' (15.2). 'There is', he says,

> one living being composed of two parts, undergoing all the experiences of soul and body, and actively carrying out whatever requires the judgement of the senses and reason, that the entire concatenation of such phenomena leads to one end so that all these things – the creation of the human being, the nature of the human being, the existence of the human being, the deeds and experiences and way of life of the human being, and the end which suits nature of this being – might be fully integrated into one harmonious and concordant whole. (ibid.)

'If there is', he continues, 'one harmony and concord of the entire living being, including the things that spring from the soul and the things that are done by the body, then the *telos* of all these phenomena must also be one' (15.3). In the same passage Athenagoras speaks of the union (ἕνωσις) appropriate to body and soul. At 15.6 he offers a rather insightful understanding of this ἕνωσις when he says '[i]t is the whole human being – not simply soul – who received understanding and reason'. 'The human being, then, who consists of both soul and body, must survive for ever; but he cannot survive unless he is raised' (ibid.). At 18.4 Athenagoras speaks of the human being as 'a composite creature' (τὸ συναμφότερον), a 'composite of soul and body' – Barnard says that he is the first Christian writer to employ the prior term[32] – and at 18.5 he says that 'the composite creature no longer exists when the soul is separated from the body'. At 21.5 he declares that '[e]ven if we grant that the passions characterize not simply the body, but the whole human being as such, and [even if we] are right in saying so because a human's life is a unity comprised of soul and body, nevertheless we shall not say that the passions belong to the soul qua soul when we examine its own proper nature with clarity'. At 25.1 Athenagoras concludes that 'the creature [is one] made up of both parts'.

The Nature of the Human

At 10.2 Athenagoras states that human beings are distinguished from purely rational natures [that is, angels and demons] and from those creatures with neither reason nor soul [that is, animals]. At 17.1 he says that this human nature has been allotted discontinuity from the outset by the will of the Creator. It 'has a kind of life and permanence characteried by discontinuity and interrupted sometimes by sleep, sometimes by death'.

The Human Being and the Just Dealing of God

At 18.5 Athenagoras says that

> [t]he soul alone should not receive the wages for deeds done in conjunction with the body (for the soul as soul is free from passions and untouched by the faults which arise in connection with bodily pleasures or with food and nurture); nor should the body alone be requited (for the body as body cannot make assessment of law and justice); it is man, the combination of both [body and soul], who receives judgement for each of his deeds.

The Soul

At 22.5 Athenagoras says that the soul needs nothing (unlike the human being, who is a needy creature, requiring food, offspring, and justice: 18.4). And, while he is clear that justice is properly meted out to the whole human being, the union of soul and body, he is equally clear that 'the individual activity of which one speaks in the case of bodily members cannot be found in the soul as it is constituted' (ibid.). The analogy here with the Cyrilline understanding of the Christ, both divine and human – where the divine, the Logos, remains always Logos – is at the very least an interesting parallel.

---

32 Barnard, *Athenagoras* (above, n16), p. 20, note 58.

The Resurrection

In the *Legatio*, resurrection is dealt with solely in the context of the charges of cannibalism and incest and not for its own sake. At 33.1 Athenagoras says that, since the Christians 'hope for eternal life, we despise the things of this life, including even the pleasures of the soul'. At 36.1, having dealt with the charge of inappropriate sexual behaviours, he suggests that no believer in resurrection would eat bodies destined to rise. One would not, he says, believe in resurrection and then eat bodies as though they would not come back to life. One would not believe in resurrection and imagine at the same time that bodies which have been eaten would not be reclaimed by their owners at the time of resurrection. Rather, he suggests, those who might commit such moral outrages are the ones who do not look to a final judgement and do not believe in resurrection, but think that the soul perishes along with the body at death (36.2). On the other hand, those who believe in a judgement and in the punishment of the raised body have every reason to act in a moral manner (ibid.). There are those, too, who cannot believe that the body, having rotted, decayed and disappeared, can be reconstituted; these regard as foolish the ones who entertain such beliefs (36.3). Yet many philosophers believe in resurrection, contends Athenagoras (but does not name them). Nothing in the teachings of Pythagoras and Plato contradicts a belief in the reconstrucrion of formerly dissolved bodes from their original elements. He does not, however, cite these philosophers as supporters of resurrection itself. He then recommends leaving aside for the time being that part of the Christian doctrine which is concerned with resurrection (37.1). It is not, of course, at the heart of his concerns in the *Legatio*. It is simply a matter collateral to his main theme.

The topic of resurrection is, however, at the heart of *De resurrectione*. At 2.3 the author acknowledges that there are those – Christians and non-Christians alike – who doubt that God is able or willing to reconstitute dead bodies (including those utterly decomposed) and to restore them to being the very same persons they had been before death. '[I]t is impossible for God, however, to be ignorant of the nature of our bodies which are destined to arise' (2.5). God knows 'every part and member in their entirety'. He knows where everything goes and 'what part of the appropriate element receives what is decomposed and dissolved into its own kind' (ibid.). He knew beforehand the nature of the elements yet to be created and from which human bodies arose; and he knew the parts of the elements from which he planned to select in order to form the human body (ibid.). 'The creation of our bodies [in the first place] shows that God's power', he says, 'suffices for their resurrection' (3.1):

> For the power which can give shape to substance regarded by these thinkers as shapeless, can arrange in many different patterns that which is unstructured and disordered, can gather into one the parts of the elements, can divide seed which is one and simple into many, can make an articulated organism of that which is undifferentiated, and can give life to that which is not alive – such a power can

> also unite what has been dissolved, can raise up what has fallen, can restore the dead to life, and can change the corruptible into incorruption. (3.2)

God both wills and is able to resurrect the dead. God can also restore to the risen bodies parts and elements which have been lost – for instance at sea, devoured by fish, devoured by animals, even eaten by members of their own species (3.3f.). Bodies which arise are reconstituted from their own parts (7.1) and can never be fused with others bodies of the same 'nature' (probably species; 7.4 and 8.2). The parts of the body 'are united again to one another and occupy the same place as before so as to restore the harmonious composition of the body and effect the resurrection and the life of the body that has died and has totally decomposed' (8.4).

Athenagoras deals, too, with the claim that raising humans from the dead is unjust and unworthy of God: unjust, namely, towards those whom God does not resurrect, particularly angels and animals (10.1f.). Yet the resurrection of human beings does no wrong to the purely rational natures (that is, to angels and demons), for it offers no impediment to their existence; and it does no wrong to those creatures endowed with neither reason nor soul (that is, to animals), for they, being soul-less, would not live after resurrection (10.2). In addition, given that animals cannot discern justice, there are no creatures on whose behalf a charge of injustice might be brought (10.4). And the work of resurrection cannot be a work unworthy of God, unless the prior and lesser work – the creation of corruptible and passible bodies – is also considered unworthy of him (10.6).

The human person, says Athenagoras, came into existence neither by chance nor without purpose (12.1). She did not come into being for the sake of the Creator or for the sake of any other creature. The human person came into being so that 'after his creation he should live and endure in accordance with the nature with which he was created' (ibid.). God did not make the human being for his own use; for he does not need anything. Neither did God make the human being for the sake of any other of his created works (12.3). God made the human being for his own sake and out of the goodness and wisdomwhich is reflected throughout creation. God made the human being simply for the survival of such creatures themselves that they should not be kindled for a short time, then entirely extinguished (12.5). The Creator has decreed an unending existence to those who bear his image in themselves, are gifted with intelligence, and share the faculty for rational discernment, so that, knowing their Creator and his power and wisdom and complying with law and justice, might live without distress eternally with the powers by which they governed their former life, even though they were in corruptible and earthly bodies (12.6).What is without purpose can have no place among the things created by God. As to that which was created simply for the sake of existing and living in accordance with its own nature, there can be no reason for it ever to perish entirely, since the very reason for its existence is encompassed by its nature and is seen to be simply and solely this: to exist (12.7).

Arguments for the resurrection of the human person, reconstituted as both body and soul, are both primary – those grounded in the work of creation – and secondary – those grounded in divine providence and the judgement of God. 'The reason derived from a consideration of the creation of human beings suffices by itself to demonstrate through a natural line of argument that the resurrection follows upon the dissolution of the body' (15.1). Human nature universally consists in an immortal soul and a body which has been united with it at its creation (15.2). Human beings are thereby composed of both soul and body.

> If there is one harmony and concord of the entire living being, including the things that spring from the soul and the things that are done by the body, then the end of all these phenomena must also be one. And the end will be truly one if the same living being whose end it is remains constituted as before. (15.3)

And,

> if understanding and reason have been given to discern intelligibles, not only substances but also the goodness, wisdom and justice of him who endowed us with these gifts, it is necessary that, where the realities because of which rational discernment has been given are permanent, the discernment itself which was given to be exercised on them should also be permanent. (15.5)
>
> It is the human being – not simply the soul – who received understanding and reason. A person, then, who consists of both soul and body must survive for ever; but a person cannot survive unless raised. (15.6)

Yet, asks Athenagoras, does death and corruption put an end to 'permanence' for the human person composed of an immortal soul but a corruptible and thereby mortal body? It is not 'worthwhile', he answers, for mortals 'to look for the undisturbed and changeless permanence that characterizes superior beings [angels]; for the latter were created immortal from the beginning and were made to survive for ever simply by the will of God, whereas humans were created to survive unchanged only in respect to the soul, but in respect to the body to gain incorruptibility through a transformation' (16.2). For 'we await the dissolution of the body as a concomitant of a needy and corruptible existence, and hope for a permanent incorruptibility to follow it. We do not regard our death as the same as the death of irrational creatures, nor do we regard the permanence of mortals as the same as the permanence of the immortals' (16.3). A 'certain of lack of continuity characterizes the "permanence" of mortals' (16.4). This 'human nature has been allotted discontinuity from the outset by the will of the Creator … it has a kind of life and permanence characterized by discontinuity and interrupted sometimes by sleep, sometimes by death' (17.1).

Athenagoras (or is it him?) concludes this work on resurrection by observing that 'the end of mortals must certainly be seen in some other state of the same composite creature' (25.2), that 'it is impossible for the same people to be reconstituted unless the same bodies are united with the same souls' (25.3).

Conclusions

What, then, of these other topics (other, that is, than God) – to which Athenagoras gives some attention? While he has much to say on matters like the Word–Son, the Holy Spirit and the Trinity, and on a Christian ethics in the *Legatio*, everything he does say in that work is intended to support his primary aim of demonstrating that Christians are not atheists but indeed are theists who believe in the one, good, uncreated and eternal God – the God who created all things and continues to provide for them, and whose oneness, goodness and provisioning are evident in his creation. Athenagors' doctrines of the Word–Son and of the Holy Spirit – and that of the Trinity itself – are intended to show both that Christians believe in a God who is one and that this God continues to engage with his creation without compromising his absolute transcendence and his differentiation from matter. (This topic is completely absent in the *De resurrectione*.) Athenagoras' treatment of a Christian ethics – though this could stand on its own – is also intended primarily in the *Legatio* to demonstrate that such living is only possible where there is a belief in the one God, who is the Creator and who continues his engagement in what he has created. Athenagoras leaves much for us to ponder upon beyond his doctrine of the one God, but it is that doctrine that is of prime importance for him here.

There are no significant differences in the treatment of resurrection in the *Legatio* and in the *De resurrectione*, notwithstanding that in the former this is merely a theme subordinate to his presentation of a Christian doctrine of God, while in the latter it is the leading theme to which all else is subordinated. In the former treatise he wishes to demonstrate that those who believe in resurrection are motivated in part by their belief in an after-life and in the God's judgement there on this present life. The latter treatise wishes to demonstrate the logic of a Christian belief in the resurrection: the belief is based primarily on an understanding of the nature and the purpose of the creation of human beings and secondarily on an understanding of a divine providence in which all must be subject, soul and body, to the judgement of God. The author argues at length in the *De resurrectione* that God is both able and willing to raise human beings and that to do so is worthy of him. He argues that the purpose of humans is existence for its own sake – existence construed as living in accordance with nature and in contemplation of God; it is not existence for the sake of God or for the sake of any other creature.. The creation of human beings is not a matter of chance, nor is it devoid of purpose. Athenagoras argues, in part because only thereby can one understand the need for the reconstitution of the whole, that the human person is a composite being, made of an immortal soul and a mortal body (rendered incorruptible through resurrection), whose union is real and interrupted only and temporarily by death. Resurrection from the dead is necessary both for the purposes for which human being was created – the contemplation of the divine and the living in accordance with one's nature – and so that the proper and righteous judgement of God might be visited upon the whole person.

Chapter Seven
Influences on Athenagoras

> By the second century AD, one in effect had the choice of adopting Aristotelian or Stoic terminology and concepts to give formal structure to one's interpretation of what Plato meant.[1]

Introduction

Berchman, in his discussion of the engagement of Jewish and Christian thinkers like Philo Judaeus, Clement of Alexandria and Origen with Middle Platonist thought,[2] examines them primarily 'within the context of ancient philosophy, and the philosophical problematics they engaged in. Specifically, what is the relation of God to the universe, how are both known, to what extent do biblical revelation and philosophical wisdom agree, and how is a reality system deduced from sacred scripture?'[3]

This could very well apply to the thought of Athenagoras, and to such a list might be added: a doctrine of God itself; the relationship of God to matter; how philosophical frameworks might be employed to organize the world of the believer; and questions of transcendence and immanence, with particular reference to the divine. If we focus on the *Legatio*, we might also identify: knowledge of and about God (5); first principles as applied by Christian thought (7); knowledge and opinion (11); ethics (11ff.); the concept of a physical and theological doctrine (13); the relationship of the Creator to the world which he has created/formed (16); daemons (17ff.); providence and the divine being (25). How and where do we detect possible influences on the development of Athenagoras' thought on these matters?

Athenagoras clearly knows his Bible but he employs it, particularly the Old Testament, somewhat sparingly. This is obvious if one compares his intentional and explicit use of scripture with the very extensive quotations from Plato (especially from the *Timaeus*), Homer (the *Illiad*), Herodotus and Euripides. He is not, it is apparent, influenced by Philo (indeed he and Philo employ many terms with profoundly different meanings and senses and it would seem evident that

---

[1] J. M. Dillon, '"Orthodoxy" and "eclecticism": Middle Platonists and Neo-Pythagoreans', in J.M. Dillon and A.A. Long, *The Question of Eclecticism: Studies in Later Greek Philosophy* (Berkeley, 1988), pp. 118f.

[2] R.M. Berchman, From Philo to Origen: Middle Platonism in Transition (Chico, 1984).

[3] Ibid., p.11.

Athenagoras may not even have known the other's work[4]); he certainly knows and appropriates some of Justin's language (although their theological and philosophical concerns are very different); his articulation of the nature of God is primarily Platonist; his choice of language for the activity of God is profoundly Stoic (particularly with respect to the Spirit pervading matter, providing coherence and unity and so on); and he uses the poets and other ancients where he thinks their witness might assist his argument. He is in one sense a Middle Platonist (one who rarely criticizes the Master and who embraces not only the language but much of the intellectual framework and presuppositions of this tradition) who will use Stoic language where it fits but does not embrace much Stoicism. Athenagoras' employment of Stoic concepts and language is evident throughout, but he is not a Stoic Christian. Where he deals consciously and deliberately with Stoicism it is more often than not to refute it. In my view he simply employs Stoic language as useful for his own purposes, putting it largely to the service of the interpretation of Middle Platonist concepts and ideas and thus to the explication and articulation of the Christian message. This is unlike his employment of Platonist ideas and language: there he clearly operates within a Middle Platonist framework and his thought is shaped to a certain degree by it in the articulation of the Christian account of God, creation and providence. He is not thereby unfaithful to the specifically Christian account – tradition and scripture; it is simply that he appears to see, for the most part, no particular inconsistencies with the Platonist tradition. That he sometimes is unfair to Plato, as Pouderon insists (and he is certainly unfair to Aristotle at a number of points); or simply often quite wrong in his interpretations and usage of Plato is not the point here.

The *Legatio*

The Scriptures

Athenagoras' major motivation for employing the scriptures in the *Legatio* would seem to lie in their ethical content, given that some 15 per cent of his direct quotations from, or clear allusions to, the gospel concern his consideration of a Christian ethics.[5] Most of these come from Matthew 5–7, from the Sermon on the Mount. He quotes or alludes to Matthew 5.28 at 31.3 and 32.2 on lust and adultery; from Matthew 5.32 (and Mark 10.11) at 32.4 on divorce; from Matthew 5.39–40 (and Luke 6.29–30) at 1.4 and 11.4 on non-resistance to violence; from Matthew 5.42 (and Luke 6.30) on Christian generosity; from Matthew 5.44–5 (and Luke

4 Yet we need also to take into consideration the evidence for some similarities in the employment of language between the author of the *De resurrectione* and Philo.

5 Marcovich claims to recognize at least 40 other possible allusions to scriptural texts in the *Legatio* but many simply consist in similarities of language or thought and nothing more. See *Athenagoras. Legatio pro Christianis*, edited by M. Marcovich (Berlin, 1990).

6.27–8) at 11.2 on Christian love of the enemy; from Matthew 5.46 (and Luke 6. 32 and 34) at 12.3 on the lack of reward for those who love only reciprocally; and from Matthew 7.12 and 22.39 at 32.4 on love of the neighbour. On the other hand, Athenagoras quotes or alludes to Baruch 3.36 and to Isaiah 43.10–11, 44.6 and 66.2 at 9.2 on the oneness of God; to Proverbs 8.22 at 10.4 on the Spirit's claim to have been created by God; to Proverbs 21.1 at 18.2 on kingly rule coming from God; and to John 1.3, 1.10, 6.46 and 7.29 and to Colossians 1.15–17 at 4.2 and elsewhere, on the notion of creation through the Word of God. At 7.3 and 9.1 Athenagoras makes much of Christian teaching being founded on a Spirit-inspired prophetic witness, but actually his use of it is scanty. It is, however, true that, when addressing those for whom the Christian scriptures could have very little authority, there is a limited value in using them. He therefore employs them more to point to the content of Christian teaching than to argue for it.

Stoicism

Pouderon says that '*la Supplique est empreinte de stoïcisme plus encore que de platonisme*'.[6] At 3.1 Athenagoras' comment that even wild beasts operate only according to the norms of nature and in the appointed seasons is pure Stoicism. For the Stoics, beginning with their founder Zeno, 'living in agreement with nature is the end, which is living in accordance with virtue. For nature leads us towards virtue' (Diogenes Laertius 7.87). The Stoics, too, employed the example of non-human animals in their acting according to their nature (and thus according to universal nature, of which individual natures are but a part) for exploring the behaviour of human animals. Long and Sedley, however, warn that 'the Stoics are not saying *we* should do these things [preserving ourselves and looking after our young] because animals do them' but rather because 'animals and humans alike are so structured that such behaviour is natural and appropriate to them both'.[7] Athenagoras' point here, however, is not, as with the Stoics, to compare human and animal behaviour and its appropriateness (though he clearly does employ Stoic language) but rather that, having suggested that Christians who do apostasize, commit cannibalism and participate in incestuous relationships are but like wild beasts, he counters his own claim that not even animals in fact act in this way. At 4.2 Athenagoras' talk of the 'impressive signs conducive to piety' in the ordering, harmony and arrangements of the world reflect both a Stoic and a Platonist framework, but one where the first component is more readily recognizable than the second. The notion of the harmony and order of the world is consistent with a Stoic worldview and, even if not inconsistent with a Platonic one either, is generally recognized as primarily Stoic in origin.

---

[6] B. Pouderon, *Athénagore d'Athènes. Philosophe chrétien* (Paris, 1992), p. 33.

[7] A.A. Long and D.N. Sedley, *The Hellenistic philosophers*, 2 vols (Cambridge, 1987), I: 352.

At 5.1, as we have seen in Chapter 4 on Athenagoras' epistemology, he roundly condemns the reliance on 'common preconceptions' for getting knowledge about God – reliance from those whom (I believe) we can identify quite safely as Stoics and Epicureans. The poet Euripides, he says, cannot himself see how such preconceptions can be relied upon, preferring instead to understand what he can of God through 'reasoned insight'. At 5.2 Athenagoras employs the language of Stoicism in his discussion of substances, predicated materials and underlying realities (ὑποκειμένας), but is not necessarily challenging Stoic thought in so doing. Yet, given his criticisms of the concept of the 'preconception' as a means of knowing God in the previous section of the chapter, that is not impossible and it is likely that here Athenagoras is employing Stoic language to debunk particular Stoic concepts. He maintains, again employing Euripides as witness, that the concept of preconception does not ensure that one can discern beneath the name of God the substrate of a particular, underlying reality which might give substance to the mere name. Athenagoras does not strictly use ὑποκειμένον as a noun here but does use it adjectivally, with οὐσίαι and πράγματα, to denote that substance or reality which underlies 'something'. He does, then, as do other philosophers, employ it to distinguish essence from accident. But here the critical matter is whether in the case of the (pagan) gods there is any 'substance' or 'reality' actually underpinning the name of 'god' given to or claimed for them. Is there, he asks effectively, evidence of 'something (τι)' actually being there? Euripides, he says, cannot see anything to give substance to the claimed reality, the name of 'god' is not predicated (κατηγορεῖν: another Stoic term) of any actual underlying reality. If there is no underlying substance behind (or below?) the name, then there is nothing there at all.

At 6.4, as part of his scheme of drawing on poets and philosophers as witnesses to the essential oneness of God, he brings the Stoics to the stand, though his employment of their conceptual framework is a classic case of praising with faint damns. He refutes their giving multiple names to the divine being as a means of giving expression to the permutations of matter through which they claim the Spirit to move, but declares that their notions of God as an artisan fire systematically producing the world and of God's Spirit penetrating the whole world mean in effect that their teaching must be that God is one and that the 'gods' are merely names for the different aspects of divine reality. The Stoics are his final witnesses in this part of his defence of Christian teaching, and they clearly come last because their evidence is not as conclusive as that of the Pythagoreans (6.1) or of Plato (6.2), but is probably only marginally worse that that of the Aristotelians (6.3). He employs the language of the Stoics to explain their teaching but does not make their position his own by way of incorporation into his own system.

At 10.3 Athenagoras again employs the Stoic language of the substrate (ὑποκειμένων) and of the entity without qualities (ἀποίου φύσεως), now in the context of the Word serving as *idea* and *energeia* of the Father and giving form to matter – although it must also be acknowledged here that the concept of formless matter being given form by divine action is also found in Plato's *Timaeus*. Yet it is clear that, while Athenagoras employs Stoic language here, he is not engaging with Stoic thought substantially. Indeed, if we take the material available both from the *Timaeus* and from Alcinous, it is possible that Athenagoras is actually employing Stoic language to interpret a series of concepts drawn from the Platonist tradition. The quotation from Dillon at the head of this chapter, on the use of Stoic (and Aristotelian) language to articulate Platonist concepts better, would seem apt here.

At 19.3 Athenagoras, dealing with the matter of the generation of the universe, makes mention of the Stoic notion of a cosmic conflagration and subsequent restoration of the world. In this and in what follows he sees the Stoic version of the Platonic distinction between the always existing, the uncreated intelligible, and that which becomes but never is, the created perceptible. He speaks of the Stoic understanding of the two causes, one active and efficacious (Providence, which at 19.4 he identifies with God) and the other passive and mutable (matter). If, he says, it is impossible for the world which is subject to becoming to remain unchanged even though it is guided by Providence, how can the gods, who also come into being, avoid dissolution? These gods, he concludes, cannot be superior to matter when they, according to some reports, derive their substance from water. Here again Athenagoras employs Stoic language, which he acknowledges as such, in order to make a key point in this treatise: that of the necessary distinction between God and matter and of the superiority of the one as the sole fiirst principle over the other, which has none of the necessary marks of a first principle. Thus here Athenagoras employs Stoic terminology in his refutation of the Stoic notion that God and matter are both first principles.

At 22.4–5, he declares – much as he had at 6.4, where he spoke of the Stoic practice of giving the names of gods to the various elements – and he declares with criticaism of the Stoic view, it needs to be said – that, if it is true for the Stoics that the supreme God is one, uncreated and eternal, that there are composite entities resulting from changes to matter and that the spirit of God pervading matter receives, in its changes, now one name (of a god) and later another, then material things ('forms in matter') will be God's body, and when all the elements perish in the cosmic conflagration the names (of the gods) will perish with them and the spirit of God alone remain. These, he says, cannot be gods whose bodies are destroyed by changes in matter. Athenagoras here exploits Stoic language to argue his case but not only does not embrace the actual Stoic position, he largely undermines it.

At 27,1f. Athenagoras employs the language of Stoic psychology, as we saw in our treatment of his epistemology in Chapter 4, to demonstrate how evil daemons employ the illusions and fantasies of weak and docile human souls, undirected by reason and with a passion for idols, to lead such humans astray. Again Athenagoras employs the language of the Stoics to make his point but manages at the same time to debunk their concepts. At 33.1 and 33.4 Athenagoras' musings on marriage and what constitutes adultery are consistent with Stoic thought, but they are also consistent with Philo and with Christians generally. The same holds for his condemnation of various forms and manifestations of immorality at 34.2, which does not suggest any particular Stoic influence.

Thus it can be seen that, while Athenagoras makes quite extensive use of Stoic language and imagery in the *Legatio*, he does not work within a particular Stoic frame of reference. Indeed, where he does engage with Stoic thought consciously it is more often than not to criticize or even to condemn it. This is particularly so at 3.1, where Athenagoras employs a commonplace notion; at 5.2, where he employs Stoic physics, and likewise at 10.3, where he speaks of the Son as the *idea* and the *energeia* giving form to unqualified matter; at 19.3, where he employs the Stoic language of the two primary causes to interpret his Platonist–Christian understanding of the divine; at 22.4–5, where he employs Stoic language against itself, to support his own position on the relationship of the divine to matter; at 27.1f., where he employs Stoic psychological language to explain the leading astray of some humans by the wiles of the daemons. At 4.2, where he speaks of the ordering and harmony of the cosmic arrangements, he employs Stoic ideas positively. At 5.1, where he condemns the use of common preconceptions as a means of apprehending the divine; at 6.4, where he refutes the Stoic practice of giving multiple names to the divine to explain the permutations of matter, and, again, at 22.4–5 he is simply critical of Stoic thought. In his dealing with Stoicism he also addresses a number of the 'philosophical problematics' identified by Berchman. At 4.2, 10.3 and 19.3 he addresses the problem of the relation of the divine to the universe, at 5.1 the problem of the knowing of or about the divine, and at 22.4–5 the problem of the relationship of God to matter (a key theme in the *Legatio*).

Others

Before moving to consider the not inconsiderable influence of Platonism and Middle Platonism on Athenagoras, we might just briefly deal with other influences. At 6.1 he employs the witness of the Pythagoreans Philolaus, Lysis and Opsimus in his argument that the Christian belief in the oneness of God is consistent with philosophical reflection. He seems comfortable in making the Pythagorean term μονάς his own, although he does not explicitly endorse the Pythagorean use of numbers. The Pythagoreans are simply convenient witnesses whom he is happy to use without much further comment. At 6.3 he likewise employs Aristotle's testimonial for the oneness of God and seems to identify the unmoved mover with the Christian God. Pouderon says that here Athenagoras '*connaît mal Aristote et sa doctrine*'[8] when he tell us that Aristotle 'brings before us one God whom they [*sc.* the Peripatetics] liken to a composite living being and say that he consists of soul and body'. Barnard declares that in this notion that the ether is the body of God Athenagoras misunderstands Aristotle – who says only that God

---

8 Pouderon, *Athénagore d'Athènes* (above, n6), p. 233.

controls the outermost ethereal sphere.[9] God's body according to Aristotle, says Athenagoras, is the ether, the planets, and the sphere of the fixed stars, all moving in circular motion, and his soul is that reason which controls the motion of the body, itself unmoved yet the cause of the body's motion (the unmoved mover). At 25.2 Athenagoras repeats the oft-stated assertion that Aristotle restricted the operation of divine providence to the heavenly realm – a notion he vigorously challenges. This, Pouderon says, is unjust to Aristotle.[10] At 12.3 Athenagoras challenges the Epicurean view that we should live as if there were no tomorrow. Like all Christians of the period, he cannot abide Epicurean thought and therefore is influenced only negatively by it.

At 19.4 and 20.1ff. Athenagoras quotes Orphic sources, but only to dismiss traditional claims about the gods, much as he does with Homer throughout the *Legatio* (but most concentratedly so in chapters 18 and 21; in the latter he cites or alludes to a passage from the *Illiad* or the *Odyssey* some thirteen times!). At 22.1 and 22.3 he quotes Empedocles on Love as the ruling principle. He employs it as being consistent with Christian teaching and is appreciative of the fact that he can draw witness from contemporary thought to underscore the point he is trying to make on the need to distinguish clearly the uncreated and eternal God from created and perishable matter. At 23.4 he draws on the testimony of Thales on the distinction between God and daemons, the former qua mind of the universe and the latter qua psychic substances. Thales is for Athenagoras yet another witness of convenience – he sustains Athenagoras' desire to point to the consistency of much of Christian thought with philosophical tradition (where this suits him). In chapter 28 Athenagoras makes use of Herodotus on the origin of the names of the gods. This historian of antiquity, much like Homer, is simply part of the intellectual world in which Athenagoras operates and is an obvious source of information for him.

Platonism/Middle Platonism

It has been proposed that Athenagoras is consciously and deliberately engaged in a conversation within Middle Platonism, and I trust I have clearly demonstrated this in Chapter 3. Here we look particularly at the ways in which Athenagoras has made use, explicitly and implicitly, of that tradition in his exploration and articulation of his primary claim that Christians are not only theists but are so in a way consistent with contemporary philosophical thought.

At 1.3, 1.4 and 15.1 Athenagoras speaks of the hostility and ignorance of the crowd (οἱ πολλοί). At *Apology* 19d Socrates, in his own defence against the charge of impiety, speaks of the hostility and prejudice of 'the crowd', and implies as much consistently throughout that defence. At 2.5 Athenagoras suggests

[9] L.W. Barnard, Athenagoras: A Study in Second Century Christian Apologetic (Paris, 1972), pp. 42 and 89.

[10] Pouderon, *Athénagore d'Athènes* (above, n6), p. 146.

that 'slanders' are spoken against some philosophers; this is repeated and more explicitly related to Christians at 3.2 and 18.2. At *Apology* 19a, 19b, 20c, 20e, 21b, 23a, 24a (twice) and 37b Socrates speaks of the 'slanders' offered against him by his accusers, slanders he is at pains to contest. Justin also speaks, at 2.3 and 3.1, of the prejudice and evil rumours spread against Christians. At 2.6 Athenagoras urges the emperors to be fair in their dealings with Christians, 'not [to] be carried away by prejudice', so that they 'will not go wrong through ignorance' about Christian belief and practice. Justin himself speaks of the emperors' possible 'ignorance of our affairs' in his *Apology* (*1A* 3.4) and speaks of beginning his 'defence of our teaching', a notion he repeats at 11.3 and 17.1. Socrates speaks likewise of making his own 'defence' at *Apology* 17c, 18a, 18d, 18e (*bis*), 19a (twice), 28a, 34b, and 35d. At 2.6 Athenagoras speaks of the emperor's love of learning and truth, while Socrates speaks constantly (*Apology* 17b, 18a, 18b, 24a, 31c, 31e, 33c and 35d) of his pursuit of the same. Justin speaks of the emperors' piety and love of learning at *1A*2.1. Thus these early chapters of the *Legatio* display very clear echoes of Plato's defence of his master but also, it must be said, of Justin's defence of the faith before the emperors.

At 3.2 Athenagoras, addressing the very matter of these alleged 'slanders', speaks of a 'natural principle' by which evil opposes virtue and of a 'divine law' by which opposites war upon one another. The phrase φυσικὸς λόγος is found also in Alcinous, where the author speaks of it as that by which we judge truth from falsehood (4.154.18), that is, the instrument by which we judge rather than the agent who judges. Dillon translates this phrase '[our] reasoning faculty working on the physical level', and Louis, '*la raison naturelle*'. Alcinous, too, speaks of 'that natural and scientific reasoning' (ὁ φυσικὸς καὶ ἐπιστημονικὸς… λόγος), which is constituted from 'simple forms of knowledge and which arises in us by nature' (*Didaskalikos* 4.155.35). Dillon declares that '*logos physikos* here almost defies translation'.[11] Athenagoras himself elsewhere speaks of Empedocles' teaching on the existence of principle of strife in all nature at 22.3 and 24.2.[12] But within Stoicism there is a clear teaching on the necessary existence and warring of opposites in nature.[13] Chrysippus in *On Providence* says that neither of two opposites can exist without the other, inferring that if there are two opposites both must exist.[14] In his *Hymn to Zeus* Cleanthes says that '[Zeus] has so welded into one all things good and bad that they all share in a single everlasting reason'. Long speaks of the 'co-existence of moral opposites in the [Stoic] concept of cosmic order'.[15] Thus Athenagoras here recognizes the existence of good and evil in the

[11] J. Dillon, *The Middle Platonists: 80 BC to AD 220*, rev. edn (London, 1996), p. 273. For a discussion of *physikos logos* see also Chapter 4 above, p. 92.

[12] See J.H. Crehan, *Athenagoras*. (New York, 1995), p.126, note 24.

[13] This is perhaps different from the teaching of Heraclitus, which posed the λόγος as that which connects opposites into a unity.

[14] F.H. Sandbach, *The Stoics* (London, 1989), p. 105.

[15] Ibid.

world and sees it, as did Empedocles and the Stoics, as a requirement imposed both by the natural order (the way things are) and by the divine order. Yet the language he employs is presumably Platonist.

At 4.1, while it is probable that Athenagoras is challenging a tendency within Platonism to place matter on the same footing with God on the grounds that matter is a first principle, for the Platonists it was normal to regard God, the Forms and matter as first principles. It is also clear that, in speaking of God as uncreated, eternal and capable of being contemplated only by mind and reason, Athenagoras is echoing standard Platonist views (*Timaeus* 28a and 52a and *Phaedrus* 247c). At 19.1 Athenagoras again employs the Platonist contrast between the uncreated and eternal and the created and perishable (*Timaeus* 27d) to make it clear that the entities divinized by his opponents are not gods. At 19.2 he then actually quotes from *Timaeus* 27d directly, to reinforce his point and to demonstrate that there is essentially no dispute here between himself and the philosophers (by which he essentially means, I presume, Plato and his school). He again alludes to *Timaeus* 27d at 20.1, when he wishes to highlight what he calls the 'absurdity' (or rather 'improbability') of his immediate opponents' theology in making of gods entities which have come into being and are thereby perishable. He alludes again to *Timaeus* 27d and to 52a (on the contemplation of God by reason) at 22.9, when he attacks these opponents yet again for seeking to divinize the elements.

At 4.2 Athenagoras speaks of the 'impressive signs to piety' evident in the order, perfect harmony and physical arrangement of the world. Now, while the language of this section could very well be influenced by Stoicism, it is possible that, in part at least, Athenagoras is also mindful here of passages such as *Timaeus* 27d and 29a – given that the remainder of the section, with its talk of the one God, Creator of the universe, true uncreated being, quite obviously reflects a passage from the *Timaeus* dear to his heart: 28c (see also 5.3). At 16.1 Athenagoras again employs Platonist language – though the possibility of Stoic influence cannot be ruled out – in describing the beauty of the world. Plato at *Timaeus* 30b and 30d describes the world as 'most beautiful', as does Alcinous at 12.1.167.9, and he describes its spherical shape from *Timaeus* 33b, as does Alcinous at 12.2.167.36 and 168.1f. Pouderon says that here we have '*la prévue cosmologique chère aux stoïciens*'.[16] At 16.3 Athenagoras again alludes to *Timaeus* 28c when he says that, if it is true, as Plato suggests, that the world is the craftsmanship of God, then one may admire the craft but worship only the craftsman – in this case God. At 16.4, when reiterating that it must be the creator that is worshipped and not the created, not matter how beautiful the latter may be, Athenagoras brings Plato in to his support, citing *Politicus* 269d, where it is said that, notwithstanding the many blessed qualities which heaven and the world have received from God, they remain corporeal and therefore cannot be free from change. They are, therefore, other than God.

---

16 Pouderon, *Athénagore d'Athènes* (above, n6), pp. 125f. and 225.

At 6.2 Athenagoras draws from a doxography to quote directly from *Timaeus* 28c3–4 on the Creator and Father of the Universe being hard to discover – one of the few word-for-word quotations of this famous passage in antiquity – and says that hereby Plato demonstrates his understanding that the uncreated and eternal God is one. Athenagoras then quotes from *Timaeus* 41a a passage concerning the Demiurge's creation of the lesser gods and declares that if Plato, who understands the Creator of the universe to be the one uncreated God, is no atheist, neither can the Christians be considered to be atheists, since they acknowledge the God by whose Word all things were created and by whose Spirit they are upheld. Rightly or not, Athenagoras takes Plato to be speaking of the Christian God at *Timaeus* 28c and 41a, and regards him as perhaps his best witness for the defence. This passage, as much as any other in the *Legatio*, demonstrates that the basic foundation and argument development which Athenagoras employs in his demonstration are Platonist.

At 10.2 and 10.3, Athenagoras' characterization of the Son of God as the Word of the Father in *idea* and in *energeia* is a combination of Platonic, Aristotelian and (possibly) Stoic concepts. While Athenagoras has been at pains to refute the notion, dear to Platonists, that matter is one of the three *archai* – declaring that matter is rather derived, created and perishable – he seems to accept that the *idea* is one of them; but he suggests that there is only one *idea*, which is the Word itself. He also, as we have seen elsewhere, speaks of other Forms; but these Forms (or εἴδη; see 7.2 and 15.4 for example) are immanent in matter and are the result of spirit pervading it and giving its formlessness form and shape. At 10.2.164.23 Alcinous says that the primal god (identified at 10.3.164.27 with the primary intellect) is the cause of the eternal activity of the intellect of the whole heaven – which, says Dillon in his commentary, is to be identified with that of the world soul.[17] The primal god/intellect is further described by Alcinous at 10.3.164.29 as everlastingly engaged in thinking upon itself in and its own thoughts; and this activity is its Form (αὕτη ἡ ἐνέργεια αὐτοῦ ἰδέα ὑπάρχει).

At 12.2, while demonstrating that Christians live the righteous and ethical life because they must one day give an account of their lives to God, Athenagoras cites *Gorgias* 523c–4a on the judgement and punishment of evil-doers by Minos and Rhadamanthys, but says that in fact not even these two or their father (Zeus) will escape the judgement of God. This is one passage in which Athenagoras would appear to offer a measure of criticism, though admittedly moderately so, of Plato. At 15.1, where he stresses the need to distinguish God from matter and to deny the latter the status of a first principle, Athenagoras alludes to *Timaeus* 27d–8a (see above) and to *Cratylus* 397a. At this place in the *Cratylus* Socrates says that, while the names of heroes and human beings might be given inappropriately (and therefore should be disregarded), 'we are most likely to find the correct names in the nature of the eternal and absolute; for there the names ought to have been given with the greatest care, and perhaps some of them were given by a power more divine than

17 J. Dillon, *Alcinous: The Handbook of Platonism* (Oxford, 1993), p. 103.

is that of men'. Alcinous declared that Plato's interest was in whether names arise from nature or by convention (6.10.160.5f.). His view, says Alcinous, was that the correctness of names was a matter of convention, though not arising from chance, but from the nature of a given thing. Thus the correctness of a name is nothing but than a convention which accords with nature. Both Alcinous (6.10.160.24f.) and Philo (*Creation* 148) recognize that it is the 'wise person' who can see into the nature of things and thus can properly grant a name to something.[18] 'He would be the best name-giver who indicates through the name the nature of the thing', said Alcinous (6.10.160.24f.), Thus the Christians who can distinguish uncreated being and the intelligible from the created non-being and the perceptible are the collective 'wise person' able to name properly, unlike the 'un-wise', the 'crowd' who are unable not only to distinguish opposites, but even to name them appropriately. Thus in this passage Athenagoras demonstrates that he is not simply using the language of those to whom he is speaking, but language which is both natural and appropriate for him. He speaks not against the background of a contemporary debate but from within that debate – or at the very least from its edge – and seeks to contribute something from his the particular perspective of his faith. At 15.4 one can see clear Platonist influence in his reference to 'material forms' (τὰ εἴδη τῆς ὕλης). This notion of 'forms of matter' finds some echoes in Alcinous too, where he says that of the intelligible objects (τὰ νοητά, as opposed to τὰ αἰσθητά) the primary are the (transcendent) Ideas while the secondary are forms in matter (τὰ εἴδη τῇ ὕλῃ) which are inseparable from matter (4.7.155.40). Dillon tells us[19] that the phrase itself is not Platonic – but rather probably Aristotelian – but the Platonic contrast between transcendent Forms and their copies, regarded as immanent forms-in-matter, can be found for instance in Seneca (*Letters* 58.16–22). In the *Timaeus* itself, Plato says of the substance (or matter) which receives all bodies (forms) and of these figures which it receives – for the former never departs from its own proper quality and thus therefore must be always called by the same name – that 'the figures that enter and depart are copies of those that are always existent, being stamped from them in a fashion marvellous and hard to describe' (50c). Here, even if not in the same language, are the transcendent Forms and their forms as received into otherwise formless matter. To confuse these would be to equate (as Plato does not) the eternal with the perishable and corruptible.

At 23.5–6, where he is speaking of daemons and seeking to show how they differ from God, Athenagoras cites *Timaeus* 40a–b in support and then quotes from *Timaeus* 40d–e on the origin of the daemons and of the gods (see also Alcinous, 14.7.171.2–15.1.171.21 and Apuleius, *De Platone* 1.11). At 23.7 Athenagoras claims that Plato has come to understand the eternal God apprehended by mind and reason and has recognized his attributes to be true being, oneness of nature and the good which is flowing from him –(here he quotes from pseudo-Plato,

---

18 *Philo of Alexandria: On the Creation of the Cosmos according to Moses,* translated with commentary by D.T. Runia (Leiden, 2001), p. 349.

19 Dillon, *Alcinous* (above, n17), p. 69.

Letters 2.312e on the three powers). Then after this preamble he asks whether Plato thought it beyond his powers to learn the truth concerning those entities who have come into being from the perceptible realms of earth and heaven. Surely not, he replies. Since Plato believed that gods could not beget or be brought forth (for what begins also ends), and because he knew it to be impossible to persuade the crowd, which accepts myths without proper examination, he thought it beyond him to tell of the birth of the rest of the daemons. Therefore he and could not say whether the gods were born or not. At 23.9f. Athenagoras quotes from *Phaedrus* 246e – on the great charioteer Zeus – and says that this reference is not to the son of Cronus but to the Creator of the universe. This Plato did, Athenagoras says, not because it was proper to address God as 'Zeus' but for the sake of clarity, given that it is not possible to tell all people of God (see *Timaeus* 28c3–4). Plato added the title 'the Great', Athenagoras continues, so that he might separate the heavenly from the earthly Zeus, the uncreated from the created, and so on.

Athenagoras' reference, at 24.3, to angels being called into being by God to exercise a particular providence over the things set in order by God – alongside God's general and universal providence – has clear (and I think deliberate) echoes of *Timaeus* 41a. In Greek philosophy, argues Pouderon, '*la partition de la function providentielle corresponde à la hiérarchie du divin*'[20]: *a double providence with Plato* (see Alcinous 15.2.171.24f.), likewise with the Stoics *(Cicero, De natura deorum* 2.164), and '*une providence unique*' in Aristotle.[21] Yet in Middle Platonism, he continues, there is a '*tripartition du divin*' which leads to a '*tripartition de la fonction providentielle*'. Plutarch (*De fato* 9–11 and 572f–4d) says that the first providence is the mind or will of the primary god, the second that of the secondary gods, and the third that of the daemons stationed in the earthly realm who stand watch over the actions of humans).[22] At first sight, Athenagoras would appear to follow the notion of a double providence; but in fact he posits three providences ('*cosmique, générique et particulière*') and fails to explicate them.[23] It is possible that the angels–daemons who have failed at their assigned tasks (see 24.4–5) are those entrusted with a 'third' providence, the watch over humankind. There the references – citations, quotations, allusions and the like – to Plato's thought and to his successors end. But these are enough to show that Athenagoras is not merely employing, exploiting even, Platonist concepts and images to make his point, as he does with the Stoics. These references, for the most part, show him participating in conversation and, to a great extent, making that conversation his own. For him Plato is effectively an authoritative text, though hardly sacred scripture, and the issue for Athenagoras and his contemporaries, who stand in Plato's shadow, is how to interpret him. Much of his employment of Plato's thought has to do with the relationship of God to the universe – see 4.1, 15.1, 15.4, 16.1, and 19.1 – a doctrine

---

20 Pouderon, *Athénagore d'Athènes* (above, n6), p. 282.

21 Ibid., p. 283.

22 Ibid.

23 Ibid., p. 284.

of God proper – see 6.2 and *Timaeus* 28c and 41a and 10.2 and 10.3 – and the notion of the Word as the *idea* of the Father, together with the problem of how one might employ philosophical frameworks to construct the believer's world – see 23.5–6 on daemons and 24.3 on angels.

One Middle Platonist whose relationship with the thought of Athenagoras could well bear closer examination is Plutarch of Chaironea. Dillon says that before Plotinus only Plutarch among the Platonists made use of the Logos concept with demiurgic functions.[24] This may have influenced Athenagoras in his own endeavour to argue for the admittedly biblical and patristic notion of creation through the agency of the Word while maintaining the key concept of the oneness of God. Russell argues that, in matters of religion, Plutarch 'belongs to the continuous tradition of Hellenic piety and Hellenic scepticism, not much affected by the great changes in religious feeling which he could sense in the world around'.[25] He also speaks of the Platonist theme of the essential reliability and goodness of God which, he maintains, is the key to Plutarch's attitude to religion.[26] This reliability and goodness of God are key features in Athenagoras' presentation of his own doctrine of God.

Conclusions to Legatio

It is clear from the foregoing that Athenagoras' understanding of the Christian doctrine of God and of the Christian life is firmly grounded in the prophetic witness, the New Testament in particular. For apologetic reasons any reliance on the testimony and authority of scripture are kept to a minimum, but they are there. Athenagoras makes use of Stoic concepts in his argumentation – as he uses the writings of Homer, Herodotus and Euripides – but does not own for himself their essential thought. His employment of Stoic language is as much to interpret and articulate Platonist thought as anything else. He does employ both the language and the theological frameworks of the Platonists and seeks, where he can, to integrate these within the biblically and prophetically informed universe which he occupies. Platonism, for Athenagoras, approaches the truth, even if it is not, in itself, the full truth. Where there is conflict, however, his loyalties are clear. He is a *Christian* Platonist, not a *Platonizing* Christian.

The De resurrectione

As in the *Legatio*, here too there are very few references, by quotation, citation or allusion, to the scriptures. An allusion to Genesis 1.26 – which is neither quoted

---

24 J. Dillon, 'Logos and Trinity: Patterns of Platonist influence on early Christianity' in G. Vesey (ed.), *The Philosophy in Christianity* (Cambridge, 1989), p. 4.

25 D.A. Russell, *Plutarch*, 2nd edn, foreword and bibliography by J. Mossman (Bristol, 2001), p. 83.

26 Ibid.

nor alluded to at all in the *Legatio* – comes at 12.6, when our author is making it clear that the human being was not created without purpose or in vain, was not created for the use of the Creator himself or for that of any other creature, but rather for its own sake and out of the goodness and wisdom of God, which is evident throughout all creation. God, Athenagoras says, made the human being simply for its own survival, decreeing an unending existence to those who bear his image in themselves (τοῖς ... ἐν ἑαυτοῖς ἀγαλματοφοῦσι) – the term ἀγαλματοῦσι is itself Philonic, as we saw in chapter one.[27] These humans are gifted with νοῦς and share the faculty of rational discernment, so that, knowing their Creator and his power and wisdom and complying with law and justice, they might live eternally, without distress, with the powers which governed their former life (12.6). Thus the image of God in which human being was created could be said to consist here in the capacity for thought and in the exercise of rational judgement.

At 23.3–4, having already made it clear in the preceding section that it would not only be incongruous but also irrational to impose obligations on human beings in this life and then to exact an account and, if necessary, to impose judgement in the next one on souls alone (23.1) – for God did not address his (ten) commandments for observation and abstinence, but to the body alone – he quotes from the Ten Commandments (Exodus 20, 12 and 14) passages on honouring one's father and mother, on adultery and on stealing (23.5): these are examples of activities of which the body is alone capable. Thus the body at least should be held accountable beyond this life for the sins of this one; and in order to be so it must survive and exist into the next, along with its associate, the soul. A use of Isaiah 22.13 and 1 Corinthians 15.32 – 'Let us eat and drink now, for tomorrow we die' – which is, for Christians, a neat (if not entirely fair) summation of the Epicurean ethics – is found both in the *De resurrectione* (19.3) and in the *Legatio* (12.3), as part of an argument that the purpose of human existence must be more profound. At *De resurrectione* 19.3, as part of his 'secondary argument for the doctrine of the resurrection' – the argument from providence and divine judgement – Athenagoras asks rhetorically whether or not human existence has a purpose. He begins his own answer by pointing to God's providential care for that which he has created. He suggests that where there is no judgement there can be no human destiny higher than that of irrational beasts, and little or no concern for piety, justice or any of the other virtues. If this be so, he continues, then the life of the beasts and wild animals would be best, virtue would be 'foolish' [or 'unreasonable'], the threat of punishment a mockery, the cherishing of any pleasure the greatest of goods, and the common δόγμα and single law for all would be the one dear to the licentious and abandoned – the law summed up by 'Let us eat and drink, for tomorrow we die'. God's providential (and thereby just) care for his creatures must therefore be exercised in this present life or in that beyond death. At 12.1 of the *Legatio* Athenagoras suggests that where one does not know that God presides over the

[27] This, as we have seen earlier, may be evidence for an Alexandrian connection for the author of the *De resurrectione*.

human race there will be no purity. Where, on the other hand, one is convinced that an account will be rendered for this life to God, one will choose moderation, for the gain of the beyond compensates for any loss (even of life) in this present existence. After quoting Plato on the punishment of evil (*Gorgias* 523c–524a: *De resurrectione* 12.2), Athenagoras challenges the notion that those who embrace an ethics based on 'Let us eat and drink, for tomorrow we die' can be accounted pious (12.3). For the Christian, this present existence is of little worth when we compare it with the one to come.

At 1.3 Athenagoras identifies two primary lines of argument in dealing with matters such as the doctrine of resurrection. These, he says, are the argument 'on behalf of the truth' and the argument 'concerning the truth'. The first is directed to, or against, those who reject a particular doctrine or dispute; this is what the contemporary rhetoricians would have called the *refutatio*. The other is directed towards those who are well disposed to such a teaching and 'who receive it gladly' (μετ' εὐνοίας δεχομένους τὴν ἀλήθειαν). The last phrase is an allusion to Luke 8.13. It is not found in the *Legatio*. At 9.1 our author repudiates the use of 'parallels' drawn by some between human creators and the divine creator: these parallels purport to show that human artisans such as potters and carpenters cannot recreate their own works once these are shattered, worn out or destroyed and that therefore God would not wish to raise dead and destroyed bodies, and indeed could not even if he wished to. Such persons, says Athenagoras, mock God and equate disparate powers. It is, in fact, more plausible and in harmony with the truth to say' 'What is impossible for mortals is possible for God' (Luke 18.27). This verse is not found in the *Legatio*.

At 8.4, in the context of declaring that any claim that cannibalism is not contrary to nature is sacrilegious (8.3), Athenagoras would appear to allude, though not necessarily so, to our Lord's statement at John 11.25, 'I am the Resurrection and the Life', when he says that the action of God effects the resurrection and the life of the dead and decomposed bodies. This scriptural text is not cited or alluded to in the *Legatio*. At 3.2 he alludes to, and at 18.5 he actually cites, Apostle Paul on the movement from perishability to imperishability (1 Corinthians 15.53). In the former passage he is speaking about God's actual capacity – allegedly denied by Athenagoras' opponents – to change the corruptible into the incorruptible; in the latter he identifies a three-stage life process for the body: this present existence, then the immediately post-death existence – in both of these the body remains corruptible – and then the resurrected existence, in which the body emerges alongside the soul as incorruptible. And again at 18.5 he quotes from 2 Corinthians 5.10 to the effect that each person, as reunited soul and body in the resurrection, will receive a just recompense for what, both good and evil, they have done in the body. Neither of these passages from the Corinthian correspondence appears by way of allusion, citation or quotation in the *Legatio*.

Athenagaoras' use of other Christian authors, as in the *Legatio*, is occasional but more marked. This is not unusual given that this writing is more clearly a part of an intra-Christian conversation. The Epistle of Barnabas declares that the coming judgement of the Lord – for glory or for destruction – necessitates a resurrection (21) and this compares with one of Athenagoras' 'secondary' arguments that divine providence requires resurrection. Justin Martyr at *1 Apology* 19 says that it is not impossible that the bodies of human beings, once dissolved, can yet, like seeds in the earth, rise again and put on incorruption. In his *Dialogue*, Justin declares that, while a belief in a 1,000 year reign of Christ is useful but not essential to Christian faith – Justin himself believes in it but many of a 'pure and pious faith' do not and are yet 'true Christians' – belief in a resurrection of the dead is non-negotiable (80). Those who deny this article of faith blaspheme the God of Abraham, Isaac and Jacob and thereby are not Christians. These are without doubt the Gnostics, or even the Marcionites. Irenaeus says that it is a matter of justice that the soul and body, as they are co-joined in this life, should thereby properly be co-joined in the 'reward' beyond this life (*Adversus haereses* 2.29.2). This compares with Athenagoras' understanding of the human being as properly and essentially a composite being, immortal soul and body. At *Adversus haereses* 5.3.2 Irenaeus declares that 'God's power is sufficient for resurrection, given that he had formed human being in the beginning'. This compares with the vigorous promotion, by Athenagoras and other Fathers, of the capacity of God to effect the resurrection, something clearly questioned, if not denied outrightly, by their opponents.

Theophilus, like Justin and Athenagoras, regards a belief in resurrection as essential to the Christian faith. 'Your faith will be reckoned as unfaith unless you believe now [in the resurrection]' (*Ad Autolycum* 1.8). In the same section he affirms the capacity of God to raise the dead. The one who formed human beings in the beginning can surely 'later make you over again', he says. He confirms this at 1.13, where he says that God 'is powerful enough to bring about the general resurrection of humankind'. One cannot speak, of course, of any influence exercised over Athenagoras by Tertullian; for the latter is situated at least a half-generation later than the former, and in a very different, western and Latin culture. Yet there is evidence for a reading of Tertullian's *De resurrectione carnis* (or *mortuorum*) alongside that of the similarly named treatise of Athenagoras; and also evidence of a commonly shaped work, of commonly inspired purposes, and so on. For Tertullian, the resurrection of the dead is the *fiducia* of the Christian. By it, he says, 'we are believers' (1). One who denies this doctrine indeed is not a Christian (3). As in the Athenagorean treatise, the primary, indeed probably sole targets in Tertullian's work are the Gnostics and/or the Marcionites. No one refuses to concede to the substance of the body its recovery from death, except those who invent, as heretics, a second deity (2). The defence of the doctrine of the resurrection of the flesh is associated with that of the oneness of God (2), and so is its repudiation. While the targets in both works are the Gnostics/Marcionites, the primary audiences are, likewise, Christians vulnerable to their arguments. It is the uneducated, the faltering in faith, the weak-minded who need to be instructed, directed and strengthened on the unity of God and the resurrection of the dead (2), so that they will not be so easily caught in the net of heterical influence (4). For the former are told quite directly that, if they hate the flesh (as the heretics do), they will have repudiated the Creator (63). But if they will only draw water from the Paraclete's fountains (primarily the scriptures, to which Tertullian devotes many chapters, unlike Athenagoras), they will never thirst for other doctrines (ibid.).

Also, like Athenagoras yet perhaps not quite so eloquently, Tertullian speaks of the human being as essentially a union of soul and body. Flesh is not only minister and servant to soul, but also associate and co-heir (7). Body and soul cannot be separated in their recompense when they are united in their service in life (8). The fullness and perfection of the Last Judgement consists in its representing the interests of the entire human person: since it results from the union of two natures, such a person must face judgement having both natures about it (8). Like Athenagoras again, Tertullian addresses the capacity of God to effect resurrection. If God, he says, produced all things out of nothing – there is no doubt (as there is with Athenagoras) that Tertullian holds on to a *creatio ex nihilo* – he will be able to draw forth from nothing even flesh which has fallen into nothing (11). Whoever can create can even more easily re-create. The restoration of the flesh is easier than its first formation. Tertullian, then, having established that flesh, once destroyed, is yet capable of restoration and that God's power can effect this, now seeks to demonstrate the cause of the restoration – a cause necessary and conformable to reason. He then offers the divine judgement of human beings as this cause (for Athenagoras, this is merely a secondary argument). The cause and necessity of resurrection lies in the requirements of the final judgement of God upon human beings, which involve the entire person, soul and body (14).

Pseudo-Justin's *De resurrectione* – possibly a third-century work and therefore not an influence on Athenagoras,[28] but a work which demonstrates, like Tertullian's, the sort of issues which engaged Christian theologians of the period – addresses a number of topics concerned with resurrection in a manner similar to that of Athenagoras. In chapter 2 the author lists, as the major objections to this article of Christian belief, the impossibility of restoring corrupted and dissolved matter, the disadvantage of saving the flesh and the claim that, with the raising of the flesh, its infirmities will also rise. In the same chapter he also identifies a two-stage process of argument: first dealing with objections and then demonstrating that the flesh will partake of salvation. This reminds one of Athenagoras' arguments *on behalf* of the truth and of those *concerning* the truth; and also of Alcinous' recognition of the process of refutation followed by demonstration (6.3.158.19f.) and of the rhetorical device of *refutatio* followed by *confirmatio*. In chapter 5, pseudo-Justin offers the standard affirmation that in the creation of human being lies sufficient proof of God's capacity to raise the dead. Here also he declares, as does Athenagoras, that resurrection of the dead is, against the claims of his enemies, worthy of the Creator. From chapter 5 to chapter 6 this anonymous autor speaks of those who are his primary audience. They are not, as they are for Athenagoras and Tertullian, faltering Christians, the weak-minded faithful vulnerable to

[28] If it is, however, from the hand of a disciple of Justin it may predate Athenagoras, but only just.

Gnostic or Marcionite-inspired doubt; they are the Gnostics themselves, whom he characterizes as unbelievers (5). He argues, from the unbelievers' own 'mother unbelief' – namely that the philosophers themselves, each in his own way, accept that matter itself (Plato), the four elements (Stoics) and the atoms and the void (Epicurus) are indestructible – that it is conceivable that God would 'be able to collect again the decomposed members of the flesh and make the same body as was formerly produced by him' (6). Chapter 8 mirrors Athenagoras' concept of human being as a composite being. The author declares that neither body nor soul can effect anything if unyoked from their communion; that neither soul by itself nor body by itself is human, but rather a 'rational animal composed of body and soul'. God has called not a part but the whole of the human individual, which is the soul and the body. Unlike Athenagoras, pseudo-Justin points to Christ's own resurrection as proof of a general resurrection (9).

Finally, it is noteworthy that for Irenaeus, Tertullian, Hippolytus, pseudo-Justin and Athenagoras the main targets in their works on resurrection are the Gnostics/Marcionites, yet both Tertullian and Hippolytus, unlike Athenagoras, make substantial use of scriptural demonstrations for their arguments.

Summary

Athenagoras' use of other Christian authors in the *De resurrectione* is, then, occasional, as it is in the *Legatio*, but more widespread. This is not surprising given that this work, unlike the *Legatio*, is placed within an intra-Christian conversation.

Argument Of these other Christian authors, only pseudo-Justin identifies a two-stage process of argumentation similar to that of Athenagoras' arguments – *on behalf of*, and then *concerning*, the truth (1.3): Alcinous' *refutatio* and *confirmatio* or *demonstratio* – when the former speaks of first dealing with objections and then demonstrating that the flesh will partake of salvation (2).

Audience and target For Justin, the target (though not the audience; for in his case that is the Jew Trypho) are the Gnostics or the Marcionites; for he says that those who deny this article of faith, the resurrection of the body, blaspheme the God of Abraham, Isaac and Jacob and are not thereby Christians (*Dialogue* 80). For Tertullian – who he cannot be a source for Athenagoras but can provide evidence of a common set of concerns and, at times, common approaches, as well as an indication of what was important for second century Christian apologists – the target (though not thereby the intended audience) of his work on resurrection are the Gnostics or the Marcionites. This is clear, given that Tertullian associates his opponents' refusal to concede to the substance of the body a recovery from death with the invention of a second God (2) and indeed he associates the defence of resurrection in body with a doctrine of the oneness of God. His primary audience on the other hand are those Christians who are uneducated, faltering in faith, weak-minded, those vulnerable to Gnostic/Marcionite arguments, who need instruction and comfort on the unity of God and the hope of resurrection. For pseudo-Justin – who, like Tertullian, cannot be a source for Athenagoras but can provide evidence of common concerns and approaches – both target and intended audience are the Gnostics and/or the Marcionites, unbelievers influenced by the philosophers (5).

Resurrection as article of faith For a number of contemporaries or near-contemporaries of Athenagoras, belief in the resurrection of the body, of the whole human being, was an essential non-negotiable article of faith. According to Justin, even if genuine Christians may, unlike himself, question the doctrine of the thousand-year rule of Christ, they cannot question the doctrine of resurrection (*Dialogue* 80). Theophilus of Antioch declares that 'faith will be reckoned as unfaith unless you believe now' in resurrection (*Ad Autolycum* 1.8). For Tertullian, the resurrection of the dead is the *fiducia* of the Christian. By it we are Christians. One who denies this belief is not a Christian (*De resurrectione carnis* 1ff.).

Human being as composite being A number of these early apologists emphasize the composite nature of human being, soul and body, both before and beyond death, and regard it as necessary for, and irrefutable evidence of, the resurrection of the whole of human being. Irenaeus says that it is a matter of justice that the soul and the body which are co-joined in this present life should be co-joined in the 'reward' beyond this life (*Adversus haereses* 2.29.2). For Tertullian, human being is essentially a union of soul and body. As I have put it before, flesh for him is not only minister and servant to soul, but associate and co-heir (7). For pseudo-Justin, neither body nor soul can effect anything if you release them from their bond with each other (8).

The power of God Most of these apologists loudly attest to the capacity of God to effect the resurrection, something which their opponents clearly deny, and link it to the original creation. Irenaeus declares that 'God's power is sufficient for the resurrection given that he had formed human being in the beginning' (*Adversus haereses* 5.3.2). Theophilus declares that the one God who formed human being in the beginning can surely 'later make you over again' (1.8 and 1.13). Tertullian says that, if God has produced everything out of nothing he will also be able to revive flesh which has fallen into nothing (*De resurrectione carnis* 11). Whoever can create can even more easily re-create. Pseudo-Justin maintains, from the evidence of the major philosophers, that God is 'able to collect again the decomposed members of the flesh and make the same body as it was formerly produced by him' (6). Like Athenagoras, he regards the resurrection of the body as 'worthy' of God (5).

Dissolved flesh to rise again? Some of the other contemporary theologians also address the capacity of the flesh, once dissolved, to be restored whole. Justin at

1 Apology 19 declares that it is not impossible for the bodies of human beings, once dissolved, to rise again like seeds in the earth.

Resurrection and providence The relationship between the resurrection of the whole human being and the providential judgement of God (judgement of good and evil) and the necessity of the former for the latter properly to take place is dealt with by a number of Athenagoras' contemporaries and near-contemporaries. The Epistle of Barnabas declares that the coming judgement of God, for glory or for destruction, necessitates a resurrection (21); Tertullian declares that body and soul cannot be separated in their recompense when they have been united in their service in the present life (*De resurrectione* 8). The judgement must address the interests of the entire human being and, given that this consists of two natures united, a person must appear in this united state before judgement. This is repeated in chapter 11.

Athenagoras' use of non-Christian sources in the *De resurrectione* is not particularly significant and occurs primarily in the area of language rather than of concept. If the *De resurrectione* is by Athenagoras, then one will have to accept some influence, at least in the realm of language, from Philo, given our author's employment of Philonic expressions like ἀγαλματοφορεῖν ('bearing an image [of God]', 12.6) and συνδιαιωνίζειν ('existing eternally', 12.6, 15.8, and 25.4). According to Runia such expressions must have come from Philo's corpus via Alexandria, as we have seen in Chapter 1 (pp. 9f.).

Evidence for the influence of Galen on the conception of active and passive functions of the living being is apparent at 5.1; of the elimination of waste from the body at 5.2, of digestive processes at 5.3; and of the operation of 'opposites' in digestion at 7.1, although, as we saw in Chapter 1, Pouderon offers a thoughtful challenge to this claimed influence. Athenagoras makes references to an 'inner (rational) law' (νόμον ἔμφυτον), which at 13.1 is part of the endowment of the human being, along with the intelligence gifted by God to safeguard and to protect the things which God has given as suitable for intelligent beings , and at 24.4 (κατὰ τὸν ἔμφυτον νόμον καὶ λόγον) it distinguishes creatures who act in accordance with an innate law and can exercise prudence and justice from those who have no share in rational discrimination. Such references can also be found in Cicero, (*De finibus* 3.6.21–2), and in Diogenes Laertius (7.87–8), where Zeno is said to have been the first to designate as the proper end of human existence: 'life [lived] in agreement with nature'.

Athenagoras' notion of the συναμφότερον of soul and body, at 18.4 (twice), 18.5 (twice), 21.5 and 25.2, derives principally from Plato. At *Timaeus* 87c–d Plato speaks of a remedial treatment for the body and the mind and declares that in order for it to be good or fair the living creature it must be symmetrical; but there is no symmetry or lack of symmetry greater than that which exists between the soul and the body. He then says that 'we must conceive of that compound (τοῦ ξυναμφοτέ ρου) [of body and soul] which we call the "living creature"'. At *Philebus* 22a and 46c he speaks, respectively, of the 'combined life' (τὰ ξυναμφότερα), of the mingling of pleasure and the mind and of the 'combination' (ξυναμφότερος) of distress and pleasure which belong to the mind and the body. At *Symposium* 209b he speaks of the 'combination' (συναμφότερον) of a beautiful body and a noble soul. At *Sophist* 250c he says that motion and rest are a 'combination' (ξυναμφό τερον), and at *Republic* 400c, in a discussion of music, he speaks of a 'certain combination' (ξυναμφότερόν τι) of the tempo of the foot and the rhythm. For the *De Resurrectione*, then, the influence of non-Christian thought is terminological more than substantial.

Chapter Eight
Conclusions

For the purposes of this work I have argued that the *De resurrectione* may be from the hand of Athenagoras and therefore I have dealt deal with both works, the *Legatio* and the *De resurrectione*, but, where possible and appropriate, quite separately. The evidence for the authenticity of the *De resurrectione* is admittedly not overwhelming, but the fact that it has been regarded as Athenagorean for over ten centuries and is so regarded by many scholars even today means that it must be treated *prima facie* as authentic and that the onus is on those who would challenge this status to make their case. At most, it is best to regard the matter as 'not proven' and therefore to stay with the *status quo*, namely the view of it as authentic. For a more detailed argument see Chapter 2.

I have argued that the context – both intellectual and historical – in which the *Legatio* was written and the contemporary *conversation* to which Athenagoras sought to contribute was that between members of the Middle Platonist tradition, and most probably within Athens itself (see Chapter 3). I have argued that it was this particular conversation, and not the one between Christian theologians over the content of the Christian *kerygma*, that provides the primary context in which Athenagoras was operating. While he does deal with the unity, the essential goodness, the creatorship and fatherhood, and the providence of God, he does not at all, explicitly or otherwise, deal with a coherent salvation economy or plan of God such as is effected in Christ and declared in the Holy Scriptures, nor with the offer of that salvation which sits at the very core of the Christian gospel. He does, however, deal very explicitly with those matters which lie at the heart of the Middle Platonist conversation: the doctrine of the two levels of reality, being and becoming; the question of whether the supreme divine entity is also directly responsible for the creation of the world; the benevolence and providence of the deity; the Forms; and the relationship between divine providence and human free will.

God, for Athenagoras, is *not* knowable (certainly not knowable *about*) through such means as the Stoic–Epicurean 'preconception', for this provides nothing of substance underlying the name of 'god' beyond the name itself; nor through that of the Stoic 'impression', which is impressed on the mind through the senses, as a seal on wax, for this leads only to delusion and to the possibility of exploitation by daemons who are the agents of the prince of matter; nor through the 'plausible' (τὸ πιθανόν) of the moderate Scepticism of the New Academy, which, like the hard-line Skepticism of the Pyrrhonists, cannot accept certain and secure knowledge. For Athenagoras, however, the notion that knowledge of God can never be *certain* is unacceptable. In this he will side with the Stoics, but not with the means by which they claim to achieve certainty – the preconception and the graspable impression. For him there is then only the witness of the scriptures and of the Spirit-filled prophets, 'played on' like musical instruments by the Spirit; and, above all, the witness of the Son, the mind and reason (and the wisdom) of the Father, the God known only (in Platonist terms) through *nous* and *logos*. As Athenagoras says at *Legatio* 7.2, the poets and the philosophers may know something about God, through the interaction of their souls and the breath of God, but their knowledge is only marginal because they do not seek to get it from its primary source, God himself. The epistemology of Athenagoras informs and in turn is informed by his theology. For his epistemology reflects both the utter transcendence of God – as the Platonists would understand it – and the engagement of this God, the Creator of all there is, with his creation, through his Word and Spirit. Thus this God is both transcendent and immanent, both wholly other and at one with his creation. Certain attributes, such as the oneness of God, can be argued for by means of logic, but such arguments, although undoubtedly effective, can only be trusted to offer more than human constructs where they are also confirmed by the prophetic witness.

Athenagoras' doctrine of God is shaped by at least two things: the concept of first principles and his consistent desire to differentiate God from matter. His doctrine of God, the discussion of which commences as soon as he begins his defence of Christians against the charge of atheism in chapter 4, looks to a fundamental distinction between God and matter. Here Athenagoras argues that, unlike in the philosophical systems of Stoics, Epicureans and Platonists, God alone (with the possible addition of the Word–Son of God) is a first principle. Matter, which is created, perishable and belonging to the realm of the sensible/perceptible – unlike God, who is uncreated, eternal, imperishable, and constitutes the realm of the intelligible – cannot be a first principle on account of its perishability and its mutability. God, for Athenagoras, is alone one, eternal, uncreated, good, Creator–Father of all there is, arranger and provider for what he has created. All this is consistent for the most part with the Christian *kerygma*, as far as it goes; but what is noteworthy in Athenagoras is the way in which his presentation of the divine being is so clearly informed by Platonist language and thought. God is alone contemplated, comprehended, indeed grasped by mind and thought. He is being rather than not-being; and this is the first time that a Christian thinker has identified the uncreated with being. He is μονάς, as the Pythagoreans would say, and he stands above matter. He is the truly divine. He is also invisible, impassible, in himself incomprehensible (ungraspable) – which is where revelation, the Word and the Spirit come into the equation – and infinite. He is encompassed by light, beauty, spirit and indescribable power, and he rules over that which he has made. He creates and sets his ministers in place, to superintend his creation. He has need of nothing from us or from anyone or anything. He is self-sufficient and seeks only (but does not need) our worship and our knowledge of him. He is Creator, constructor and artisan. He is the active cause insofar as he is providential. He is immortal, immovable and immutable. He neither changes nor decays, as matter does. He is true being and of one nature. He is the supreme entity, he is absolutely transcendent, as the Neo-Pythagoreans and Neoplatonists later would require him to be, but he remains engaged with that which he has created. This is the genius of the exposition of the Christian *kerygma* which Athenagoras assists to come to life.

Athenagoras deals with other themes in the *Legatio* which, while for the most part they are subordinated to his doctrine of God, are yet not insignificant in and of themselves. In his treatment of a doctrine of the *Word–Son of God* he is clearly concerned in the first place to provide an explanation of how God, in a manner consistent with monotheism generally and with the transcendence required of the God of Plato, the Middle Platonists, and the Neo-Pythagoreans, might remain utterly transcendent and separate from his creation – as he is for those Middle Platonists for whom of course God is also the creator of the universe – and yet engage with that creation. Therefore the Word, in a manner consistent also with the biblical and patristic witness, is the divine entity (though not separate from the Father) through which the universe is created, ordered and arranged; it is that through which the universe is ruled, and that through which the ministers created by God for the providential care of the universe are put in place. The Word also, as the Son of God, is the mind, reason and wisdom of the Father and thereby the means by which God can be known. The Son is also both the *idea* – qua image in which the creation is created – and the *energeia* – as the very activity of God engaged in that creative process – of the Father. These images are exclusive to Athenagoras among Christian theologians and mark out his thought as distinctive within the tradition. The incarnation, as indicated in Chapter 5, is dealt with only in the most marginal manner. This is a not an issue for Athenagoras in his treatment of the charge of atheism, and it is one which would probably have raised more problems with his addressees than he was then prepared to deal with at that point.

In his treatment of the *Spirit/Holy Spirit*, Athenagoras is again concerned to articulate the way in which the supreme Creator–Father–God can remain transcendent and outside his creation and yet be fully engaged with it. Therefore the Spirit in Athenagoras' view performs certain functions. First, the Spirit inspires – it 'plays' the prophets like musical instruments, so that their utterances are authentically divine. The Spirit, for Athenagoras – and the imagery and language here are pure Stoicism – is also that divine entity (again, not separate from the Father) who both provides for the unity of Father and Son and upholds and gives coherence to all those things which are created by God through his Word. The Spirit is, presumably, the 'breath of God', through affinity with which the souls of the poets and philosophers are enabled to acquire some, admittedly peripheral, understanding of the nature of God. The Holy Spirit, active in those who speak prophetically, is an effluence of God which flows forth from him and then returns like a ray of the sun. The *Trinity*, dealt with most extensively in chapter 10, is again intended in its treatment to serve the higher purpose (here) of defending the Christians against the charge of atheism. Yet this treatment is not without value in and of itself. A high level of sophistication is evident and Athenagoras demonstrates a solid grasp of the issues involved, particularly within the context of a philosophical conversation. At 6.2 he sees the work of God as a co-operative endeavour between God (the Father), the Son as an agent of creation, and the Spirit as an agent giving coherence to the creation. At 10.2 he speaks of the Spirit providing unity and power to the union of the Father and the Son, and at 10.5, of their unity and of their diversity in rank. At 12.3, in the context of his discussion of a Christian ethics, he declares that, in their living out the Christian life, Christians are guided solely by their knowledge of God, a knowledge which is constituted by the unity of the Son and the Father, the communion of the Father and the Son, and the unity of Spirit, Son and Father and their very diversity when united. These things are repeated at 24.2, where Athenagoras speaks of the unity and diversity (in rank) of Father, Son and Holy Spirit, of the Son as the mind, reason and wisdom of the Father and of the Spirit as an effluence like light from fire.

Athenagoras' treatment of a Christian *ethics* is characterized by at least two features. First, he presents the mode of living of the Christians – an ethical life characterized by moderation, concern and affection for the other, and a preference for the next life over this one – as being accompanied by the knowledge that in our living now we are not unobserved by God; this is a fact which will affect our transition to the life beyond. Thus Christian living is a testimonial both to the existence of God and to the nature of that God, whose attributes will be reflected in a life lived in faith to him. Second, in his ethical reflections Athenagoras also deals with the fact that, while some humans, like some angels, choose to serve God faithfully, in a manner consistent with their appointment, and thereby live the virtuous life, others, again like some angels, do not, and thereby live a life of vice. This, says Athenagoras, is a matter of free choice, a free will given the creature by the creator, and, in the case of those who fail to be faithful, simply an example of the willingness of daemons associated with the prince of matter to exploit the weakness and frailty of the human soul which is not turned toward God and the things of heaven.

Finally, we look in summary at the question of the influences at play in the thought of Athenagoras. We have seen how he understands himself to be acting in a manner faithful to the biblical and prophetic witness and how this is evident particularly in his dealing with a Christian ethics. Yet his employment of scripture is infrequent and not at all as frequent as that of Homer, Herodotus and other pagan authorities. His intended audience, however, would not have been swayed by any attempt to employ the scripture as his principal authority. He is also clearly influenced by earlier Fathers, particularly by Justin Martyr; but one ought not to make more of this than the evidence warrants.

Athenagoras is influenced in his choice of language and imagery by the Stoic tradition, but he chooses more often to repudiate it or at least to lessen any suggestion of a reliance on its thought and substance. Stoicism provides part and parcel of the intellectual language of the day; some would suggest that in the second century (though not later) this is the dominant philosophical school or tradition. Yet it is Plato, or more correctly his later interpreters, like Alcinous,

Plutarch, Apuleius and others, who influence not only his choice of language but the very intellectual framework in which he operates. In choosing to defend the Christians against the charge of atheism and to portray them instead as convinced and convincing theists, he not only employs the language of others in order to get his point across, but indeed embraces the symbols and the substance which underlie these linguistic forms and contentedly makes them his own. His presentation of God in terms which are consistent with Platonism and acceptable to its followes – as one, as eternal, as being, as intelligible and so on – is not simply a strategy of employing the language of those with whom he is in conversation; this is indeed the language with which he is most clearly comfortable. In the second half of the second century, Athenagoras of Athens, philosopher and theologian, chooses to engage primarily, not in the conversation then current among Christian theologians of his time, about the nature of the Christian *kerygma*, but rather in a conversation carried among Middle Platonists, a conversation which was taking place at that time very much in Athenagoras' own city of Athens and was principally about the divine being. He does not, despite appearances, fawn over the emperors, but he simply employs the normal rhetorical approaches of his day as he faithfully engages the philosophers with the message of the gospel. His participation in that conversation, his epistemological stance and his acknowledgement of their sources of knowledge both inform and are informed by his presentation of a doctrine of God and of the Word and Spirit, a doctrine by which he manages to refute the charge that Christians are atheists, demonstrating instead that there is no segment of ancient society more believing in God than they are.

Bibliography

Texts and Translations

Alcinoos: Enseignement des doctrines de Platon, edited with introduction and commentary by J. Whittaker and translated by Pierre Louis, Collection des Universités de France (Paris: Les belles lettres, 1990).

Alcinous. The Handbook of Platonism, translated with an introduction and Commentary by J. Dillon (Oxford: Clarendon Press, 1993).

Athenagoras. Embassy for the Christians. The Resurrection of the Dead, edited, translated and annotated by J.H. Crehan, Ancient Christian Writers No. 23 (New York: Newman Press, 1955).

Athenagoras. Legatio pro Christianis, edited by M. Marcovich, Patristische Texte und Studien Band 31 (Berlin: Walter de Gruyter, 1990).

Athenagoras. Legatio and De Resurrectione, edited and translated by W.R. Schoedel, Oxford Early Christian Texts (Oxford: Clarendon Press, 1972).

Athénagore. *Supplique au sujet des chrétiens et Sur la Résurrection des morts*, edited and translated with an introduction by B. Pouderon, Sources Chrétiennes, No. 379 (Paris: Les Editions du Cerf, 1992).

Cicero. De natura deorum. Academica, edited and translated by H. Rackman, Loeb Classical Library (Cambridge, MA: Harvard University Press, 1951).

Diogenes Laertius. Lives of Eminent Philosophers, 2 vols, edited and translated by R.D. Hicks, Loeb Classical Library (Cambridge, MA: Harvard University Press, 1972).

Philo of Alexandria: On the Creation of the Cosmos according to Moses, translated with commentary by D.T. Runia (Leiden: Brill, 2001).

Plato. Timaeus, Critias, Cleitophon, Menexenus, Epistles, edited and translated by R.G. Bury, Loeb Classical Library (Cambridge, MA: Harvard University Press, 1929).

Plato. Republic, edited and translated by P. Shorey, 2 vols, Loeb Classical Library (Cambridge, MA: Harvard University Press, 1937 and 1935).

Reference Works

Philosophy

Algra, K. et al. (eds), *The Cambridge History of Hellenistic Philosophy* (Cambridge: Cambridge University Press, 2005).

Armstrong, A.H., 'Pagan and Christian traditionalism in the first three centuries A.D.', *Studia Patristica* 15 (1984): 414–31.

Berchman, R.M., *From Philo to Origen. Middle Platonism in Transition* (Chico: Scholars Press, 1984).

Bos, Abraham P., '"Aristotelian" and "Platonic" dualism in Hellenistic and early Christian philosophy and in Gnosticism', *Vigiliae Christianae* 56 (2002): 273–91.

Dillon, John, 'The Academy in the Middle Platonic period', *Dionysius* 3 (1979): 63–77.

—— 'Plutarch and second century Platonism', in A.H. Armstrong (ed.), *Classical Mediterranean Spirituality: Egyptian, Greek, Roman* (World Spirituality vol. 15), (London: Routledge & Kegan Paul, 1986): 214–29.

—— '"Orthodoxy" and "eclecticism": Middle Platonists and Neo-Pythagoreans', in John M. Dillon and A.A. Long (eds), *The Question of Eclecticism: Studies in Later Greek Philosophy* (Berkeley: University of California Press, 1988): 103–25.

—— 'Logos and Trinity: Patterns of Platonist influence on early Christianity', in G. Vesey (ed.), *The Philosophy in Christianity* (Cambridge: Cambridge University Press, 1989): 1–13.

—— *The Middle Platonists: 80 BC* to *AD 220*, rev. edn (London: Duckworth, 1996).

Drozdek, Adam, *Greek Philosophers as Theologians. The Divine Arche* (Aldershot: Ashgate, 2007).

Huffman, Carl A., *Philolaus of Croton: Pythagorean and Presocratic* (Cambridge: Cambridge University Press, 1993).

Jones, K.M., 'The Ideas as the thoughts of God', *Classical Philology* 21 (1926): 317–26.

Laidlaw-Johnson, Elizabeth A., *Plato's Epistemology. How Hard Is It to Know?* (New York: Peter Lang, 1996).

Loenen, J.H., 'Albinus' metaphysics: An attempt at rehabilitation. I: The inner consistency and the original character of Albinus' interpretation of Plato', *Mnemosyne* IV, 7 (1954): 111–22. IV, 9 (1956): 296–319.

Loenen, J.H., 'Albinus' metaphysics. an attempt at rehabilitation. II: The sources of Albinus' metaphysics', *Mnemosyne* IV, 10 (1957), 35–56.

Long, A.A., *Problems in Stoicism* (London: Athlone Press, 1971).

—— *Hellenistic Philosophy: Stoics, Epicureans, Sceptics*, 2nd edn (London: Duckworth, 1986).

—— *Stoic Studies* (Cambridge: Cambridge University Press, 1996).

Long, A.A. and D.N. Sedley, *The Hellenistic Philosophers*, 2 vols (Cambridge: Cambridge University Press, 1987), Vol. I: Translations of the Principal Sources with Philosophical Commentary; Vol. II: Greek and Latin Texts with Notes and Bibliography.

Mansfeld, J., 'Three notes on Albinus', *Theta-Pi* I (1971): 61–80.

—— 'Compatible alternatives: Middle Platonist theology and the Xenophanes reception', in R. van den Broek et al. (eds), *Knowledge of God in the Graeco-Roman world* (Leiden and New York: Brill, 1988): 92–117.

—— 'Alcinous on fate and providence', in J.J. Cleary (ed.), *Traditions of* Platonism: *Essays in Honour of John Dillon* (Aldershot: Ashgate, 1999): 139–50.

Oliver, J.H., 'Marcus Aurelius and the philosophical schools at Athens', *American Journal of Philology* 102 (1981), 213–25.

—— Marcus Aurelius. *Aspects of Civic and Cultural Policy in the East.* Hesperia Supplement XIII (Princeton: 1970).

Reydams-Schils, G., *Demiurge and Providence: Stoic and Platonist Readings of Plato's Timaeus* (Turnhout: Brepols, 1999).

Rich, A.H.M., 'The Platonic Ideas as the thoughts of God', *Mnemosyne* IV, 7 (1954): 123–33.

Russell, D.A., *Plutarch*, 2nd edn, with foreword and bibliography by J. Mossman (Bristol: Bristol Classical Press, 2001).

Sandbach, F.H., 'Phantasia Katalēptikē', in A.A. Long (ed.), *Problems in Stoicism*, rev. edn (London: Athlone Press, 1996): 9–21.

—— 'Ennoia and Prolēpsis in the Stoic theory of knowledge', in A.A. Long (ed.), *Problems in Stoicism*, rev. edn (London: Atholone Press, 1971): 22–37.

—— *The Stoics*, 2nd edn (London: Duckworth, 1989).

Schofield, M., 'Preconception, argument and God', in M. Schofield et al. (eds), *Doubt and Dogmatism: Studies in Hellenistic epistemology* (Oxford: Clarendon Press, 1980): 283–308.

Sharples, R.W., 'The criterion of truth in Philo Judaeus, Alcinous and Alexander of Aphrodisias', in P. Huby et al. (eds), *The Criterion of Truth: Essays Written in Honour of George Kerfred together with a Text and Translation (with Annotations) of Ptolemy's On the Criterion and Hegemonikon* (Liverpool: Liverpool University Press, 1989): 231–56.

—— *Stoics, Epicureans and Sceptics: An Introduction to Hellenistic Philosophy* (London and New York: Routledge, 1996).

Skemp, J.B., 'The Timaeus and the criterion of truth', in P. Huby et al. (eds), *The Criterion of Truth: Essays Written in Honour of George Kerfred together with a Text and Translation (with Annotations) of Ptolemy's On the Criterion and Hegemonikon* (Liverpool: Liverpool University Press, 1989): 83–92.

Spanneut, Michel, *Le Stoïcisme des pères de l'Eglise: De Clément de Rome à Clément d'Alexandrie*, Préface de H.-I. Marrou (Paris: Editions du Seuil, 1957).

Tarrant, H., *Scepticism or Platonism? The Philosophy of the Fourth Academy* (Cambridge: Cambridge University Press, 1985).

Vogel, C.J. de, 'A la recherche des étapes précises entre Platon et le Néoplatonisme', *Mnemosyne* IV 7 (1954): 111–22.

Athenagoras

Alfonsi, L., 'Motivi tradizionali del giovane Aristotele in Clemente Alessandrino e in Atenagora', *Vigiliae Christianae* 7 (1953): 129–42.
Barnard, L.W., 'The Embassy of Athenagoras', *Vigiliae Christianae* 21 (1967): 88–92.
—— 'The Old Testament and the authorship of Athenagoras' *De resurrectione*', *Journal of Theological Studies* 15 (1967): 432–3.
—— 'Notes on Athenagoras', *Latomus* 31 (1972): 413–32.
—— Athenagoras: A Study in Second Century Christian Apologetic. *Théologie historique* 18 (Paris: Beauchesne, 1972).
—— 'The authenticity of Athenagoras' *De resurrectione*', *Studia Patristica* 15 (1984): 39–49.
Barnes, T.D., 'The Embassy of Athenagoras', *Journal of Theological Studies* 26 (1975): 11–14.
Buck, P.L., 'Athenagoras's *Embassy*: A literary fiction', *Harvard Theological Review* 89 (1996): 209–26.
Diels, H., *Doxographi Graeci*, 3rd edn (Berolini: W. de Gruyter, 1958).
Festugière, A.J., 'Sur une traduction nouvelle d'Athénagore', *Revue des études grecques* 56 (1943): 367–75.
Geffcken, J., *Zwei griechische Apologeten* (Leipzig: B.G. Teubner, 1907).
Grant, R.McQ., 'Irenaeus and Hellenistic culture', *Harvard Theological Review* 42 (1949): 41–51.
—— 'Athenagoras or Pseudo-Athenagoras', *Harvard Theological Review* 47 (1954): 121–9.
—— 'The chronology of the Greek Apologists', *Vigiliae Christianae* 9 (1955): 25–33.
—— 'Some errors in the *Legatio* of Athenagoras', *Vigiliae Christianae* 12 (1958): 145–6.
—— *The Early Christian Doctrine of God* (Charlottesville: University Press of Virginia, 1966).
—— 'Five Apologists and Marcus Aurelius', *Vigiliae Christianae* 42 (1988): 1–17.
Keseling, P., 'Athenagoras', in *Realexikon für Antike und Christentum* (Stuttgart, 1950), I: 881–8.
Lona, H.E., 'Bemerkungen zu Athenagoras und Pseudo-Athenagoras', *Vigiliae Christianae* 42 (1988): 352–63.
—— 'Die dem Apologeten Athenagoras zugeschriebene Schrift "De resurrectione mortuorum" und die altchristliche Auferstehungenapologetik', *Salesianum* 52 (1990): 525–41.
Malherbe, A.J., 'The structure of Athenagoras, "Supplicatio pro Christianis"', *Vigiliae Christianae* 23 (1969): 1–20.
—— 'Athenagoras on Christian ethics', *Journal of Ecclesiastical History* 20 (1969): 1–5.

—— 'The Holy Spirit in Athenagoras', *Journal of Theological Studies* 20 (1969): 538–42.

—— 'Athenagoras on the Location of God', *Theologische Zeitschrift* 26 (1970): 46–52.

Mansfeld, J., 'Resurrection added: Ihe Interpretatio christiana of a Stoic doctrine', Vigiliae Christianae 37 (1983): 218–33.

Marcovich, M., 'Athenagoras, De resurrectione 3.2', *Journal of Theological Studies* ns 29 (1978): 146–7.

—— 'On the text of Athenagoras, De resurrectione', *Vigiliae Christianae* 33 (1979): 375–82.

Pouderon, B., 'L'Authenticité du Traité sur la résurrection attribué à l'Apologiste Athénagore', *Vigiliae Christianae* 40 (1986): 226–44.

—— *Athénagore d'Athènes: Philosophe chrétien* (Paris: Beauchesne, 1989).

—— '"La Chair et le sang": Encore sur l'authenticité du Traité d'Athénagore', *Vigiliae Christianae* 44 (1990): 1–5.

—— 'Athénagore chef d'école à propos du témoignage de Philippe de Side', *Studia Patristica* 26 (1993): 167–76.

—— *D'Athènes à Alexandrie: Etudes sur Athénagore et les origines de la philosophie chrétienne* (Quebec: Bernard, 1997).

Runia, D.T., 'Verba Philonica, αγαλματοφορεῖν, and the authenticity of the *De* resurrectione', *Vigiliae Christianae* 46 (1992): 313–27.

—— 'Platonism, Philonism, and the beginnings of Christian thought', in idem, *Philo and the Church Fathers* (*Vigiliae Christianae*, Supplement XXXII) (Leiden: Brill, 1995): 1–24.

—— 'God of the philosophers, God of the patriarchs: Exegetical backgrounds in Philo of Alexandria', in idem, *Philo and the Church Fathers* (*Vigiliae Christianae*, Supplement XXXII) (Leiden: Brill, 1995): 206–18.

Ruprecht, L.A., 'Athenagoras the Christian, Pausanias the travel guide, and mysterious Corinthian girl', *Harvard Theological Review* 85 (1992): 35–49.

Schoedel, Wm. R., 'Christian "atheism" and the peace of the Roman Empire', *Church History* 42 (1973): 309–19.

—— 'Apologetic literature and ambassadorial activities', *Harvard Theological Review* 82 (1989): 55–78.

Scholten, C.,'Athenagoras', *Lexicon für Theologie und Kirche* (Freiburg: Herder, 1993), Vol. I: 1143.

Schwartz, E., *Athenagoras libellus pro Christianis. Oratio De resurrectione* (Leipzig: J.C. Hinrichs, 1891).

Vermander, J.M., 'Celse et l'attribution à Athénagore d'un ouvrage sur la résurrection des morts', *Mélanges de Science Religieuse* 35 (1978): 125–34.

Winden, J.C.M. van, 'The origin of falsehood', *Vigiliae Christianae* 30 (1976): 303–6.

Zeegers vander Vorst, N., 'La "Prénotion Commune" au chapitre 5 de la Legatio d'Athénagore', *Vigiliae Christianae* 25 (1971): 161–70.

—— 'La Paternité Athénagorienne du De resurrectione', *Revue d'histoire ecclésiastique* 87 (1992): 333–74.

Other

Countryman, L.W., 'Tertullian and the regula fidei', *Second Century* 2 (1982): 208–27.
Daniélou, Jean, *Gospel Message and Hellenistic Culture* (London: Darton, Longman and Todd, 1973).
Edwards, M. et al. (eds), *Apologetics in the Roman Empire. Pagans, Jews and Christians* (Oxford: Oxford University Press, 1999).
Gavrilyuk, Paul L., *The Suffering of the Impassible God. The Dialectics of Patristic Thought* (Oxford: Oxford University Press, 2004).
Giunchi, M., 'Dunamis et taxis dans la conception trinitaire d'Athénagore (Leg. X.29; XII.21; XXIV.9)', in Pouderon, B. and Doré, J. (eds), *Les Apologistes chrétiens et la culture grecque* (Théologie Historique 105) (Paris: Beauchesne, 1998): 121–34.
Grant, R.M., *The Early Christian Doctrine of God* (Charlottesville: University Press of Virginia, 1966).
—— *Greek Apologists of the Second Century* (Philadelphia: Westminster Press, 1988).
May, Gerhard, *Creatio ex nihilo: The Doctrine of 'Creation out of Nothing' in Early Christian Thought* (Edinburgh: T&T Clark, 1994).
Osborn, E.F.O., *The Beginning of Christian philosophy* (Cambridge: Cambridge University Press, 1981).
Pannenberg, W., *Basic Questions in Theology*, Vol. 2 (London: SCM, 1970–73).
Rankin, D.I., *From Clement to Origen: The Social and Historical Context of the Church Fathers* (Aldershot: Ashgate, 2006).
Rist, J.M., *Augustine: Ancient Thought Baptized* (Cambridge: Cambridge University Press, 1996).
Wartelle, A., 'Quelques remarques sur le vocabulaire philosophique de Saint Justin dans le *Dialogue avec Trypho*', in B. Pouderon and J. Doré (eds), *Les Apologistes chrétiens et la culture grecque* (Théologie Historique 105) (Paris: Beauchesne, 1998): 67–80.

Index